MW00856105

The Autobiography of an
African Princess

THE AUTOBIOGRAPHY OF AN AFRICAN PRINCESS

Fatima Massaquoi

Edited with an Introduction by
Vivian Seton,
Konrad Tuchscherer and
Arthur Abraham

First published in 2013 by
PALGRAVE MACMILLAN®
in the United States—a division of St. Martin's Press LLC,
175 Fifth Avenue, New York, NY 10010.

Where this book is distributed in the UK, Europe and the rest of the world, this is by Palgrave Macmillan, a division of Macmillan Publishers Limited, registered in England, company number 785998, of Houndmills, Basingstoke, Hampshire RG21 6XS.

Palgrave Macmillan is the global academic imprint of the above companies and has companies and representatives throughout the world.

Palgrave® and Macmillan® are registered trademarks in the United States, the United Kingdom, Europe and other countries.

ISBN: 978–0–230–60958–7

Library of Congress Cataloging-in-Publication Data

Massaquoi, Fatima, 1904?-1978, author.
     The autobiography of an African princess / by Fatima Massaquoi ; edited with an introduction by Vivian Seton, Konrad Tuchscherer, and Arthur Abraham.
        page cm
     ISBN: 978-0-230-60958-7 (alk. paper)
        1. Massaquoi, Fatima, 1904?-1978. 2. Vai (African people)—Social life and customs—20th century. 3. Vai (African people)—Germany–Social conditions—20th century. 4. Vai (African people)—United States—Social conditions—20th century. 5. Liberia—Social life and customs—20th century. I. Seton, Vivian, 1950–editor. II. Tuchscherer, Konrad, 1970- editor. III. Abraham, Arthur, 1945–editor. IV. Title.

DT630.5.V2M37 2013
966.620049634092—dc23   2013017229

A catalogue record of the book is available from the British Library.

Design by Newgen Knowledge Works (P) Ltd., Chennai, India.

First edition: November 2013

10 9 8 7 6 5 4 3 2 1

Contents

ILLUSTRATIONS

FOREWORD

Hans J. Massaquoi
Author of *Destined to Witness: Growing Up Black in
Nazi Germany* and
nephew of Princess Fatima Massaquoi

Had it not been for my Aunt Fatima, I would have been completely cut off from my African roots. A student in her early twenties in pursuit of an academic career at various German institutions of higher learning, Aunt Fatima was a frequent visitor to the tiny apartment that my German mother and I occupied in one of Hamburg's modest working-class neighborhoods. Often, during her visits, she would take me on small excursions during which she regaled me with some of the most fascinating stories about life in Africa, which instilled in me the wish to one day go to Liberia and see for myself. Through her, I also learned more about my brilliant grandfather, Fatima's father (Momolu Massaquoi), with whom my mother and I had lived until his departure to Liberia in 1929, and whom I adored and greatly missed.

Due to the rise of racist National Socialism and the approach of World War II, Aunt Fatima left Germany in 1937, and after studies in the United States returned to Liberia, where she built a stellar academic career. I didn't catch up with her until 1948 when my father arranged to have me join him in Monrovia. When my father and I had difficulties living in harmony, who came to my rescue? Aunt Fatima. She invited me to stay at her home until I could make more suitable arrangements. I accepted her kind offer and stayed with her, her husband, and their infant daughter, Püppchen (Vivian Seton), for a couple of weeks. During that time, I was fascinated by the breadth of her intellectual interests and by her experiences as a widely traveled student. Once again, my aunt inspired me to see more of the world for myself. Eventually, she wished me luck and bon voyage when in the spring of 1950 I headed for the United States to build my own career as a journalist.

The last time our paths crossed was in 1971 when I was sent to Monrovia to cover the funeral of Liberian president William V. S. Tubman, and I took the opportunity to drop in on my aunt for a long chat. Again, I was impressed by her command of a vast array of subjects. Clearly, one of the most educated women I have ever known, my Aunt Fatima obviously inherited her father's keen intellect and his love of education.

ACKNOWLEDGMENTS

The editors are grateful to a number of people who have helped us along the way with assistance and advice. These include Nickole Sharp, Cristina Ridgeley-Mones, Ekaterini Melidoniatis, Marie-Caroline Causin-Von Zieten, Linnie Folk-Rosenthal, Tombekai Sherman, Renee Ennix, Dr. Coyness Ennix Jr., Rea Brändle, Afrika Hayes-Lambe, Professor Robert Hill at UCLA, Beth Howse in Special Collections/Archives at Fisk University Library, Prof. Dr. Rainer Hering at Landesarchiv Schleswig-Holstein—Prinzenpalais (Germany), Dr. Tina Campt of Duke University, Dr. Eckhard Breitinger at the University of Bayreuth, Prof. Dr. Adam Jones at the University of Leipzig, Professor Henry Louis Gates, Jr. of Harvard University, Professor Dirk Philipsen of Virginia State University, the late Hans Massaquoi, and the late Prof. Dr. Ernst Dammann.

We would also like to thank our editors at Palgrave, Christopher Chappell and Sarah Whalen.

We are grateful to our families—the Setons, Massaquois, Abrahams, and Tuchscherers—for patiently seeing us through this project.

INTRODUCTION

The Vais may have a song to sing, a parable to utter, a prayer to offer or a law to interpret—all of which may be necessary elements in the progress and enlightenment of mankind.

—*Momolu Massaquoi*[1]

Princess Fatima Massaquoi was descended from royal lineages of the Vai people of both Sierra Leone and Liberia. She was born in southern Sierra Leone about 1904,[2] daughter of Momo IV (Momolu Massaquoi) who wore the crown of the Gallinas, and she died in Monrovia, Liberia, in 1978. Her autobiography was written between the years 1939 and 1946 and examines her life experiences in Africa, Europe, and America (see figure 0.1). She lived an extraordinary life on all three continents, and her story records everything from insider views of traditional life and societies in Africa, to her experiences of intense racism in Nazi Germany and the segregated American south. During her journey she plays her violin for royalty and presidents, entertains Marcus Garvey with her poetry, crosses paths with leading intellectuals and entertainers, and even attends Nazi rallies.

While she was a student in the United States, she began writing her life story as a class project for a social psychology course at Fisk University in Nashville, Tennessee, in 1939. From that point it grew until she completed it in 1946 as a student at Boston University. Her account reflects three important segments of her life. The first part (1904–1922), contains her recollections of her infancy in southern Sierra Leone and her early childhood and school experiences in Liberia. The second part (1922–1936) relates her life as a young woman coming of age in Nazi Germany, very much in the public eye as the daughter of the sociable Momolu Massaquoi, Liberia's consul general to Hamburg, Germany. Under the pressure of increasing racism in Germany, and with the help of her father's friends, she traveled to the United States. The third and final part of her story (1936–1946) records her observations and experiences in the United States and concludes as she prepares to return to Liberia.

It is unfortunate that she did not add the natural fourth part of her life story, her life and work in Liberia, where she made great contributions to

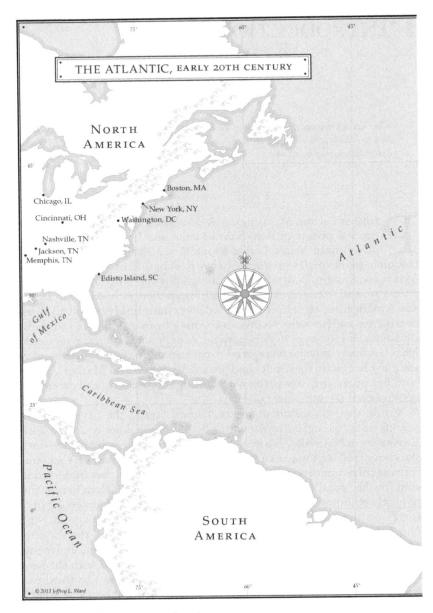

Figure 0.1   Map of the Atlantic

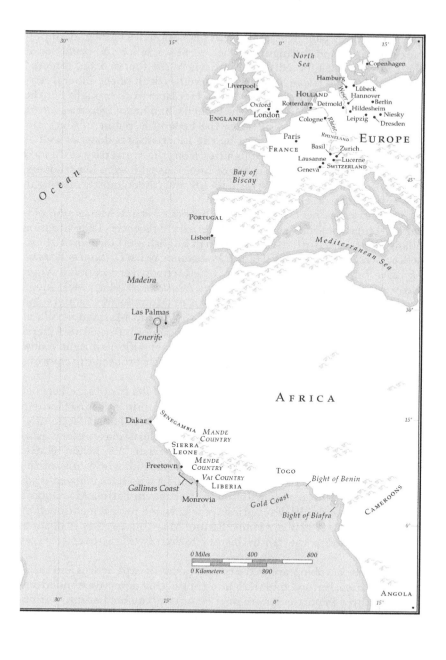

her country's development. She served her nation in a number of important capacities and distinguished herself as a scholar and professor at the University of Liberia (1947–1972), where she founded and directed the Institute of African Studies and served as dean of the Liberal Arts College until shortly before her death. Her later work brought her the Bronze Medallion of Molière by the French Chamber of Deputies (1956), the Iron Cross by the president of the Federal Republic of Germany (1962), the Grand Star of Africa by the Liberian president, as well as an honorary Doctorate of Humanities from the University of Liberia (1973). She influenced generations of Liberians who were her students, and an account of her interesting later life and career, mostly missing in this action here, deserves to be written.[3]

Very little has been known publicly about Fatima Massaquoi, outside of Liberian circles that is, until relatively recently. That situation changed, perhaps, with the publication in English and German of a bestselling book by her nephew, Hans J. Massaquoi, titled *Destined to Witness: Growing Up Black in Nazi Germany* (the German version being *Neger, Neger, Schornsteinfeger!: meine Kindheit in Deutschand*). Hans Massaquoi, born in Hamburg in 1926, was the son of Momolu Massaquoi's son Al-Haj. He and his mother, Bertha, lived at the Massaquoi villa at Johnsallee in Hamburg until Momolu Massaquoi returned to Liberia in 1929. In his book, Fatima Massaquoi appears with her bright yellow leopard-skin coat and "Afro so huge it would have aroused the envy of a Fiji Islander."[4]

Hans Massaquoi also recounts the racial insults his "Tante Fatima" received on account of her relationship with a prominent young German man, and how she reluctantly agreed to buy Hans his Nazi action figures—Hitler, Göring, and Goebbels—for his Christmas present. Also mentioned in Hans Massaquoi's book is his cousin "Püppchen" (Little Doll), Fatima Massaquoi's daughter and only child, who is one of the editors writing here. Indeed, for those readers who have enjoyed reading *Destined to Witness*, they will find in the pages of Fatima Massaquoi's autobiography colorful descriptions of events and people mentioned by her much younger nephew Hans. Fatima Massaquoi's story is in some sense a prequel to the family history related by Hans over 50 years later.

While the autobiography covers a vast array of experiences and situations in Africa, Europe, and the United States that deserve extended discussion, three in particular are important to note here because Fatima Massaquoi alludes to them but never fully contextualizes them in her writing. The first was an accident in her childhood in Monrovia that injured her hands, suffered in the course of a punishment administered by her stepmother, Ma Sedia. Fatima had been accused of taking something from a food storeroom and was punished by having to stand on a box with her hands tied above her with a hanging rope to keep her hands aloft. She fell from the box, alone in the storeroom, with no one hearing her cries for help, and the rope brutally ripped the flesh and twisted the bones in her hands. She forgave Ma Sedia, who she loved dearly, yet her hands were a painful reality that she was forced to deal with for much of her young life. These required constant medical attention, which curbed her activities such as playing the violin. The condition of her hands also prioritized her position among Massaquoi children for inclusion in the trip to Germany in 1922. Fatima was very self-conscious of her hands throughout her young life and always made it a point to hide the scars on her hands in photographs.

Secondly, by the end of her stay in Germany, she does not explain the circumstances of her father's sudden departure from Germany for Liberia in 1929 after being recalled from his diplomatic position, and what subsequently transpired once back home. Briefly, Momolu Massaquoi, who was in failing health, was recalled because leaders in government (the True Whig Party) feared he was secretly collaborating with the opposition (the People's Party). Additionally, he was suspected of not being in full support of the defense of Liberia amid international accusations of slavery and forced labor.

When he returned to Liberia, he assumed the position of postmaster general. He declared his intention to run for president in 1931 against his close friend Edwin Barclay, who held the position upon King's resignation in 1930. This resulted in a dramatic backlash against him and the entire Massaquoi family. Intimidated by Massaquoi's popularity, Barclay sought to criminalize him. Although he failed, he succeeded in preventing him from contesting via a series of lawsuits that continued long after, until Massaquoi's death in 1938. But Barclay did not stop there. After winning the presidency, he sought to obliterate Massaquoi by getting his achievements and services to the state expunged from all public records and history books. But Massaquoi's monumental record could not be wiped out; it has continued in public memory and in oral history. Barclay stayed in power until 1944, when William V. S. Tubman became president.[5] Only then could Fatima return home without the fear of political persecution, but by then her beloved father had already died.

Lastly, Fatima refers to her great great grandfather, King Siaka, perhaps the greatest of the Vai kings "whose fame is still legendary in the Gallinas." Yet outside the confines of the text there has remained a keen sensitivity, even regret, in the Massaquoi family concerning the involvement of their forebears in the slave trade that sent tens of thousands of captives across the Atlantic Ocean into bondage. King Siaka and his son Prince Manna were directly involved in this trade, and some of the now famous Amistad captives passed through their hands.[6]

In this book we have striven to retain as closely as possible the original voice of Fatima Massaquoi, yet render that voice in an easily readable way. Massaquoi's typescript draft contains hundreds of strikeouts and notes in the text and margins, making the editing process a challenging one. We have attempted as best as possible to incorporate such changes as Massaquoi intended, and likewise have corrected obvious typographical, punctuation, and grammatical errors in order to make the text readable and modern. Likewise, we have given modern standard spelling to peoples and places to avoid confusing the reader. While we attempted to avoid any substantive changes in the narrative, at several points we were forced, for purposes of publication and readability, to cut from the original writing. We are confident that in this process the integrity of the original has been preserved.

English was not Fatima Massaquoi's first language. In her early years she spoke Mende and Vai, and while she learned English as a schoolgirl in Liberia, her English was surpassed by her fluency in German and French learned as a student in Germany and Switzerland. At the time of her writing, the literary language which influenced her most was German, and at times she appears to translate her thoughts directly from that language. On the other hand, she often gives literal translations in English of African expressions that may appear curious to a Western audience.

Massaquoi occasionally inserts her own footnotes in her text and our editorial footnotes have been sequenced into the original footnotes, in all such cases appearing in square brackets followed by "*Eds.*" In sections where she includes songs or poems in Vai or Mende we have left off her attempt to provide phonetic transcriptions, which were difficult to read in the original. Original page numbers in the manuscript have not been followed to allow smoother reading and avoid the irregularities in pagination, with missing pages or duplicated page numbers. In order to present the book in an organized fashion, we have had to break up certain sections into smaller chapters and use a standardized format for letters, quotes, and subtitles.

Fatima Massaquoi was known by several names throughout her life. She was called "Famata" in early life, a Vai and Mende contraction of Fatimata derived from the Arabic form "Fatima." As she describes in her autobiography, she was named after her grandmother, Queen Famata Sandimani. While in Germany, she began using the standard Arabic form, "Fatima," for her name. In 1948 she married Ernest Freeman, whose original Vai name, "Fahnbulleh," had been changed to "Freeman" while he had been in school. Instead of adopting her husband's Western-sounding name (considered a "slave name" by her family), she reverted the name to "Fahnbulleh." Her new name, post autobiography, became "Fatima Massaquoi-Fahnbulleh." Her husband also changed his name to "Fahnbulleh." Most of her friends, students, and colleagues, however, simply called her "Madame."

Fatima Massaquoi-Fahnbulleh lived her life until the day she died with a single regret, that her autobiography relating her experiences and observations in her early life was left unpublished. Five years before her death, in 1973, she suffered a stroke. At that time she was living in Monrovia, Liberia, along with her daughter, Vivian, and her son-in-law and two grandchildren. It was this decisive event that led Vivian to arrange through her mother's colleagues at the University of Liberia to have the autobiography microfilmed, with the thought in mind that this small step would ensure a measure of permanency and exposure for the monumental work.[7] By this time the manuscript totaling over 700 typewritten pages and over 203,000 words, was suffering the ill effects of the tropical environment. The title she gave to this work was "Bush to Boulevard: The Autobiography of a Vai Noblewoman." The original manuscript can no longer be traced, and it is thought to have perished in the Liberian Civil War, which lasted from 1989 to 1997. The editors here relied on the microfilm, viewed in both its positive and negative forms, which allowed us to read from very dark and very light pages.

The story of the genesis of the autobiography is an important part of the autobiography itself, as readers will see from one of the late chapters of the book. It was by no means a rosy experience or memory, but it did produce the felicity of this work. Fatima Massaquoi's first attempt to write about her life began in 1939, in a social psychology course at Fisk University taught by Chinese scholar Dr. Bingham Dai, who assigned the work as a class project. She was encouraged to continue with her writing, subsequently working with Fisk professor Mark Hanna Watkins, who at the time she was assisting with linguistic studies. However, for most of the time, their relationship limped through a dramatic clash over broken promises but perhaps more crucially, over issues of "intellectual property." In 1943, Watkins who had never been to Liberia or any part of Africa, published an article on the exclusive male society of the Vai, drawing his information from Massaquoi's autobiography and private letters exchanged between her and her brother, Siaka.[8] While Watkins later claimed that he had received full authorization from Massaquoi as an "informant," and had even purchased the letters from her, she maintained that the first she knew of the publication was when a friend brought it to her attention, and that she never would have agreed to sell her family letters to Watkins. According to Massaquoi, the relationship was finally severed when she perceived that Watkins intended to publish her autobiography, which he was reading and editing, under his own name. This resulted from a published report, in another journal later that year, which included the title of Massaquoi's book with only Watkins name attached to it.[9]

Massaquoi took up the complaints she had with Fisk authorities, beginning first with several of her professors, and eventually with the Fisk president and even the Fisk Board of Trustees. On the verge of financial destitution and fearing that the Fisk authorities would get her deported, she sought legal representation on the matter, only to be denied help by one lawyer after another once they learned who the high-powered Fisk individuals involved in the dispute were. Finally, she met a sympathetic lawyer who would argue on her behalf, local civic and political leader Coyness L. Ennix, known for his flamboyant style and cigar smoking. With his help, no lawsuit became necessary.

As Massaquoi left Nashville for Boston, she was awarded a master's degree for a thesis on "Nationalist Movements in West Africa" (a thesis topic she proposed but never wrote). More important, perhaps, was the satisfaction of repossessing all her original autobiographical writings. Watkins retained the material he had gathered from Massaquoi for a Vai dictionary, along with several Vai stories and songs he had recorded from her. He also retained a short and incomplete version of Fatima Massaquoi's autobiographical account, dealing with the early period of her life in Africa, written in his own hand on the reverse sides of used examination booklets, infused with his own edits and notes.[10]

Fatima Massaquoi clearly rejected her characterization as a passive informant in her collaboration with Watkins, as she had for years worked with leading German scholars—including August Klingenheben, Diedrich Westermann, and Ernst Damann—on scientific studies of the Vai language and even taught the language for five semesters at the Seminar für Afrikanische Sprachen at the University of Hamburg at the invitation of the renowned professor Carl Meinhof. Indeed, she went on to publish a number of items relating to Vai language and culture[11] as well as teach in the field, and her obituary credits Watkins only with having *assisted her* in compiling a Vai dictionary, which was a "marvelous achievement."[12]

With the help of longtime family friend, the internationally acclaimed musician Roland Hayes, Fatima Massaquoi moved to Boston to begin course work toward her PhD. While at Boston, the Fisk misadventure continued to haunt her, as the issue of her autobiography consumed and frustrated her greatly. Without completing her degree at Boston University, she accepted a professorship in Natural History and Foreign Languages at Liberia College in 1946, which became the University of Liberia in 1951. For the first time since 1922, Fatima returned to her home and to her family.

Massaquoi's daughter, Vivian Seton, also known as "Püppchen," is today the primary Massaquoi family conservator. Vivian inherited from her mother a wealth of personal artifacts belonging to her grandfather Momolu Massaquoi, which Fatima acquired directly from him or from his late wife Rachel Johnson (Ma Sedia). Included in this collection are some of Momolu Massaquoi's writings and letters to prominent individuals, as well as diplomas and clothing (including his often-photographed diplomatic uniform worn in Germany). These items, along with Fatima Massaquoi's own library, diaries, and other belongings, are safely housed by Seton in the United States.

Perhaps the most important part of this rather vast treasure is the collection of hundreds of black-and-white photographs—many of them taken professionally in studios—of various members of the Massaquoi family in Liberia, Sierra Leone, Germany, Switzerland, and the United States. Most of these photos have never been viewed publicly. They include family photos, as well as those of prominent individuals—royalty, presidents, well-known academics, politicians, and entertainers. The photos contain rare shots of Africans in Germany and a rare gem of Marcus Garvey's lieutenants being entertained at the Massaquoi dinner table in Hamburg. A glimpse of these important historical photographs was offered in Hans Massaquoi's *Destined to Witness*. Several of the photographs from this collection were reproduced, including the portrait of Momolu Massaquoi wearing the crown of the Gallinas and the evocative cover photo of Hans as a young schoolboy wearing a swastika on his chest, which are all of great historical interest.

The publication of this book brings closure to a dream that went unfulfilled, until now that is, which was Fatima Massaquoi's desire to see her story brought to the world. It also brings closure for another woman, her daughter, Vivian, who promised her mother that one day she would make that dream a reality. The project might perhaps never have been realized if not for the urging of Konrad Tuchscherer, who over the years has engaged in field research on the Massaquoi family in the Gallinas, the Sierra Leone section of the Vai, which straddles the modern Sierra Leone-Liberia border, where members of the Massaquoi family still live and the history of the Massaquoi crown is still very much remembered. In the course of his research on the indigenous Vai and

Mende scripts, he visited the birthplace of Princess Fatima Massaquoi and traveled the roads that she once walked. For many years he has felt that Princess Fatima Massaquoi's autobiography provided vivid insider accounts of Africa as well as a unique narrative of experience outside the continent, and his diligence made this project possible.

Finally, it was the hard work and timely involvement of Arthur Abraham, the leading historian of Sierra Leone that ultimately made the completion of this book possible. Abraham, in his fieldwork and archival research over the last 30 years, had examined the life and career of Fatima's father, Momolu Massaquoi, and published about him. He brought his great insights and expertise to the project. At a time when the project was languishing, Abraham generated the steam to push the project through to its final realization. His relentless efforts to restructure the manuscript to meet the publisher's requirement, without losing any substance, gave consistency and better structure to the narrative by reorganizing material to align with chapter themes, even sometimes changing chapter titles to better reflect the chapter content, etcetera.

It is a sanguine note on which to conclude that nearly 70 years after the completion of her autobiography, Princess Fatima Massaquoi's story finally enters the public domain, which thus fulfills her dying wish.

Notes

1. Momolu Massaquoi, "The Vai People and Their Syllabic Writing," *Journal of the African Society*, Vol. 10 (1911), p. 466.
2. For a discussion of Fatima Massaquoi's year of birth, see p. 13, note 18 below.
3. For short biographies of her later career, see: Mary Antoinette Brown-Sherman, "Profile of a Fallen Daughter," *Palm*, Vol. 9, Nos. 5–6 (1979), pp. 33–35; Raymond J. Smyke, "Fatima Massaquoi Fahnbulleh (1912–1978): Pioneer Woman Educator," *Liberian Studies Journal*, Vol. 15, No. 1 (1990), pp. 48–73. Massaquoi's former students have often drawn attention to her influence on their lives and careers—see, for example, the interview with Liberian ambassador Rachel Gbenyon-Diggs in Marilyn Séphocle, *Then, They Were Twelve: The Women of Washington's Embassy Row* (Westport, CT: Praeger, 2000), p. 93.
4. Hans Massaquoi, *Destined to Witness: Growing Up Black in Nazi Germany* (New York: HarperCollins, 1999) and *Neger, Neger, Schornstein!: meine Kindheit in Deutschland* (Bern: Scherz, 1999). In the English version, see pp. 60–63 for a description of Fatima Massaquoi.
5. For a full treatment of Momolu Massaquoi's return to Liberia and his subsequent bid for the presidency and the backlash, see Raymond J. Smyke, "Massaquoi of Liberia: 1870–1938," *Genève-Afrique*, Vol. 21, No. 1 (1983), pp. 73–105.

6. See Adam Jones, *From Slaves to Palm Kernels: A History of the Galinhas Country (West Africa) 1730–1890* (Wiesbaden: Franz Steiner Verlag, 1983), pp. 56–61 on King Siaka and p. 117 for King Siaka's family tree. For King Siaka's relationship with the Amistad captives, see Marcus Rediker, *The Amistad Rebellion* (New York: Viking, 2012). See also Arthur Abraham, *Mende Government and Politics under Colonial Rule* (Freetown: Sierra Leone University Press, and London: Oxford University Press, 1978) and *The Amistad Revolt* (Freetown: USIS, 1987).

7. "Writings and Papers of Fatima Massaquoi-Fahnbulleh, Institute of African Studies, University of Liberia, Monrovia, Liberia" (Bedford, NY: African Imprint Services, 1973).

8. Mark Hanna Watkins, "The West African 'Bush' School," *American Journal of Sociology*, Vol. 48, No. 6 (May 1943), pp. 666–675. Massaquoi's complaints to Fisk authorities that Watkins had drawn from her autobiographical notes and letters without permission were never pursued once she left Fisk. The article would prove to be the most influential of Watkins's career, subsequently reprinted three times: Charles S. Johnson, ed., *Education and the Cultural Process* (Chicago: University of Chicago Press, 1943), pp. 38–47; Solon T. Kimball, ed., *Readings in the Science of Human Relations* (Tuscaloosa: University of Alabama Press, 1950), Vol. 2, pp. 451–460; and George Spindler, ed., *Education and Culture: Anthropological Approaches* (New York: Holt, Rinehart and Winston, 1963), pp. 420–443.

9. "Official Reports and Proceedings," *American Sociological Review*, Vol. 8, No. 4 (1943), p. 67.

10. The title of this appears as "Morning Beam: The Autobiography of a Vai Noblewoman: The Education of an African Girl in Three Cultures." An attached note reads: "written by Fatama Beendu Sandemanni (1911/12–), daughter of Momolu Massaquoi, a Vai and Liberian statesman, and Massa Mbaalo, a Mende; written as a project for a class in Anthropology taken under Charles S. Johnson, in which the students wrote an autobiography." This material is held in the Charles S. Johnson Collection, Special Collections, Fisk University, Nashville, TN (but the reference to Johnson is incorrect, the professor was Bingham Dai, and the course was "social psychology"). The linguistic material collected by Watkins from Massaquoi, including sound recordings, are held in the Archives of Traditional Music at Indiana University. Without Massaquoi's further assistance, Watkins was never able to publish any of his research on Vai.

11. Fatima Massaquoi-Fahnbulleh, "The Seminar on the Standardization of the Vai script," *University of Liberia Journal*, Vol 3, No. 1 (1963), pp. 15–37; Fatima Massaquoi-Fahnbulleh, *Fatu's Experiences* (New York: Frederick Fell, 1953); Fatima Massaquoi-Fahnbulleh, *The Leopard's Daughter* (Boston: Bruce Humphries Publishers, 1961).

12. Mary Antoinette Brown-Sherman, "Profile of a Fallen Daughter," *Palm*, Vol. 9, Nos. 5–6 (1979), p. 34. A reference to the Vai dictionary, without Watkins name attached to it, appears in "State College Gets New Professor," *The Weekly Mirror* (Monrovia), Vol. 17, No. 42 (October 25, 1946), p. 1.

CHAPTER 1

MY BIRTHPLACE, ETHNICITY, AND PARENTS

I t was in Gendema, then the capital city of the Gallinas, that I first saw the light of the world. The Gallinas is a territory inhabited by the Vai people, who occupy territories in southeastern Sierra Leone and western Liberia (see figure 1.1). The term Gallinas, which applies only to that portion of the Vai country that is situated in Sierra Leone today, is derived from the Portuguese word *gallinha* (hen), and the name was probably given to the territory because of the great number of guinea fowl found there by Portuguese sailors.[1] The original inhabitants of the country themselves call this territory Massaquoi, and this name was chosen because a member of the Massaquoi family played the most important role in its founding, and a Massaquoi has sat on the throne of the country since its foundation. Another name by which it is known is Jayaloɔ (Jayaloh), a contraction of Jayalɔlɔ which means Jaya's country, after one of the kings.

According to Vai traditions of origin,[2] there lived a great king in the Mande land whose name was Kamala,[3] nicknamed Jomanni, who was very adventurous and enterprising, always looking for new places to conquer. It happened that one day a group of the king's special hunters, who had made their way deep into the forest after traveling several years, heard a great roaring noise, to investigate which they climbed up to the top of a mountain. They discovered that from this summit they could see a great distance over the surrounding area. In one direction they saw a large body of water so expansive that there was no visible land beyond it. They hastened to return to their homeland to tell King Kamala that they had seen the "end of the world." Thereupon the king sent them back with more hunters to obtain more information concerning what they had seen. The spot on which the hunters stood when they beheld the ocean they called Koiji (salt water), where grew a town by the same name and even to this day is in existence.

The people with whom the hunters came in contact were the Gola people,[4] who lived near that body of water and scraped salt from the rocks that had been left there by the ocean. With these Gola, the hunters exchanged some dried meat for salt and departed. When the hunters had reported all that had happened on their journey, the great Mande king Kamala assembled all of his people and asked the hunters to narrate their experiences. Then the leader of the hunters stood upright and recalled

Figure 1.1   Map of Vai country

their fights with crocodiles, leopards, and other animals, in which many of them died, leaving only seven to return to the Mande country.

Perceiving fear in the eyes and faces of his people, King Kamala immediately asked: "Who is going to open the road leading to sundown (the west)?" But no one spoke. Then, Kamala the Younger looked in the direction of his father and seeing that his father wanted him to do one great deed that would show that it was he, indeed, who had begotten him (for with the Vai the children of great people are known by their deeds), stood up and said: "Father, I am going to lead the way to the shores of the great water to the west."

Thereupon rose the sons and nephews of the other Mande kings, eleven in all, and they spoke one by one: "We are also prepared to follow Kamala the Younger in opening the way to the ocean." Then Kamala the Great ordered: "Let the head of each country [territorial division] supply ten cavalries equipped to carry provisions for the trip. Each cavalry must consist of twenty-five warriors." The outfit of Kamala the Younger consisted of 3 cavalries with 50 horses. There were in all 13 regiments, making a total of 316 warriors with 140 horses.

On the following day at dawn they assembled all the horses, provisions, and equipment for the trip. Then Kamala the Great took his *banjalo* (warrior sword) and a big spear and gave them to his son saying, "if in truth it is I who begot thee, then go straight to the shores of the great body of water in the west allowing nothing to stop you or cause you to turn back until you have reached your destination." He turned to his nephew and said, "You are going to be the leader of these people. Stand at the head of all these warriors and lead them until you have reached the ocean." And his nephew accepted the challenge, or, as the Vai say "laid his hands under them."

The Mande people departed in two batches; the first comprising one regiment with ten horses and their riders left on the first day including Kamala and his cousin. Their journey led them into a great forest called Kambo. If one stood at its foot and looked up, one would gain the impression that the mountain extended all the way to the skies. On that mountain lived all kinds of fierce animals that fought the traveling Mande, and many of the people perished in the struggle. Besides, the paths in that forest were very narrow, and the hunters knew only one path. Consequently, the travelers became greatly disturbed and said to Kamala: "We cannot enter deeper into this forest. We are not willing to die in such a wicked manner. Therefore we are going to sit at what seems to be the entrance to this dense forest and find another way to the west. Whichever side of the mountain we find to traverse we shall pass by that way."

There they stopped, at the foot of the mountain, where they built a big town. They spent four years there, during which time other Mande men and women, apart from the warriors, joined them. It was during that period that children were born to them by the women who had come there. The people living not far from the foot of the mountain had also given them wives, who also bore them children. When the feet of those children became strong and able to carry little things, the group left that town to continue their journey.

During all this time Kamala the Great had heard nothing of his son, so he sent people in search of his son saying, "Go in search of my son, and when you hear of him, please return and clear my head (i.e., let me know); go straight to him before returning to me." Those messengers traveled long and far before they reached Kamala the Younger. They spoke to him saying, "Your father Jomanni is worrying very much about you because he has heard no news of you." When the traveling comrades of Kamala saw the messengers, some of them wanted to return to the Mande country. But Kamala the Younger told them that he could never return to the Mande country before reaching the sea. Then he turned to the messengers and said, "Return and tell my father that on the fourth day of the new moon, I shall enter the forest. If God be willing I shall see the ocean before returning to the Mande country." Then he assembled all of his people and told them that he would be departing when the new moon appeared. They all showed great fear, but Kamala paid no attention.

On the fourth day the new moon arose, Kamala's herald announced to all that they would depart the following day. Then Kamala called all the heads of the various countries together and asked them: "Who is going with me into the forest tomorrow?" Whereupon, his brother Ngolo, who had followed him, and his cousin, who had been entrusted with leading the armed men, stood up and said that they would continue to follow him. But the other heads said that they were afraid and could not go if they were to enter the dense forest.

Kamala felt hurt, but he said nothing. Hastily he mounted his white horse, and before leaving, turned to his comrades and said: *won kono mbe taala fai* (wait here for me; I shall go forward). Turning his back on them he made his way into the forest. Those who remained became the *Kono moenu* (waiters), and those who advanced became the *Fai moenu* or *Vai moenu* (the forward goers). Thus originated the names for the Kono and the Vai peoples, who to this day remain separate ethnicities.[5]

There were several adventures with wild beasts in the forest, Kamala himself reportedly slaying thirteen leopards while his younger brother earned the sobriquet Fangaloma because he was stronger than a chimpanzee. The valor of Kamala's spear-bearer also earned him the name Kiyatamba. When they came out of the forest, Kamala changed his bearing and did not continue in the direction of Koiji.

On their arrival at the coast, the inhabitants of the country appeared intimidated, for they had never before seen so many people coming out of the forest at one time. The rulers then asked of Kamala, "Have you come to declare war on us or have you come to trade?" Kamala replied, "I have not come to declare war, nor have I come to trade or to seek anything whatsoever. I have come to see the ocean." The kings of the land thereupon accepted Kamala (i.e., they put their hands under him) saying, "Then this land has nothing evil for you." The kings then gave them guest houses and had food prepared for them.

While talking to the kings of the land, Kamala heard the roaring noise and surmised that someone was bringing war upon him. He quickly instructed his spear-bearer to get all the warriors to follow him, leaving the rest behind. As he mounted his white horse, Fangaloma and Kiyatamba and their officers all followed him. They traveled a day and a half before reaching the ocean. At the moment just before the sun stood directly over their heads, Kamala's horse ran straight into the ocean. Since Kamala was still sitting on that horse, it turned back to the shore. It repeated this action seven times. So did the other horses which had been following. Then Kamala threw up his spear and planted it in the ocean sand, shouting "*kalalase…kalalase*" (the spear has reached). Kamala had reached the object of his journey. The Mande people built their first town where Kamala thrust his spear. That town remains to this day and the Vai people still call it Kaase, a contraction of the Mande *kalalase*.

Kamala himself remained in Kaase and sent for his carriers and bearers of burden baskets. As soon as they arrived, they went to the lakes. It was at that same time that he crossed the Kee and Kpaale rivers and reached the spot where his father's original messengers founded the town of Koiji, which still exists in the Gbema section of the Vai country.

After sometime in Gbema country, he crossed the Gbeya river, known today as the Mano river, where he met people who honored him by giving him all kinds of animals, wives, and a place to live in. This place was called Telebo (sunrise) by our father Kamala, because he himself had come from the place where the sun rose. It is from this town that the entire Teewoh country (morphed from Telebo by locals) received its name. The Teewoh country is situated exactly between the Gbema (Gbeya) and Mafa rivers.

Kamala's younger brother Ngolo, who acquired the name Fangaloma, settled in Teewoh, and he and Kamala founded the town of Gbese in that country. Gbese then became the capital of the Teewoh and the seat of the Fangalomas, who later became the Fahnbullehs, for Fangaloma's nephew, was Fahnbulleh, the very first of the Fahnbullehs. Our fathers have told us that Kiyatamba also settled in Teewoh. Many of the Mande people first settled in Teewoh, but many of them left and spread through-out the rest of what is known today as the Vai country. The other countries[6] that they first settled in were Gawula, Tombe, and Mofe.

Kamala's own son remained in Kaase until he founded Jayaloh. His descendants became the Massaquois, because when his horse first reached the ocean, his herald cried out, *mansa mu i la goi, mansa mu i la goi* (you are a great leader, yea, a great leader). From this has derived the present form, Massaquoi.[7]

The Massaquois became kings of Jayaloh, which expanded westward as far as Fuendu wu, and is variously known as Jayaloh, Massaquoi, the Gallinas, even Jaiahun in British colonial records.[8] It is situated between the Mabesi Lake and Vinja and the Kpaale (Moa) rivers. The territories that exclusively belong to the Vai country are the following: Jayaloh, at first ruled by the Massaquois alone, but following a split later in the Massaquoi family, became divided into two kingdoms or families, Massaquoi and Kpaka; Peli Sowolo, ruled by the Jadoibes; Gbema and Teewoh, ruled by the Fahnbullehs; Sombo Daa, Gola and the Daseni Konee, and Gawula governed, respectively, by the Kiya Solus, the Kiya Howo, and the Mofes.

All of these countries were family kingdoms. When the leader of one of these kingdoms became stronger than the rest of his colleagues, he would be elected head of the combined kingdoms. Thus the strongest of the kings became king of the whole of the Vai country, a position frequently held by the Massaquoi family.

Since the days of Kamala, the route between the coast and the Mande country has been through Gonwolonama, Gonwolo, Jondu, Bopolu, and finally Musadugu, which is the beginning of the Mande country. Important metropolises grew in Vai country. Gendema is capital of Jayaloh.[9] Failoh[10] and Maalema are the capitals of the Sowolo[11] country. Ngalinga is the capital of the Gbema country. Gbese is the capital of Teewoh, while the capitals of Gawula are Gonwolonamalo and Jondu. Finally, the Tombe country has Mande and Towoso as capitals.[12]

From the time of the coming of the Mande to the present day, some 600 to 800 years are estimated to have gone by. This number my people have estimated by the redwood, the *kpato*, and the cotton trees. These trees are planted for the purpose of determining centuries, since their branches die at fairly regular intervals.[13] The trip from the Mande country to the coast must have taken place before the year 1200 AD. This assumption is based partly on the fact that those who came could not have already been acquainted with Islam, otherwise they would have given some of the towns and countries they founded Islamic names, since they have the habit of basing events on phenomena with which they are acquainted.[14] Vai is one of the few languages of Africa with its own indigenous writing system. The Vai script was invented by Dualo Bukele, a spiritual chief of the nation, and completed and compiled by my father between 1911 and 1926. It is a syllabic script capable of representing objects as well as words in almost any language. Each syllable of a word is represented by a symbol.[15]

The foregoing is one of several legends that the Vai tell of their origin. No claim is made here that it is the authentic one. I myself happen to know two others, one of which is very similar to the one I have given, and the other resembles it in several aspects. These legends were told to me in childhood, first by my father's oldest sister, Mother Jassa Kpaakpaa of Njagbacca, later by my uncle, Dr. Lamini Massaquoi, at one time physician at the government hospital in Monrovia, Liberia, and a little prior to that medical advisor and teacher at the Muhlen-Mission in Liberia, which is under the auspices of the Lutheran Church of America. When I visited Uncle Lamini's home he would always quench my thirst for stories. A very old man in Jondu, whose name was Boakai, also told me the story. Finally, my father and brothers related to me the narratives. Aside from these, the story is contained among those recorded by Herr Professor Dr. Klingenheben[16] of Hamburg University, whose sources were my brothers and father.[17]

At the time of my birth, my father, Momolu IV, wore the Gallinas Crown.[18] My grandfather was King Al-Haj or Lahai. His wife, my grandmother, was Queen Sandimanni, a name she acquired on account of the great things she did for the *Sande* society.[19] Of her valor, the late Honorable G. W. Ellis, secretary to the American Legation in Liberia had this to say:

> Taradoba was the favorite wife of King Arma, who died from a wound received in battle. The Capitol of his kingdom was at Bendoo. King Arma had a very ambitious brother who was king over a large number of people northwest of the Vai country, and upon the death of the former he usurped his throne and made himself king over the Vais. Taradoba with five or six hundred warriors of her dead husband took possession of a southern province. By the new king of the Vais three attempts were made to subdue her, but she successfully repelled each invasion. It is said that she commanded her troops in person, distinguishing herself with such valor and success that one might fittingly refer to her as the Jeanne d'Arc of the Vais. She ruled for many years, and her son, Momolu Massaquoi, educated at Central Tennessee College, is now king over the Gallinas.[20]

The neighbors of the Vai, the Gola, gave her the nickname of Taradogba (Taladogba), which means "brave" in their language. Grandmother Famata (Fatima Sandimanni) is said to have learned the art of warfare from her own father. Many of the elders of the tribe, whom it was my good fortune to meet, were delighted to relate what pleasure they had in the bravery and ability in the art of warfare that she demonstrated.

She fought many wars, some say eight altogether. Her youngest son, my father, was born on a battlefield at a place called Kpassalo, which Büttikofer writes as "Passawo."[21] The town is thus named because of this event, since *kpa* means mark, trace, spur, and *lo* means inside. It is unusual for a woman to have a baby on a battlefield when she herself is fighting and leading her army. Legends about her are widely told in the Vai country. One contribution that grandmother made to the Republic of Liberia as a whole was (according to my father's accounts) the introduction of the tax system, which the Liberian government later adopted and uses even to this day for the taxation of the native elements of the population.

My paternal grandfather King Al-Haj or Lahai, was grandmother's junior in age. She was his first wife, and he, her third husband. It is said that grandmother never followed him to the Gallinas where he lived, because her duties were to administer the Liberian side of the Vai country, and, he, the Gallinas country. She respected and admired his art of warfare so much that she married him. Grandfather Lahai was the son of King Jaya (spelled also as Jaia and Jaiah) of the Gallinas and grandson of King Siaka (also spelled Ciaka), whose fame is still legendary in the Gallinas.[22]

My father, Momolu IV, as he is popularly known in the Vai country, was the first of my grandfather's, and the youngest of my grandmother's, children. The positions of my grandfather and grandmother thus made my father the inheritor of two thrones, that on the Liberian side of the Vai country as well as the Gallinas. Both grandparents, therefore, were desirous of giving my father a fitting education. Since the vast majority of Vai people are Muslims, one can easily understand their disinclination toward seeing him receive a Christian training. Grandmother herself had taught my father the Koran as well as the Vai script.[23] Her intention was later to train him in the art of commerce and warfare that he would need to govern his people.

Fate, however, has a way of interfering with plans of parents for their children. As my father narrated to me, Bishop Penick[24] of the Protestant Episcopal Church of America was appointed bishop of Liberia, and in soliciting the aid of African monarchs for his work in Africa, he and Mrs. Penick visited grandmother. Both father and the Penicks immediately loved each other. Mrs. Penick brought some candy to Njagbacca, where grandmother was living, and gave father one or two pieces every day. Father enjoyed being on hand every morning to receive this precious gift from his new foreign friend.

Thus, when the bishop and his wife left, he missed them greatly, but even greater was his curiosity to know where this beautiful woman lived and where she acquired the sweets from. So, on subsequent visits, father, still not being able to persuade his mother to let him go to the mission in Cape Mount, simply ran off. He was between eight and ten years of age when he entered St. John's school. Thus was the beginning of the bishop's ambition to "save the boy's soul." One missionary gave this account:

> An important feature of missionary work in Africa is the influence of Christian schools on African royalty....A few influential African monarchs have been converted to the Christian life; but thousands of their sons have become Christians through the Church school...One of these, Momolu Massaquoi, comes from a line of powerful African rulers. His father was Prince Lahai, son of the great King Jiah. His mother was Queen Sandimani. As is customary among the Vai nobility, Massaquoi's parents spared no pains to prepare him for an influential position. At the age of six he began the study of Arabic as well his own Vai language. When, at the age of ten, he entered St. John's School, Cape Mount, he could read and write his own tribal language and was fairly well grounded in the Koran.[25]

During the time father was at St. John's School in Cape Mount, he proved so diligent that Bishop Penick made special arrangements for his further studies in America. But grandmother opposed these plans. She then took him to Monrovia, to live with a highly respected and cultured Americo-Liberian family,[26] and to attend Liberia College. As Liberia College at that time did not accept children of indigenous parentage, the family made father work as a house servant, in spite of the fact that grandmother from time to time brought such goods as rice, ivory, palm oil, chicken, cattle, etcetera. My aunt Jassa, grandmother's oldest daughter, often told me how utterly shocked they were when they visited Monrovia once and found father in rags among pots and casseroles in the kitchen. This story is not being narrated out of prejudice as many children from the indigenous population have lived in and been brought up by Americo-Liberian families with excellent results. Grandmother, however, took father home. But he did not remain with her for long as he ran away a second time. On finding out he was leaving for America (in 1892) she told him that he would never see her again, and he never did. But while he was in America, she still contributed to his support by sending him ivory and other commodities, which he converted into money.

In America, father first attended schools in Boston and New York. But he was desirous of becoming better acquainted with Negro America, and Bishop Penick assisted him in entering the then Central Tennessee College, which later became Walden University. It was under the North American Methodist Mission Board.

He traveled widely, from Canada to the Pacific Coast, lecturing about Africa. Some of these tours were with Dr. Hubbard, who was at the time soliciting funds for the Meharry Medical College.[27] He told me several times how much time he spent in Dr. Hubbard's home in Ohio. Father also lectured under the auspices of the Episcopal Board. He was chosen in 1893 to give the opening address at the World Exhibition held at Chicago under the auspices of the Congress of African Ethnology, choosing as his topic "The Evangelization of Africa." This address was so well received that it opened possibilities for further study. For example, he was offered a scholarship to attend Oxford University by an English clergyman who heard him. He later took the opportunity, studied for a while at Oxford and London, and toured through Europe.

Shortly before the beginning of the year in which father was to complete his studies at Central Tennessee College, the situation in Liberia called for his return to Africa. The *Sofa* war[28] came to his mother's territory, and accompanying her army, she was mortally wounded. Momolu felt he could reach home in time to defend his homeland, and so left abruptly before graduation only to discover on arrival that his mother had died and the territory had been devastated. He did not take over rulership of the territory immediately, but preferred to take over his old school, St. John's, at Grand Cape Mount as principal. He was the first African to hold that position, and he stayed there for six years. During that time, he tried in vain to contact his American girlfriend Maude, believing he needed her assistance to advance Western culture in ruling his people.[29]

While at Cape Mount, father wrote many articles about the school, how the surrounding communities saw it, and what the school was capable of doing for the Vai nation in general. Here is a typical quotation of the progress made in those days:

In 1877 there were not five men in the Vai territory who spoke decent English; to-day hundreds of young men and women express themselves well in that language. In that year there was not a single man who could read the Roman character; to-day nearly all business letters, petitions and other diplomatic documents from Vai Kings and merchants are written by Vai boys and girls in civilized language. In 1877 there was not a single Christian among us; to-day we have hundreds in the fold of Christ.[30]

It was at Cape Mount that father conceived of plans for better roads, industrial schools, etc., for the interior of the nation. The untimely death of grandfather Lahai, however, ended father's career as teacher, principal, and missionary, for the affairs of the Gallinas fell upon his shoulders.[31] (Thus, after six years at the school, he took the Gallinas Crown in

Sierra Leone in about 1903. But his efforts to reclaim all the traditional Vai state the British had fragmented led to a serious rift, resulting in the British removing him in 1906. He returned to Liberia and for the next 25 years, held several important government portfolios).

Because African social customs and organization are very different from those of the West, it is possible for a man to inherit a wife, and in some circumstances the relationship will be purely social. Besides, all the wives of a person's father are "mothers." Thus, my father's wives, (my mothers) are and were, in chronological order: Mother Soko Sando, Mother Zoe, Mother Yaawaa, Mother Massaa Barlo, and Mother Beendu. My biological mother was Massaa Barlo.

Mother Massaa was the daughter of the chiefs of the Bali district.³² Maternally, her mother's home is in Dia on the Liberian side of the Vai country, making her a Vai on her maternal side. Grandmother Jassa, my mother's mother, is supposed to be maternally a Gola, and on her paternal side a Vai. Grandfather Barlo was from Bandajuma. I do not know much about my maternal relatives because I left them when I was quite young, but I shall discuss my contact with them in a following chapter. The fact that a child belongs to the patriarchal line has hindered me from discovering much about my maternal family and from being able to write about them with very much accuracy as I can about the Massaquois.

I don't know when my mother was born or the date of her marriage to my father. But she and her older brother, Mbimba, now in Pujehun, were born in the Bali District of Sierra Leone. Both were children and Mother Massaa had not joined the *Sande* during the time of the *Gulu Gutu* War (the Hut Tax Rebellion in Sierra Leone) in 1898. The above reference is made only because we Africans do not as a rule keep records, but approximate dates by the association of events. Mother Massaa and Uncle Mbimba, then, were old enough children during this period that when the war came to their section, they were able to flee with the women into the forest without being carried, while the men did the fighting.³³

My mother spoke both Mende and Vai and she could also read and write the Vai script. As a Muslim, she also knew Arabic. She had joined the *Sande* women's society because it was the traditional school for girls to receive training that would prepare them for the responsibilities of African womanhood and for motherhood.

Notes

1. For a brief history of the Gallinas country: see S. M. Despicht, "A Short History of the Gallinas Chiefdoms," *Sierra Leone Studies*, Vol. 21 (January 1939), pp. 5–13. [Also Adam Jones, *From Slaves to Palm Kernels: A History of*

the *Galinhas Country (West Africa) 1730–1890* (Wiesbaden: Franz Steiner Verlag, 1983). *Eds.*]

2. [A part of the "Mande Diaspora," in which interior Manding peoples moved coastward, via trade and warfare; known alternatively as "Mani Invasions." *Eds.*]

3. [Anglicized to "Kamara the Great." *Eds.*]

4. [A West-Atlantic, Mel-speaking people, who were the indigenous inhabitants of the region prior to the arrival of the Vai. *Eds.*]

5. [The Kono people are today found primarily in neighboring Sierra Leone and they tell a similar story about how they "waited" while their brothers (later, Vai) ventured to the coast in search of salt. Linguistically, the Kono and Vai languages are "a dialect pair" that are mutually intelligible. *Eds.*]

6. [Traditionally, a country is a distinct territorial unit of a larger ethnolinguistic space. Today, following colonial practice, they are called chiefdoms. But they still translate from the local languages as countries. *Eds.*]

7. [Another tradition relates that on reaching the sea, one of the followers shouted in excitement *"Mansa, koi!"* meaning, "King, behold the sea." *Eds.*]

8. [*Massaquoi* later became the title for the Vai kings of the Gallinas. *Eds.*]

9. Since about 1917, the capital was moved further inland to Blama Massaquoi, which is about 15 miles inland.

10. [Today Anglicized to Fairo. *Eds.*]

11. [Today Anglicized to Soro. *Eds.*]

12. If any important names of families and cities have been omitted in this connection, it is not done intentionally. It is hoped here also that any Vai person reading this and not finding his or her family name and capital city mentioned will pardon me, as it is impossible to give in this narrative all the names and towns in detail. I personally still consider them a part of the unit of the Vai people and would never intentionally leave out any of them, for we are all one. The difficulty, however, is that it is impossible for one person to retain too much data without a written document. Besides, there is no one on this side of the globe who can be used as a source for supplementary names and data. I have therefore contented myself with such materials that I am measurably certain of.

13. I have this assumption and reasoning from my late father, who was partially responsible for my becoming acquainted with the story, and since he was considered an authority on Vai life and culture, I have thought it necessary to use his impression.

14. [Although there have been several estimates of the time of Vai arrival on the coast, it is now generally accepted by historians of the Upper Guinea Coast that the Vai were already settled on the coast before the mid-fifteenth century, before the first European adventurers reached there. *Eds.*]

15. [For information on the Vai script and Momolu Massaquoi's relationship to it, see chapter 5, endnote 13. *Eds.*]

16. [Klingenheben was a well-known Africanist scholar and close family friend of the Massaquois. *Eds.*]
17. The above-mentioned persons varied very little in relating details of the story. That is probably why I remember it almost literally.
18. [A missionary report says Fatima was born about 1911 or 1912, but this is unlikely as Momolu was a Liberian government official at that time. He ruled Gallinas from about 1902/3 to 1906 when he fell out with the British colonial administration in Sierra Leone and was forced from the throne. He then crossed into Liberia and for the next quarter of a century held important government positions. If Fatima was born when Momolu was ruler of Gallinas, and if she was about two years old when her father sent her away because of the problems he was having with the British colonial administration, then the more likely year of her birth is ca. 1904. A point repeatedly raised by Fatima Massaquoi throughout her narrative is her uncertainty concerning her birth date. *Eds.*]
19. *Sande* will be discussed at length in another connection.
20. G. W. Ellis, *Negro Culture in West Africa* (New York: Neale Publ. Co, 1914), p. 74.
21. [Johan Büttikofer, *Reisebilder Aus Liberia* (Leiden: E. J. Brill, 1890). *Eds.*]
22. [King Siaka, the most famous Vai king, consolidated the Vai state in the early nineteenth century, a task continued admirably by his son, Mana. Jaya was Mana's brother, but he was old and blind when he inherited the throne. He proved to be weak and effete, which provided ample opportunity to fuel political rivalries. Momolu Massaquoi's attempt to reassert the old power of the Vai state led to serious friction with the British colonial administration and his subsequent deposition in 1906. See A. Abraham, *Mende Government and Politics Under Colonial Rule* (Freetown: Sierra Leone University Press, and London: Oxford University Press, 1978); Jones, *From Slaves to Palm Kernels. Eds.*]
23. [The Vai script is today primarily a male prerogative, and it is uncommon for a woman to write the script. However, the script has at times appeared in connection with the female initiation society, with inscriptions on society masks. *Eds.*]
24. [Charles Clifton Penick (1843–1914) was the third missionary bishop of Cape Palmas and Parts Adjacent from 1877 to 1883. *Eds.*]
25. Walter H. Overs, "Momolu Massaquoi: An African Prince," in *Sketches in Ebony and Ivory* (Hartford, CT: Church Missions Publishing Company, 1928), p. 8.
26. [The descendants of freed slaves from the United States who founded Liberia in 1822 under the auspices of the American Colonization Society are called Americo-Liberians. *Eds.*]
27. [George Whipple Hubbard (1841–1921), the founder and first president of Meharry Medical College. *Eds.*]
28. [The *sofa* were mounted warriors of the great Mandinka empire builder Samori Toure, who in the latter part of the nineteenth century created an empire from the Ivory Coast west to the Atlantic Ocean in Guinea. The French imperialists wanting the same territory fought him for seventeen

years with the collaboration of the British and he finally surrendered in 1898. *Eds.*]
29. Letter in care of Mrs. Maude P. Stewart, formerly Miss Mansfield, of Chicago, Illinois, to whom I am deeply indebted for letting me use it. [See also, C. O. Boring, "Massaquoi and the Republic of Liberia: An Echo of the Parliament of Religions," *The Open Court* No. 3 (March 1913), pp. 162–168. For a slightly garbled report of Massaquoi's return, see "Two African Monarchs Summoned Home from Their Studies in America," *The New York Sun* (July 29, 1894), p. 7. *Eds.*]
30. Momolu Massaquoi, "Africa's Appeal to Christendom," *Century Magazine* (April) 1905.
31. [The records show that Lahai died in 1890, and Lahai's "small father" (father's brother, i.e., "uncle" in Western culture), Momoh Fofi, Jaya's brother, ruled until about 1902 or 1903 after whom Momolu Massaquoi took the crown. *Eds.*]
32. [Present-day Bari Chiefdom, Pujehun District, Sierra Leone. *Eds.*]
33. [The Hut Tax War is known by several names in different parts of the country—Bai Bureh War in the north of Sierra Leone, after the warrior who led the resistance, and the *puu-goi* (white man's war) in southern Mende areas, etc. *Eds.*]

CHAPTER 2

MY BIRTH, AND CUSTOMS ABOUT CHILDBIRTH IN THE GALLINAS COUNTRY

Among the many things that have struck me while traveling and becoming acquainted with peoples of other cultures are the striking differences in values and perception of events occurring in the daily web of life. With regard to childbirth, I have observed that in the West, only two persons who are concerned when a child is expected, the husband and wife, whereas with my people, all of the community is concerned. While a woman in Western culture visits a doctor for physical and biological health reasons, in my culture a woman visits many kinds of specialists for a variety of reasons.

The naming of children is a reflection of the events happening during the period. A child is named after a particular event. The child very often represents the event itself. Phenomena such as lighting, thunderstorms, bad crops, and good crops, too much rain causing floods or too much sun and heat, all influence the life of the child in the thinking of my people. If a child is born during a great storm, then a very tremulous time for that particular community can be expected with the likelihood of the child being warlike or troublesome.

Dreams are also important, and people worry about their dreams and possible interpretations when children are expected, and in a general sense even for the group as a whole. I did not know much about this as I was quite young, but I have noticed that in many instances dreams in my culture have meanings just as in Western culture. Loss of teeth, like bleeding, means illness or death, while bleeding or blood in Western culture, I notice, sometimes means money. Flesh or meat of any kind denotes worry, trouble, or even illness or death. The snake means treachery and so on. Good dreams are those of abundant crops, fruit and fruit-bearing trees, and a clean house. Because there is such an abundance of dreams and meanings attached to them, there are professional dream interpreters.

As the Western woman consults a doctor, so does the Vai woman, but for different reasons. It is also not the same kind of a doctor who is consulted. In my culture, what the woman looks for, in case no illness of any kind accompanies her pregnancy, is whether or not she can expect a good *jinana* (ghost or spirit) or an evil one. But if she does not feel well, she visits a *boli-kai* (traditional healer or medicine man), who can be a woman, and who makes medicines from herbs.

The type of doctor consulted often depends on the religion of the parents. All of them consult a sand reader or sand cutter. He predicts what kind of "spirit" the mother is bearing. Expectant mothers also get anxious about the fate of the child since they want to know what the child will grow up to be—a great warrior, an important person, ruler, or so. The sex of the child is also told where for instance the parents have only had boys and want a girl, and also what to do so that it will be a girl. This is also done if the mother particularly wants a male child. The reader also sometimes states how and what name to give the child in accordance with what he sees. In some cases, a dead ancestor who was angry with the expectant mother or father might need to be reconciled, and the child represents that ancestor in every respect and is often then named after the dead relative. The question of the connection between the dead and the living is, in my opinion, definitely a part of the religion of my people, which Westerners call "ancestor worship."

There are of course other prognosticators who are consulted, such as the *wuju*, a magician who uses *juju* (magic), and the *mɔli-man*[1] or *mɔli-kai*, who is an Islamic priest. The magician prevents harm from coming to people and can perform mysteries, great deeds, and the like. Evil deeds sometimes, of course, are expected to be in his power. The magician and the mɔli-man have the power to conduct and carry on various forms of ordeals. They serve long apprenticeships to gain proper experience before they can practice on their own.

The mɔli-man typically writes passages from the Koran on a slate, which is washed off, and out of this, a *dasimɔ* (amulet) is made.[2] This amulet is worn wherever the evil is assumed to dwell, and wearing it will either prevent the evil from nearing the person, or will make it leave him or her. Those sharing the Islamic faith believe in this, just as the Christians believe in the sign of the cross at baptism. It is symbolic for them to wear these charms. The sand reader, on the other hand, can only read at certain intervals and at certain constellations of the planets and stars for various purposes, but I know very little of this.

The custom among my people is to separate wives from their husbands during pregnancy, but my mother did not go home to her mother when she expected me. I was never told the reason, and so one will be surprised to know that I was born in Gendema. Two or three months before, mother's older sister, Hawa, had come down to be with her and to represent her family on the occasion. Also, father's half-sister,[3] Mother Jassa Kpaakpaa, came up from the Liberian side of the Vai country for the occasion, accompanied by one or two of her daughters.

Many prognosticators were consulted concerning my birth, for I was to be born after a number of boys in a row. These were chronologically:

1. Hawa: a girl, married the late Varney Papa, Chief of Pala, before I was born.
2. Alhaj or Al-Haj (Arabic form of Vai name, Lahai): named after my father's father. His nickname is Gbabai, or Gbabey.
3. Jaiah or Jayah (civilized name[4] Clarence Lawrence): connected with the army of Liberia and now district commissioner of the Kru Coast.
4. Manna or Suamanna or Asumanna: named after Prince Manna, once king of the Gallinas, who was a brother to father's father.
5. Jawa or Jalawa (civilized name is Edwin): named after President Edwin Barclay.
6. Bey: named after Hon. T. E. Beysolow, father's cousin and former associate justice of the Supreme Court of the Republic of Liberia.
7. Ibrahim, or Abraham (Arabic and Christian forms of Vai name, Boima): nicknamed Kpana.
8. Nathaniel Vaali (another form of Varney/Vaani)
9. Fatima Sandimanni (Arabic form of Vai first name, Famata): nicknamed Jebeh.
10. Samuel Ciaka (Siaka): nicknamed Goyo.
11. Sarah Anne Sie: nicknamed Kobo.
12. Tawe (girl, died in infancy).
13. Momolu Dasia (died in infancy).
14. Arthur Momolu Tonie: self-styled nickname Abut.
15. Leone Germainia Kenuja (girl, died in infancy).
16. Friedericus Tango (called Fritzi).
17. Fascia Rachel.

Those are my siblings,[5] and we shall discuss their names later.

As I have mentioned, my father had gone to a Christian school against the wishes of grandmother. He always told me that he never forgave himself for doing so. Although she had sent him goods and helped to support him while he was in the United States, he often wondered whether she ever forgave him since he never saw her again. He had never dreamed of her or felt her spirit around him. Before I was born then, people who knew her began dreaming of her frequently. Father himself had such dreams. Once he dreamed she came to him but would not show herself. As soon as she would get close to him, she would fall on her face. He could only see the white veil she wore, wrapped around her head and shoulders. Mother Jassa, grandmother's oldest daughter, also had a similar dream. But one day, father related, he saw grandmother clearly, and she told him that she was coming back to him in the flesh to comfort and console him and then disappeared.

So I was supposed to be the reincarnation of grandmother herself. Nobody can imagine how much such a circumstance obligates those from whom great things are expected. I tremble sometimes at the mere thought, even though they are only dreams. Father and his sister later certainly told me all this because they too expected something of me.

Meanwhile, mother too had visited all the people who had in their powers to tell her my future. She was, in the intervening time, also showing all the symptoms of how women in her condition should act: peculiar temperament, extreme fondness for certain persons, and hatred and intolerance toward others. The target was Mother Jassa's father's older sister who had come down to be near her for the occasion. Mother Masaa is said to have become extremely fond of Mother Jassa all of a sudden. Her explanation for this was based on the popular belief that the person who is extremely hated or liked is the one whom the child will resemble most. Mother Masaa is said to have insisted on sleeping in the same house and bed with Mother Jassa. She is said to have followed her everywhere. There was nothing Mother Jassa could do to get my mother to go anywhere and leave her during the day. She clung to Mother Jassa daily. Mother Massa wanted me to resemble Mother Jassa. And I did not come far away from that I am told. I am told by father and many people who knew my grandmother that I bear the image of my father's mother. Even Europeans who knew her used to constantly tell me this. And, if Mother Jassa resembled her own mother—my grandmother— then Mother Massa's efforts and wishes were not in vain.

So, mother did not go to her own mother or other maternal older female relatives to have me. She remained in Gendema, the city that had almost become Europeanized. There were about a dozen or so white people living there who had factories[6] selling items as cloths, salt, tobacco, cutlasses, axes, pipes, enamel wares, and other goods. These items were exchanged for raw material such as piassava, palm oil, palm kernels, ivory, coffee, cacao, and quite often, gold and animal skins. My father too, due to his Western training, not only built good roads and established an industrial school, but also a "castle" for himself, a large rectangular structure constructed of imported materials. It had two wings in which some of the women, and sometimes guests, lived. The high middle section was his own living quarters and reception rooms.

This castle became the subject of a song in the Gallinas country, which shows that the people were keeping up with what father was doing, even though it was in jest. The interesting thing about people who are being governed by any administration is that they tend to joke sometimes, even of the things they are proud of:

> *I lia puu, puumosia ti ngi gbowaa*
> *I yaama mbei, i katawaa loa*
> *yaada yaada yaaa yaadaa*
> Refrain:
> *Momo Fo Gendema katei loo*
> *kpatei le.*
> *Yaada Gendema katei loo*
> *kpatei le.*[7]

Although as the song says Momolu IV's castle is his riches, I was not born in it. In Africa, the men live by themselves and entertain in their homes, while the women live in surrounding houses or "huts." I was born in the hut built for mother, in which, I have been told, she and Mother Kula lived. But Mother Soko Sando also told me that mother was much younger than she was and had been living with her. Both Mother Kula and Mother Soko Sando later told me about the roles they played at my birth. Mother Soko Sando to this day is particularly fond of me. Also I remember that when we were in Germany, she would never miss sending me special things like hand-woven clothes, earrings, and other nice things which little girls usually delight in having. I am very attached to both of these mothers, but especially Mother Soko Sando, since Mother Kula died a long time ago.

I was born in a *kuuii* (bath house).[8] I am sorry that I am unable to give the reader any definite date of my birth, as there are many controversies about it. But the time of my birth was around noon, at the stroke of thunder, followed by a flash of lightning, which the people in the area understood to mean something big was happening. One interpretation was that I would be great and do great things for my people. The other was that it meant disaster, a *daate* (pot breaker). This is a bug hill or little shapes of pots formed by ants on fallen trees. Used in connection with people it means an individual who spoils things he or she touches.

A flash of the lightning and the roar of the thunder—yes, the occult forces of nature had spoken in the middle of the day to announce the birth of a child. My poor gentle mother, worried, she too consulted those in authority on such matters. She is said to have cried over the meanings of good or bad omens. Since she was a Muslim, she naturally sought a dasimɔ to protect her child against evil spirits. The nature of my birth did something to me. While I am usually afraid of nothing, I remain afraid of lightning to this day.

Birth customs among the Vai and Mende peoples as a whole are similar to other neighboring peoples. When the woman gives birth, she is said to be struggling between life and death, "against death for life." The *maavoli* is her lady in attendance who would correspond to your midwife or even doctor. This midwife is assisted by many other experienced women of the community. The relatives are anxious, and as soon as the birth has been successful, they all shout *Hoyoo!* This is a hurrah, bravo, kudos, hailing the new born stranger.

The midwife is rewarded by the child's father and relatives with kola. The kola nut is symbolic in rituals in so many ceremonies and phases of African life. Traditionally, the nut or nuts are given, about a dozen of them as the custom and circumstance may demand. But the kola can also consist of intrinsic gifts. Sometimes tobacco or anything valuable that is given is called kola. Mother Jassa brought me then into the world and she was assisted by Mother Soko Sando and perhaps others.

In Africa, the greatest day that a woman can have is the day when she gets a child. Everyone honors her, including the husband, bringing gifts of all kinds. Not having children is often considered a disgrace and there is even a term to describe the condition—*kpema* (barren), which literally means "does not continue on." Although this is considered a shame, people show great sympathy toward those who have no children. Every effort is usually made to bring about conception. Medicines and all sorts of herbs prescribed by various doctors are used to help women who happen to be thus unfortunate.

After a child is born, the afterbirth is brought into the house and buried in a hole by the fireside. The baby is not allowed to leave the house until it has received its name. Before the introduction of Islam and Western civilization, the naming of a child took place after four days for boys and three days for girls. Now, the child is brought out of doors after eleven days whether it is male or female. The umbilicus for a boy is usually planted with the kola tree to render the child as invaluable to his people and make him as intrinsic as the kola nut itself. The umbilicus of a girl is usually planted with the banana tree, symbolizing fruitfulness and gentility.

With regard to naming, usually after a duration of eleven days, the parents consult extensively, and it depends as much on the religion of the parents as on special circumstances in the family or community. Children are also usually named after dead relatives, especially the immediate grandparents. After that, other relatives are honored, sometimes dead brothers and uncles and aunts. Also, sometimes children are named after the aspiration of the parents, or after close friends or honored personalities of the nation. This system places a great obligation on children as they constantly try to live up to their names.

Family names are usually not often used, though people know them. The reader has perhaps wondered at my calling my mother Massa Barlo all through this narrative. But you see according to our custom, my mother has to carry her maiden name all her life. She has the right to use my father's first name, as Massa Momolu, to distinguish her from others bearing that first name. But never the name Massaquoi, which her children have the right to use.

During the period of eleven days, my parents, like other parents, were trying to decide on a name for me. My father once told me that whereas the birth of my siblings was celebrated for a day, mine was commemorated with three, as he was united in spirit with grandmother for coming to him in the flesh. People came from all over with gifts to honor mother on her day. Europeans trading in the area were said to have brought many gifts. The name my parents decided to give me was that of my grandmother of course.

Grandmother's name was Fatima (Famata) Beendu Sandimanni, and this was the name that I received in full. I do not use the name Beendu and dropped it long before it got into any papers. I was not given a nickname during the eleven days of waiting. Usually, if the parents are Muslims, the people have the habit of calling the baby, if a boy, Mɔli, and if a girl, Titi, which is a Creole term meaning little girl.

As everything else in African life is connected with a ceremony or a ritual, so is naming a baby. In my case, Mother Jassa, grandmother's oldest daughter, had come to be with mother at the time. Usually the person who names the child gives his or her name to the child. But of course grandmother was dead. So the next best thing was her oldest daughter. The person naming the child is the only one who has the privilege to be the first to take the child outdoors.

The people made a *dɛɛ*,[9] (a sort of mush out of rice flour), which was sacrificed to Allah for my health and prosperity. This was then turned over to Mother Jassa and she ate a piece of it and then said, "I name you Fatima, in honor of my mother…may you be great even as she was." This she said into both my ears each time she came out of doors with me. She went out and came into the house three times, each time saying the same thing in my ears. If the Vai and Mende had not been somewhat Islamized, Mother Jassa would have had to chew the kola nut and then administer it lightly into my mouth before saying the words she spoke. This is the strict ancient custom prevailing among the people, and there are many who still adhere to it. I have of course pretended to have remembered what she must have done.

There are other groups of neighboring people whose customs are different. For example, among the Sherbro and Krim of Sierra Leone, names are laid down or handed down traditionally. These names vary according to order of birth, so that when one hears the name of a child, one need not search for the constellation of birth.[10]

I remember nothing whatsoever of my life in the Gallinas because my mother's mother came to fetch mother and me at father's request. For, at the time when I was about 18 months or two years old, father was having trouble with the British government and did not want mother and me around. Most of the older boys had been sent to various relatives and others to school.

As mentioned, I remember only what people have told me of my babyhood and life in the Gallinas. I am said to have never talked like a baby and to have spoken quite a few months before I could walk. So I must have walked while I was in the Gallinas. The only things of these baby talks that I remember and that I am supposed to have spoken was to call my brother Al-Haj, whose nickname was Gbabai, "Dabai" and Jaiah, whose nickname was Gbukei, "Dudu," which I call both of them to this day.

There is one thing which Mother Jassa's daughters—Jeneba, Hawa, and Famata—told me I am supposed to have said to my mother, who was usually very quiet and said very little unless she was spoken to, but cried whenever something did not please her. When she got worried and wept because of the trouble father was having, I am supposed to have said, "*Mu hei mu kɛkɛ lɔ*," which they, exaggerating as people always do, translated to me in this manner: "Why don't we women sit and look at father. He is quite able to take care of the situation instead of crying and weeping about it like a weakling." Actually, the expression only says: "Let us sit and look at father." This also shows me that I must have spoken both Vai and Mende simultaneously, because the above expression is in Mende, and I was always under the impression that I only spoke Vai at the time.

In Germany, father used to tell me what a crybaby I was when we were in the Gallinas, and how I used to scream with no one able to pacify me but him. People used to console him saying that I would become a great singer. But these things are blank in my mind. Had it not been for a later visit, I would know nothing of the Gallinas but the name.

Notes

1. [Anglicized to "mori man." *Eds.*]
2. [The washed off verses of the Koran are used as *lasmami* to rub and/or drink. The *dasimɔ* or *lasimɔ* which is the actual amulet, is made out of the written verses of the Koran on parchment, which are tightly wrapped, sometimes carefully stitched in leather, that is then worn on the wrist, arm, neck, or sometimes on the ankle. *Eds.*]

3. [Half-relations are not known in African family terminology and organization. It is a very Western concept that Fatima uses here apparently because she had been living in the West for many years. *Eds.*]
4. [In Liberia, "civilized" is used to denote "Western" with the undertones of superiority. *Eds.*]
5. [In 1958, Fatima Massaquoi learned of another sister, born in 1929, and not listed here. Her name was Fasia Jansen, daughter of Elli, who was Fascia Rachel's (number 17 in the list of siblings) nurse. The father was Momolu Massaquoi. When Momolu Massaquoi's wife, Rachel (Ma Sedia) discovered the pregnancy she forced Elli Jansen (Jansen being her later married name) to leave the Massaquoi home. Fasia never met her father as she was born after Momolu Massaquoi returned to Liberia in 1929. Elli named her daughter Fasia after Fascia Rachel who had been in her care. Later, in 1958, Fasia Jansen made contact with the Massaquois in Liberia through Liberian diplomatic channels, and Fatima kept up a regular correspondence with her through the years. Fatima first met her sister Fasia in 1960 in Hamburg, with Vivian Seton witnessing the meeting; Vivian remained in regular contact with Fasia until her death in 1997. Fasia Jansen, like her cousin Hans Massaquoi (Hans was a grandson of Momolu Massaquoi, the son of Al-Haj Massaquoi and a German mother), suffered in Nazi Germany. She overcame great odds to distinguish herself as a dancer and peace advocate, being awarded the *Bundesverdienstkreuz* (German Medal of Merit) in the 1980s. For interviews with Fasia Jansen, see Tina M. Campt, *Other Germans: Black Germans and the Politics of Race, Gender, and Memory in the Third Reich* (Ann Arbor: University of Michigan Press, 2004). *Eds.*]
6. [Trading stores from the nineteenth century down into colonial times were called "factories" and their managers, "factors." It is really a misnomer. *Eds.*]
7. [The song is in Mende and a free translation is: "He went to the Western World and the Westerners confused him /made a fool of him /made him lose his senses; he came back and built a large compound... massive, massive. Momolu IV of Gendema built a compound... just wealth." This song was probably to poke fun at the ruler, a perfectly legitimate freedom but only expressed during major celebrations when licence is given to ridicule anyone. But then it may create a tradition that carries on. *Eds.*]
8. *Kuuii* is a Vai [and also Mende] word for the place where baths are taken. It is usually built at the back of huts and homes and is more or less an enclosure. The word *jakuwu lo*, a person's home, is synonymous. The German word "Innenhof" is a good translation for it as there seems to be no accurate English word to translate the term.
9. ["Lɛwei" in Mende. *Eds.*]
10. [Here Fatima Massaquoi includes lists of names in Sherbro and Kono, which we have not included. The names are sequential, and denotative for the first born, second born, etc. It is also a custom of the Kissi people. *Eds.*]

CHAPTER 3

LIFE AND CUSTOMS IN THE BALI (BARI) COUNTRY OF SIERRA LEONE

The use of terms such as "tribes," "natives," and the like that Westerners use to describe Africans is pejorative, and Africans dislike it. These are all expressions you have invented to undermine us and whatever authority we hold. If I use these terms then, it is only done so that you might understand me.

Regarding my mother's home, all I remember is that some of her people were Vai on her maternal side. My maternal grandfather's family, that is to say my mother's father's family, were Mende and ruled in Bandajuma in the Bali [Bari] district of Sierra Leone. Grandfather lived in Bandajuma while grandmother followed her sons to live in a place called Teleyoma. I want my reader to understand that whatever I am writing here about my first environment and impressions in life is subject to error as I was very, very young.

If I remember correctly, my Uncle Mbimba had been instrumental in opening up the town or in reopening it for residence. He is a Muslim and he and some cousins, one Mabu and a lady by the name of Nangbe, had been rulers of the town, what would correspond to your mayor here. Teleyoma was a twin town with Samatia, both situated on the Tɛli-yei (Black river) in Mende, hence Teleyoma meaning "beyond the Black river." Samatia was sandy and afforded many opportunities for a person to catch jiggers. I remember whenever mother took me there, she would examine my toes for them before putting me to bed, an act which displeased me very much indeed, because, if there had been jiggers, the procedure to remove them was painful.

Teleyoma had about 40 or 50 houses built in circles as can be seen from figure 3.1.[1]

The town had a circular arrangement, divided into four quarters. In the center was the mosque where people prayed and at other times held meetings. Surrounding the mosque were four kitchens, one for each

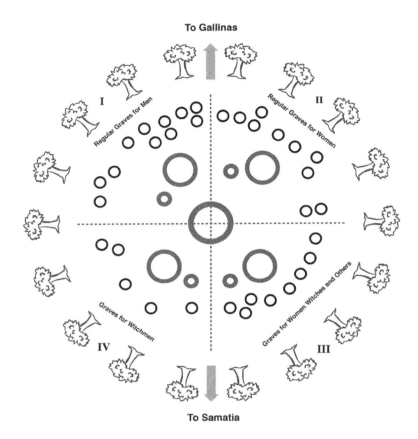

Figure 3.1   Sketch of Teleyoma Town

quarter of the town, and equipped with one or several hearths, the attics serving as storage or reservoirs. People used them during the dry season when it would be too warm to cook in the huts. The mosque and the kitchens had open sides with dwarf walls containing two entrances opposite each other. Residences were on the periphery and beyond that, land for cultivation. Although farming land is apportioned according to individual needs by the town chief, the land belongs to the people and the chief is only a trustee.

The homes of my family were in the second quarter. The hut to the front near the regular graveyard is where grandmother and her daughters lived, as well as the wife of one of my uncles. The other two houses opposite belonged to my mother's brother, Uncle Mbimba. He prayed in one and he slept in the other. The other relatives of mother, as well as Chief Nangbe (a woman), had their homes in the first quarter. Mother's sister Hawa had her home in the third quarter, with homes of other people in the second quarter dividing us.

There are a few people and events that I recall from my childhood that are not chronological, but perhaps the chronology here does not matter as much as the fact that they took place. There was grandmother Jassa (not to be confused with my father's sister Jassa in Gendema), mother's sister Hawa, Uncle Mbimba, mother, Mother Soko, Uncle Sammi and Mother Kanda. That takes care of the immediate members of my family.

Mother Hawa married an old king who died soon after and was now married to a young man whom the family did not approve of, and so slighted her. Uncle Mbimba is a Muslim priest, and is now living in Pujehun. Aunt Soko lost her husband, but she is now married with several children according to letters I received. Aunt Kanda got married shortly before I left. "Kanda," by the way, is a type of bitter manioc, and, as the name suggests, Aunt Kanda must have been the most unattractive one in the family.

One of the early events that I remember, not without a certain amount of curiosity and pleasure, was the death of my grandmother. I really did not know what it meant to die. I had an idea grandmother was probably sleeping or might come back some day to tell me some stories. I also remember that mother was not home when her mother died. I think they said that she had gone to visit father. A messenger was sent after her, but she arrived shortly after grandmother died. Grandmother was fair in complexion with sandy hair and little flat breasts from which I sucked milk, actually only the action of doing so, for it was the most difficult thing to wean me.

Mother had just arrived in time to sit before the corpse and weep. Every morning all the women came together and wept with outstretched feet on the ground. This lasted about 40 days, the usual period of mourning. The women would come at daybreak and after weeping for a while, would go get water from an earthen pot and wash their faces, then return and shake the hands of mother and her sisters. One morning I noticed that one of the women, after squeezing her eyes ever so much, could not bring forth any tears. She went and took the cup and wet her eyes, went sobbing to mother and shook her hand. I promptly remarked that the wetness of her eyes were not tears, but water. Mother of course reprimanded me for this rudeness.

Women who were nearly grandmother's age prepared her body for burial. The body was opened up, as was the habit, to find out evidence of witchcraft. The women came rejoicing and declaring that the inside of grandmother's stomach was clean. The women thereafter bathed and dressed her, and wrapped her in a white cloth. The body was then turned over to the men, who did the burying. We did not attend the funeral. Several days later, mother took me to see grandmother's grave on the road, not far from our house. It was under a kola tree, the earth light in comparison to the other darker places where those were buried who had died previously.

During all the period of mourning, all family members had their hair shaved. Mine was shaved, too. They only wore sacks and old clothes. After sometime these were exchanged for white clothing. The women rubbed their bodies daily with ashes while the wailing went on, but the men did not. I remember this part of the story only too well because I did not want to have my hair cut and screamed and struggled while Uncle Mbimba shaved it. Neither did I want the ashes on my body. But such were the customs, and I was living there and had to adhere to them whether I wanted to or not.

It was the custom in the case of the death of a ruler, that sometimes the head was detached and kept sacred to be turned over to the next ruler. With the coming of Islam many of these customs changed. But for everybody, the mourning period lasts about 40 or 42 days. During this period, it is believed that the spirit of the deceased is not settled. At the end of the mourning period, a great feast takes place, which, depending on the means of the family, can last up to three days.

When the time came to celebrate my grandmother, I woke up to find my mother not there to bathe or dress me, since she had gone to help make preparations for the feast. But a girl who was looking after me told me that mother had said that I should wear a *vanja* (a beaded apron worn around the waist). There was also a pretty red-yellow-black striped cotton squared head cloth for me to tie as a bandana on my head. Above the beaded vanja, I wore several strings of silver twisted chains which one of my uncles had worked for me. I also wore matching bracelets, two on each wrist, earrings and chains around the neck, all made by the same uncle in the same pattern. I was dressed then quite to befit the occasion, and was led to mother who was playing in the procession. I hardly recognized her as she was dressed up in a fashion that I had never seen before. She wore a purple velvet wrapper with blouse and head cloth to match. All were embroidered with gold. How beautiful she was, I thought.

There was drumming and dancing and masquerade displays with all kinds of artists displaying their skills. Mother was playing the *saassaa*[2] with a group of other women. Seeing how gorgeous and beautiful mother looked while playing the saassaa, I thought there was no other profession in the world for me but to learn to play this instrument. Later on, Uncle

Mbimba who was only too grateful for my caprices, made me a saassaa. It is, by the way, only a gourd or calabash at the round top of which a hole is made. The women then string some shells, sometimes beads, and attach several strings of threads in a bundle at the top. The bundles of threads at the top are held in the left hand, while the right hand holds the lower narrow end of the gourd. By shaking this, the rhythm is produced. With my saassaa, a new world opened for me, and I did not rest until I had the rhythm to at least one song. With time, my knowledge of playing the saassaa has increased, which many of you have heard when I have appeared on your programs in America. My uncle further indulged me by playing the *mbaka* (hand organ), whenever I would be playing the saassaa. I had become a musician! At least so I thought.

Hawa was Uncle Mbimba's wife who had lived in our hut with us. He only had this one wife, by the way, as he was a priest and did not have time for any more. Besides, he had the obligation of looking after his mother and sisters, and perhaps this also did not leave him as much time to devote to his own family. Unfortunately, Hawa died in childbirth not long after grandmother died. When Hawa's feast was held, the people cooked rice with chicken and threw it on the grave. On another day of the feast, a sacrifice was offered and also placed on the grave.

The purpose of this was probably to appease the spirits and help strengthen them to be good custodians of the town. But at the time I thought that the people expected Hawa to come out and eat the food especially as the best parts of the chicken had been placed on the grave with a cup of water. So I would steal out to the graveyard to see Hawa come out and eat. When she did not appear I took a piece of the chicken, and told my mother Hawa did not want it, much to her disgust and fear. Although I never did see Hawa as I had hoped to, I did see my grandmother once. No one believes it of course.

One excellent example of my vivaciousness in early life was demonstrated when the district commissioner (DC) visited our town. These colonial officials, all British, administered the districts. They were very powerful and greatly feared. News came that the DC, nicknamed *Ngombukaabu*,[3] was coming to our town to collect taxes. This particular commissioner was dreaded by the people and they made all kinds of preparations to hide what they did not want him to see or know.

The people of Teleyoma were apprehensive when his visit was announced. They set about cleaning the town, and discussions were held as to who should remain in town and who should hide. People like Uncle Mbimba and the lady king of the town Nangbe, among others, of course had to stay. Mother came to my bed on the eve of his coming and told me that we had to get up early the next morning to go to the farm or forest. I asked who Ngombukaabu was, and why I, the daughter of Momolu IV who bore the name of the Vai queen, had to run away from him. I said I was not going.

When mother woke me up next morning, I put up a big scene until Uncle Mbimba came and said I should stay with him. Ngobukaabu was late arriving. Nangbe received him and while she was making her tax declarations, I asked to be permitted to go and see what a white man was. I went and stood with my two hands on Nangbe's knees, while she and the other leaders of the town discussed business and looked from one to the other. Although Nangbe, Uncle Mbimba, and others spoke English, all this business was discussed through an interpreter. Ngobukaabu said something in Mende to me, and I replied that I did not like him, because he was feared and hated and made my people pay taxes. But I earned my first or second whipping. I say here first or second whipping because there is another incident that I will relate after this, which also brought me a whipping and I don't remember which was first or which was second.

Another whipping that I received in childhood in the Bali District was also for speaking out what I thought. It had been rumored that a woman had had a baby with a chimpanzee. Everyone came and told mother about it. African babies are usually not hairy, but this woman's baby child might have been unusually hairy. One day, the girls had taken me to the river to bathe. On our way back, I saw the woman in question, walking and leaning on a walking cane while doing so. She asked for help from one of the girls, but I told the girl not to help her, since it served the woman right to have a chimpanzee baby. I had completely forgotten the incident when one night Uncle Sammi appeared looking for me, very angry. Before anyone could answer, he was at my bedside, took me out of bed by my two feet and carried me out of the hut and gave me a good whipping. I was very angry and did not want to have anything to do with Uncle Sammi, but mother explained how badly I had hurt the woman and told me to go apologize to her the next day.

Mother Hawa is now dead; she died around 1926. Uncle Sammi died in about 1926 or 1927. Mother Kanda is still married to her same husband. Uncle Mbimba, married to his same second wife, is living in Pujehun, and has several children of his own now. I sometimes wonder what he will say about my remembering so much of the life I had in the Bali district when he had been the supporter of the family, and what a grand job he did indeed. A long, long time ago, Dia-molle finished his training with my uncle Mbimba and returned to his own mother and father in the Vai country in Liberia. Mother Soko is living in Funikolo, in Massaquoi chiefdom and has several children. I am to take care of her daughter, Kula, if I should ever be fortunate enough to return home before she gets too old. I don't know the whereabouts of anyone else I happened to mention.

My own mother, Massa, the mother who never tired to look after her *Ngeledando* (the child from the mouth of the skies), died in 1938—since I have been in America. We separated like this: while playing in the sand, she came and said she had something to tell me. "You are fast becoming my great lady and you have to promise me that you will not be sad or cry over what I am going to tell you." Now, father wanted me—the man we both loved. She told me then, on that memorable day, that Aunt Teneh (Tɛɛnɛɛ) Massaquoi was at the house and she had come from father to fetch us. She said that perhaps she might not be able to go, because of her family, but that she wanted me to go because father could do so much more for my welfare than she could ever do, just as he was doing for my brothers.

Aunt Teneh spent a few days in Teleyoma while the family debated whether or not I should be sent to my father as mother had suggested. The reason why they had to debate was because among my people, one of the greatest opportunities that a husband has of showing his love and appreciation for his wife and her family is the time when she loses a relative. When grandmother died, father did not participate in the feast or as they call it, to "pull the cry." Neither was there any representative. What had happened is that father was too busy adjusting to life and work in Liberia and he asked his cousin to attend the feast on his behalf. This relative simply kept all the goods and never appeared on the scene. Aunt Teneh told me later in life that she was quite embarrassed when she arrived in Teleyoma to fetch mother and me, to find the family so full of resentment. She told them that father did not know that the cousin, Mambu by name, never reached the place. Not that I disbelieve Aunt Teneh Massaquoi or father, but late in life I made it my business to have the man verify the fact of father's having sent him.

Aunt Teneh, a man by the name of Ngulufuuo, and another by the name of Bala had been the delegates that father had sent to fetch us. They and Uncle Mbimba, Uncle Saami's wife, mother, and I then made the trip to Bandajuma, where grandfather was ruling. On our way to Bandajuma, mother showed me a little town by the name of Gawula and told me that she had once lived there a few months and that that is the place where she should have wanted me to be born.

We arrived at Bandajuma, and I thought I had seen nothing so picturesque. On a hill on the other side of the river stood the residence of the king of the district. The people living there had their homes on the hills and below was the valley with a stream that separated one section of the town from the other. Aunt Taweh was buried in the middle of the town as she had been the favorite wife of the chief of the district. Mother, who had gone to her funeral, showed us where she had been buried.

Aunt Teneh, Uncle Mbimba, and mother then went to talk to grandfather. He wouldn't hear of mother's going back. He was angry that mother could consider going back to father who had insulted her and her whole family. Thus it was decided that mother, by this token, had become theirs and father had no more claims on her. But mother was pleading for me to be allowed to go to father, even if she could not go to him against the wishes of her folks. She made all kinds of threats about what she would do if they did not allow me to go to father, and finally they agreed that I could go.

It is useful at this point to explain some cultural elements involved in such conflicts. A wife always belongs to her family.[4] That is why she does not change her name when she marries. When anything happens, for example, if the man violates the law, the family has a chance to take the wife back. So, this is what happened. Although Uncle Mbimba and the rest of the family had liked father very much, many a time both Uncle Mbimba and mother would sit and tell me what father would like me to do in a given situation—what they wanted me to do was never in their minds. This could not be said of grandfather. Grandfather and others, I understood later, had really resented father's European education. He thought father unwise for not getting along with the colonial officials in Sierra Leone. Perhaps it would be interesting to know what the conflicts were that caused him to abdicate the throne of the Gallinas,[5] and to look further into what he and some of his friends have had to say on the matter.

The conflicts that father had with the British authorities could be summed up in the fact that he had been trained in Western culture and had the ambition of training his people along Western lines. This of course would have spoiled much of the trade in the colony as well as undermine the authority that the colonial government exercised in the area.[6]

The traders in the Gallinas bought goods such as palm oil, piassava, palm kernels, cacao, ivory, and other materials from the Africans in the area, but paid very little for them. They then sold the goods for about eight or ten times what they paid. Father then found out what was being paid on the world market for the goods and made a law that no African in the place should sell his goods directly to Europeans. From that point, goods were to be sold to him and he would in turn sell them to the European traders. As he paid the Africans more for the goods and in turn demanded more from the European traders, the former responded splendidly. This of course embittered the traders greatly.

Another thing that annoyed Momolu IV was the fact the British officers in the area were in the habit of disregarding important cultural norms and taboos. I was told of an incident when a commissioner disregarded certain African customs and laws. The grove where the men's organization of the Poro (*Pɔlɔ* or *Pɔɛɛ*) is in session is very sacred. Nonmembers cannot trespass there and have to announce themselves by shouting. Otherwise the *kpowa* (noninitiate) will be caught and initiated if he is a man. If the trespasser a woman, she disappears forever.

This particular district commissioner had the habit of violating these rules, which was reported to father frequently. When the commissioner was caught, father himself, a member of the Poro with rights to initiate a person, initiated the European. This incident has been memorialized in the song: *Momo Fo waa, i DC waa pɔɛɛ ma* (meaning in Mende, " Momo IV came, and he initiated the District Commissioner into the Poro").[7]

These examples of father's tension with the colonial authorities are only a few of those that caused him to resign. The ultimate cause was that father had been charged with having more sympathy with Liberia than Sierra Leone. His own paternal brothers are supposed to have reported his celebrating the 26th of July, the Liberian Independence Day, at which time he invited his Liberian relatives and friends to celebrate. Such are but a few of the incidents that I remember people telling me. I personally believe that father was living much ahead of his time.

Through mother's sobs, it was decided that I should go to father. Uncle Mbimba then bade us farewell in Bandajuma and we departed. But before leaving the subject of this uncle, I would like to say a little more about him in connection with his relationship to his sisters.

Uncle Mbimba took over the responsibility of his sisters who returned home. He supported mother and me entirely, which is the duty of the brothers, if their sisters who go to *Kaiwoo* in Vai or *Hinweehun* in Mende (marriage) should return home. His wife lived with us, as is usually the case. But it was Uncle Mbimba's duty to do what the men had to do for all the womenfolk. It was he who got the land for our farms, cut down the trees and shrubberies, and then turned the land over to the women for sowing the crops. For, a remnant of the ancient African spiritualistic religion holds that only the women and the earth are sisters, since they are the only two that are capable of reproduction by nature. Since the female species and the earth are sisters, they are therefore sympathetic to each other, and only what the woman sows can grow abundantly. Not that what the man sows will not grow at all. But it will not grow in abundance. Uncle Mbimba not only wove the clothes that these sisters wore but also represented them before the law. I here take leave of him for the period, but not without great gratitude and a depth of appreciation for his solid and sincere sense of duty. For I cannot remember when mother, any of my aunts, or I stood in want of anything that was needed to live in our culture and environment with this uncle around.

On leaving Bandajuma, I was subdued by the magnificent roads and beauty of the African soil. Each town was cleaner than the next as we traveled westward. Many were deserted, with inhabitants gone to their farms. Sometimes all that would remind us that we had reached towns and cities would be the banana trees, clean houses, crowing of the cocks, occasional barking of dogs, still winds, and children playing.

Mother and I became quite close on the way, for, until she took leave of me, I traveled in her hammock. All the time she was advising me on how to act and what to do. She seemed to have had a dreaded fear of father's feeling that she had neglected me. She told me of her love for father. I am reminded of a little incident, when a handsome man named Lansana from Samatia whom the family wanted mother to marry after divorcing father, came to Teleyoma. He stood in mother's way in the open kitchen when I was playing around. I saw my mother take the burning wood out of the fire, and, asking him again and again to leave and never come back, she whipped his face with it. I never forgot it. And who says that an African cannot love? I am asking this question because I have often read such statements in your books when speaking of Africa. All I can remember about the woman I am privileged to call my mother was love and devotion as well as understanding for the man who was the father of her children. So we traveled farther and farther away from Teleyoma through Bali country to the Gbeya (Mano) river.

But let us see what news I have had of what became of Teleyoma. A classmate of mine from Germany wrote me while in Africa that Teleyoma was now in ruins, with all the people having moved elsewhere or gone to Samatia. This was in 1934.[8] A brother of mine, Nathaniel Va-Ali, informed me almost simultaneously that Teleyoma and Samatia had merged.

So mother and I with all our baggage, after spending the night with some cousins in a nearby town called Jambibu, stood on the banks of the Gbeya, which separates Liberia from Sierra Leone and thereby also separates the Liberian Vais and Mendes from those of Sierra Leone. To this point, mother and I had had such good times together all through the years that I had not really realized that she would not be with me. I had enjoyed the envy of her cousins all through Bali country where we stopped, when they had asked her about her beautiful daughter. They had all wished I could be theirs. All of this of course had made mother feel better about the parting.

On the light brown sand of the river we stood, waiting to get into the canoe to be crossed over to Liberia. Mother took me up into her arms. She told me not to cry. She further told me to tell father to send for her as soon as he could, for, she could not live without me. A thing which he did later, but her family thought it was too late and that he had had to be reminded of his duty. Well, I guess one has to adhere to the customs of one's environment no matter where one goes or what else one becomes in life.

Even today, I sometimes still see my mother standing across the Gbeya, watching us as we crossed the river. Sometimes when I think of the waves of the river, it seems to rise before my eyes, dashing the canoe away from the shore where my mother stood. Sometimes they seem to say, I can never let you land on her side again. I still see mother across the river. I can hear her sweet gentle low voice whispering in my ears when she picked me up and gave me her last advice. For, I never saw her again. The Gbeya separated us then, and, death later separated us forever.

Notes

1. [Recreation of original hand-drawn map by Fatima Massaquoi. *Eds.*]
2. [Vai: *saassaa* (Mende: *seiguleh*) is a musical instrument mostly played by women, which may have originated with the Sande society. It is made out of a gourd with stringed beads tied around the big end with a rope handle to enable the player to hold the two ends of the instrument firmly and shake it rhythmically. *Eds.*]
3. [This was the nickname of W. D. Bowden who was DC of Bandajuma and later Panguma districts, and like all DCs at the time, greatly feared. He was so nicknamed on account of the manner of his walking, as if on burning grass. The name later came to symbolize his dress, especially the wide-legged khaki shorts he loved. Today *ngombukaabu* simply refers to shorts with ample legs. *Eds.*]
4. [Among the neighboring Mende and other groups, it is the opposite. The woman, once properly married and given in hand, remains in the family of the husband even after the husband dies. *Eds.*]
5. [Momolu IV was deposed by the colonial administration in April 1906 and given only eight days to go into exile. *Eds.*]
6. [The best scholarly treatment of the 1906 downfall of Momolu Massaquoi is in Arthur Abraham, *Mende Government and Politics under Colonial Rule* (Freetown: Sierra Leone University Press and London: Oxford University Press, 1978), pp. 188–194. According to Abraham, "The colonial administration considered Momolu Massaquoi a dangerous chief. He persistently tried to reclaim the other dismembered sections of the Gallinas...As an educated African—particularly an African educated in the United States—Massaquoi was inevitably suspect to the colonial authorities, who feared such people." (p. 194). *Eds.*]
7. [Considering the fact that the DCs were practically small gods, it is more likely that he was initiated with his full consent. *Eds.*]
8. [A reference to Richard Heydorn, Fatima's German boyfriend, who conducted linguistic research in Liberia prior to World War II. *Eds.*]

CHAPTER 4

LIFE AND CUSTOMS IN THE VAI COUNTRY OF LIBERIA

From Jambibu we traveled in little canoes along the Njagbacca Creek to the town of Njagbacca. This town holds an important position in the life of the Vai people as it was the home of Queen Sandimanni during whose reign development, cleanliness, and discipline prevailed all over, as we have learned from Büttikofer.[1] Njagbacca is also important in that it forms a boundary between the Gawula and the Teewoh districts of the Vai country. Everyone in the town spoke both Vai and Mende, as did most of the Vais in the Teewoh District. But the town itself was somewhat of a disappointment to me. We arrived there in pouring rain. Everyone knows how much rain and gloomy weather can influence a sensitive mind. These were those big drops of African rain, which can look beautiful, but can soak you to the skin and make you feel as if your last hour on earth has come.

As our canoe was anchored, I heard father give orders that I be taken to Mama Jassa. The creek to Mama Jassa's house, though not far, seemed ever so long. The town, in the rain, was muddy and in the town square was a ditch of water, where something green seemed to have set in. The houses in Njagbacca were very clean but not many in number. There were about thirty huts and two guest houses, two factories (trading stores), two bungalow-type houses called *pani kens* and *goongenken,* the difference being that the former is covered with corrugated iron sheets.

The Vai family is similar to neighboring groups, but very different from those amid Western culture where family is simply the man, woman, and children and is mainly monogamous. Among my people who are mainly Muslim, a man can marry as many as four wives if he can support them. But family extends beyond husband, wife/wives, and children and includes other relatives as well.

Generally, any older man in the community is called "father" by the children, and sometimes by the grownups. Among my people, age demands a great deal of respect, and it extends even to situations when a person is just a year older, [and has to be addressed appropriately]. All fathers' brothers and cousins are fathers. By the same token, all older women in the community are called mothers by their juniors. All fathers' sisters, who are called here female cousins, are mothers and so are all of mothers' sisters. The matter of calling older people generally "mother" and "father," when not related, corresponds to the German habit of having very small children call all older persons "Onkel" and "Tante."[2]

The only uncles are the mother's brothers, while the father's brothers are fathers. This is partly due to the fact that the woman after marriage retains her maiden name so that people may know her taboos. Her children have no rights in her family except that the uncles always owe the child the "goat's head." This goat's head may consist of anything intrinsic or the heads of other animals, except the cow, the head of which is never supposed to be consumed by people of noble birth.

The uncle provides his sisters' sons, his nephews, with wives, and sometimes, they can retain their uncle's daughters as bail. That is, they can keep them from marrying until the uncle has fulfilled his duty. The nieces never get this debt paid off and hence the uncle eternally owes the nephews the "goat's head," with the result that the nephews can often demand anything the uncle has as goat's head. The nephews then, are allowed to take their uncles' daughters in "goat's head marriage."[3]

The brothers of an individual are not just confined to being the children of the parents as in the West. All the cousins as far as can be traced are considered brothers. The Vai expression for this is *nomo,* which means a person with whom one is on an equal basis, but if older must be addressed as *ngɔɔ* (ngoh). The same explanation goes for a sister too, except that the Vai term for sister is *nomo-musuma,* a female sibling or *nomo-kaima,* a male sibling. Perhaps to understand these terms better, one has to think of the German word *geschwister,* to have their exact or equal translation.

A person's in-laws are his or her *demina* or *demiaa.* Those are his wife's or her husband's brothers and sisters. This in-law relationship has restrictions or taboos, quite different from the habits and patterns of Westerners. A man may not go into the home of his mother-in-law and avoids her as much as possible. But of course a wife has much to do with her mother-in-law, for both she and her husband often live with his mother for awhile. Often also, the daughter-in-law is trained by the mother-in-law.

A man's wife is not only the woman he is married to but all of her sisters and so-called cousins as well. As in the days of the ancient Hebrews, when a man's wife dies, he usually marries the wife's sister or cousin, the reason being that marrying a relative may provide the child, if there is one, with a mother who will treat him better than a totally strange woman will.

A grandfather is the father of the mother or father of a person. Both the paternal and maternal great-uncles are grandfathers, since the paternal uncle is father, the paternal grand-uncle is naturally grandfather. Only the maternal uncle is the uncle. Grandmothers are the same as in the Western sense, but great-aunts are grandmothers.

My father's oldest sister, my aunt, with whom I stayed, was Mama Jassa. Both my father and she were children of Queen Sandimanni, but by different fathers. Mama Jassa was much older than father and in fact nursed him because father was born on the battlefield and grandmother had to continue fighting. So, all my brothers and sisters call her grandmother, *mama* in Vai, although I called her Mba Jassa, which means Mother Jassa, while I was with her.

Mama Jassa inhabited one of the large huts in the town. Her son, Habibu,[4] who was a Muslim priest, Mina,[5] the town chief, and Mother Soko Sando all had beautiful huts. Apart from other members of the family, there were also "domestic slaves"[6] living in Njagbacca the time I was there. Father left me with Mama Jassa, while he proceeded to Monrovia, hoping to settle there permanently. My brothers, Siaka and Bey, went with him to attend school there. Although Habibu was a priest, he had only one wife, but Chief Mina had many. Some lived in pairs, others alone, and still others lived in the hut with Mother Jassa and me. There were also some traders in Njagbacca, who did prosperous business.

Mama Jassa and her daughters received me cordially. Life in Njagbacca was quite different from what it had been in the Bali country with mother and her folks. There, I had spoken Mende chiefly, although I learnt Vai from my mother. At first, I had Mama Jassa and the people in Njagbacca believing that I only spoke Mende. But my little secret was exposed when someone said something about my mother and I replied in Vai. In Njagbacca, I had to find new playmates as I was lonely. Then I discovered consolation in Mama Jassa's garden. Each day I would go there early and talk to my mother until Mama Jassa stopped me for fear of being kidnapped by foreigners and sent out of the country and sometimes into slavery. But I missed my mother badly. I wanted the same hairstyle that she had; I refused to have the head-cloth she had given me washed for fear the touch of her hands might be washed away. The vanja, or little beaded apron, she had made for me remained sacred; even after the threads rotted I kept the beads under my pillow.

But my condition did not last very long. Mama Jassa had many children and grandchildren as well as great grandchildren, and she knew how to handle the situation. I was told that I was her mother, who had come back to life again and should be near her, since the daughters only came on visits occasionally. Now, she said, everything here belongs to the two of us. My brother Manna had been hers before I came, but he had been sent off to school in Sierra Leone, and I had come to take his place. Thus, Mama Jassa and I shared a special friendship. Even her daughters, when they came to visit, felt that she was spoiling me.

Being so small, I had no heavy duties while in Njagbacca. There was a Gola girl in town to play with me, and she and I had to keep the grass and weeds off the grave of Grandmother Famata Sandimanni. Besides, as Mama Jassa was very forgetful, I had to remind her where she laid her keys. I had to remind her how many kinds of hens we had at the farm, the cocks, the cows, the sheep, the goats, and anything that had anything to do with her memory. Mama Jassa, like father, always addressed me as "mother" and always sought my opinion before she did anything.

The web of life cannot be described without bringing in Mama Jassa's daughters and their children. Apart from the foreign factories (stores) in Njagbacca, one of which was owned by a white man, and another, owned by a foreign firm, there was a Creole man from Sierra Leone, by the name of Bickersteth, who married Famata, oldest daughter of my brother Mina, Mama Jassa's oldest son. They had a son, Sammi, who was about my age. There was Famata Sheriff, married to a Mr. Tamba in Jondu. Another daughter was Jenneba Sheriff, who was married to Chief Laya of Fali on the Gola border and she had three sons.

Sister Hawa Sheriff is Mama Jassa's third daughter. She is married to Chief Tammuzuu of the Gawula District whose home is in Tiennimanni. Her children are: Varney Tammuzuu (name given in the mission school is Nathan Varney Gray), whom we nicknamed Moli Piece. Sister Hawa is the only daughter of Mama Jassa who herself had daughters. Mama Jassa's last daughter was Sando Sheriff. She was married to the Chief of Gbayokolo, by the name of Varney. She had one child during the time I was there.

In addition to these daughters who often came with their children and sometimes husbands, to visit, there were other relatives in Njagbacca. There was Moana, a "cousin," and his wife, Kaata, and Habibu's wife, Hawa, and Ballah Sandimanni, father's nephew, and his wife, Saata, and their son Momolu Sandimanni. There was also Ballah Sandimanni's brother, Momolu Sandimanni, who had no wife and children at the time.

Thus, life in the town of my grandmother was by no means dreary. Whereas I had been an only child in Teleyoma, I was now one of many.

When Mama Jassa's grandchildren came, they usually lived in our hut. They thus became my playmates. We ate out of one dish as was the custom, and it came with rules, similar to the Western good and bad table manners. People must wash their hands first before eating, collecting the food from the bowl with the hand. The food must be in the middle of the four fingers and the hand must not be pushed too far into the mouth. It is quite an art. I sometimes wish I could see the person accustomed to eating with a fork and knife try it.

Mama Jassa's home was the center of activities. Everyone came there for advice. Also, there was not a child in the community—that is to say, in the neighboring towns as well—at whose birth she and Mama Soko, and Mina's oldest wife (whose name I have forgotten), did not assist. People cooked there, people borrowed, they sobbed, they laughed. My poor mother just would not remember who took or borrowed what. So, I was responsible for reminding her and the family members did not like it.

Because the Vai are agricultural people, they live chiefly off the products of their farm labor. People set out to work very early before the sun got too hot. Farming is done during the rainy season; in the dry season there is no rain. In the rainy season, it pours daily, the rivers are flooded and crops and vegetation grow in abundance. But it is the worst season of the year. People usually live on what has been stored up. Men cannot go hunting and women cannot fish. Hence, there is usually a scarcity of everything.

It is generally believed by foreign visitors that the men in Africa do not work, but in fact there is a strict division of labor in the economic system. Since certain labor tasks have to be accomplished during a certain time or season of the year, the men are usually free when they complete their work. After the rains, comes the harvest season, and the men do no type of work on the farms. In February, the men begin to prepare the farm. They clear and prepare the land, plough and sow, and then turn the farm over to the women by April. The children, male and female, keep the birds away from picking the grains off the ground or others from eating the mature rice later. When the women take over the farm, the men do other work such as constructing the huts and weaving, hunting, and have a time of leisure in general. Hence it is not true that men do not work.

The Vai have several kinds of towns. There is the town proper, *sanja*, and there is a sort of half-town, and finally the village or *daa*. The towns are seats of the principal leaders of the population and also meeting places for conferences and festivals. The half-towns are not as permanent as the towns. They are occupied by people who do farming. These half-towns, if fertile enough, often eventually grow into a town, while others become depleted and the population is forced to move to another new opening of virgin soil in another part of the country.

From the half-towns, one can then go to villages or farms to grow crops. But all processing work, such as producing palm and palm kernel oil, growing cotton, etcetera, are done in the half-towns. In smaller quantities, crops like cassava or manioc, coco yam, sweet potato, or banana are grown around the big towns—they correspond to an orchard or garden in the Western world. But the farms produce these and others on a larger scale. The main crops that the Vai raise are rice, manioc or cassava, sweet potatoes, and many others for which I know not the English names.

We went to the farm daily then; the women had to do so. At our farm, I was usually bored, for, aside from picking sand or stone out of the rice to cook, I had nothing to do but fall asleep, especially when it was hot. Aside from going to the farm and returning home at night, the daily life in the family was pretty regular. It is not like life here at all. Mama Jassa was anxious to teach me everything she knew. I had to stand around in the mornings when we arose and see how the cooking was done. I had to watch the boiling of the pots and see the ingredients that went into them.

Not only did I have to observe the things that a well-bred girl had to observe, but often Mama Jassa would take me on one of her herb excursions and show me this and that herb, telling me their names and usages. I remember one of them in particular which she used for colds. It had white looking buds with tiny black spots on them, which the Vai call *jambaajamba*. This particular herb she used for people with minor stomachaches, headaches, and the like. The leaves of the same herb she often used for people with constipation and the like, and kept a pot boiled with it almost daily.

Mama Jassa told me once that she had had a dream and that Grandmother Sandimanni from the world of the spirits had shown her a herb to cure a disease that my favorite cow had had. And, oddly enough, she went out that morning and brought the herb to cure the cow. It did. All of this of course impressed me greatly.

There is something that happened early one morning that gave me a great and new interest while in the Vai country. I awoke early to go into the *kuuwu* (bath enclosure). On that remarkable morning, I chanced upon one of Mama Jassa's daughters, who had come home for confinement, bring her baby into the world. The women that day in the kuuwu had forgotten to close the door to the house and I had thus been able to surprise them. This annoyed the older people very much, for, although I was led back to the house right away, I had seen enough to ask questions.

Persistent questioning led Mama Jassa one day to sit down and explain everything before I was satisfied. It is not this event that is significant as such. But the reactions it awakened in me. For, in the ensuing evenings, I remember going around carrying my saasaa as my baby. When asked why I did it, I retorted that I wanted to learn how to sleep with a baby, because some day I am going to have a little boy and I didn't want to roll and crush him up.

The baby whose delivery I had partly seen became my baby. He was the first child I had asked somebody to tie to my back. Even to this date he likes me more than most of Mama Jassa's other grandchildren. I asked my sister, the mother of the child, whether I could not have him for my very own. Whenever I wanted to go off and play with the other children, she would call out to me: "Come and play with your baby," or "Come and play the saasaa for your baby," or "Sing a lullaby (*dondoidon* in Vai) for your baby."

After I was sent away from the kuuwu, I watched everything that was connected with the mother and the baby. They brought what I now know to be the afterbirth and buried it in a hole in the earth inside of the hut. Over that hole they laid a mat upon which mother and child slept. This was near the fireplace. I asked Mama Jassa why it was done. She replied that it was to keep away evil or witchcraft from harming the mother or baby.

I tried my best to keep track of the spot where the afterbirth had been buried. I asked Mama Jassa what she had done with mine, since she had assisted with my birth. She described the place exactly, and in later years, upon a visit to Gendema, I was able to trace the spot, and those who knew about it agreed that it was the right place. It also created a sentimental response in me—there I stood, beholding the very spot where mother and I had spent my first days on earth... I wondered what she must have felt while nursing me those first days and what I had been like.

While I had kept up with everything that was being done in Njagbacca relating to my baby, I had not kept up with what had been done to his umbilicus. I did see Mama Jassa putting drops of a leaf on it, a deed which she explained was to enable it to fall off easily. Otherwise, I know not what was done to it. You may wonder here why something should have been done to it. Well, the fact is that my people are in the habit of giving mother earth something back in return for the life she yields. If a boy, the umbilicus is usually buried with a tree, one which is symbolic of valor, truth, strength, and courage. An illustration of this is that my own father's umbilicus was buried with the *oan-kon,* (cotton tree) at Kpaasalo.

Kpaasalo had been a battlefield for one of grandmother's wars. It had been the very battlefield upon which she gave birth to father, her last child, and courageous as she was, had been able to send her boy to her daughter, Mama Jassa, for nursing so she could continue the fight. What was expected of the child? He was to trace, mark the spot with his birth—hence, *kpa* (sore, wound, spur, trace, mark), *sa* (to put, to lie down), *lo* (inside). This spot surely must have been good for coming generations to live. Hence, the foundation of the town. Hence, a brave and vigorous child.

For many reasons, I am inclined to believe that this battle was in 1872 and that father must have been born on the fifth or sixth of December. The problem here is that Africans keep up with events and history pertaining to the whole community, and not the individual. It may also be because we Africans tend to give mothers credit for the birth of a child. I remember once when we were living in Germany, Ma Sedia and some of her friends got together to give father a birthday party. He did not like it at all. He thought it a sin, as do the Vai, for the child does nothing to come into the world.

With regard to my baby, I observed it daily. The baby was fed its mother's breast milk as often as it liked, unlike how babies are fed on this side of the globe. At three or four months, it was fed crushed bananas and rice-water, drained off the rice when boiling it for the adults. Gradually, he was given harder foods, much sooner than in the West. The fact is that my people feel that a child should not be brought up very delicately because if a child should die, it is better in childhood than live as a burden to the community, as happens in your asylums and your prisons.

The mother in my culture is to know no bounds in caring and waiting on her child. Hence the Vai proverb *Den wolo kinaa, ke soke ya den la kowa a wa ton ko kinalee ba ja lo* which means having a child is sweet, but working for your child is the sweetest thing in motherhood. This in essence is motherhood. In return, it is the highest duty of the child to always, at all times, and in all places, protect and respect the name of the mother. I am reminded in this respect, when we were playing in Njagbacca, how Mama Jassa's grandchildren, when they got angry with me, would call my mother a Mende or some such trifle, which sounded abusive. A man would fight to death for the honor of his mother if someone abuses her or uses foul language against her.

There are other thoughts and ambitions which the observation of my baby awakened in me. Just as how during the feast for my grandmother I had seen mother play the saassaa, and then wanted to become a saassaa player, I now wanted to become a medicine woman in the village and cure people like Mama Jassa did. My plans for the time when I would become a woman ran thus: I was going to marry a great warring king. For him, I would have at least four children, perhaps more, three boys and one girl. Since my husband was going to die early in war, I was not going to remarry. I was going to carry on his war instead, just as grandmother, Queen Sandimanni, had done. For, in this way, I would at least deserve having been given her name. Then after winning his wars I would settle down and cure the sick. Thus I had to begin then, learning about the herbs.

I did learn a great deal about herbs as I said before. One day, "my baby" suffered a spell of nausea. Immediately I went and got some herb and gave him. His mother became frightened when I told her. But she calmed down when she heard what it was and that it had helped. Well, all of this is a child's paradise, with beautiful gardens—colorful ones that have all the splendid sceneries of nature. It takes sometimes only reality to make the colors fade, as even the sun withers the real flowers.

In the daily course of life, food plays an important part. Since foods differ all over the globe, let us look at some of the ways Vai women find their way to the hearts of their husbands and children. As I have said, my people grow a number of items on their farms. The palm trees give them an abundance of food and cash. The palm fruit produces palm oil, which is used as oil for food, cosmetics, and for soap products. The seed of the palm nut gives us the palm kernel, which is exported, but also produces its own kind of oil used in foods. The coconut gives us oils for foods as well as soaps. The piassava, coffee, cacao, rubber, and other items we also grow for export. But my people grow a whole lot more mainly for subsistence.

Now, before we describe some of the Vai dishes, we have to bear in mind that different people have different modes of life and philosophies. I have noticed that although people here are intolerant of the things other people do, they very often have philosophies and customs that vary from the pattern. Often, you pick up the papers and read of the great insanitary conditions among other nationalities of the world, or hilarious accounts of their gluttony. What has probably happened is that in many ways the "civilized man's" life has become so complicated that he has lost track of the fact that nature provides a large reservoir of food to provide for the needs of children. In an effort to make life as easy as possible so that he can search for money, he has to be re-taught by his scientists about these reservoirs and the benefits for the human body. If man lives near nature, his nutritional needs are provided for amply.

Vai staple food is rice, and there is a legend about it. A Vai king fell ill and refused to eat anything that his subjects would offer him. One day, a strange woman was passing and she asked to be allowed to cook something she had with her for the king. The woman cooked rice and the king ate it. Every time the king felt hungry, he would call *nkolo*, which means "give me once more." The food the woman cooked for this king became *kolo,* which is the Vai term for the uncooked rice even today; it is something that must be given once more.

Any African or Vai girl more specifically, around six years of age, can cook rice, which is eaten with many delicious vegetables and sauces. There are different types of vegetables which are usually prepared with fish, fowl, or meat, fresh or dried, and palm oil or palm kernel oil is added. There is a special dish called *paŋɔaa* or *ponwaa* prepared by steaming vegetables like okra or okra leaf on top of rice that is cooking. It is then mixed to give a green and white appearance. With this dish, a meat, fish, or fowl gravy is prepared by frying these and then adding water and onions, pepper and salt, and boiled.

In all the cases, where these sauces and vegetables are prepared, it is not simply placed over the rice. The Vai woman is very artistic in serving the dishes, especially when these dishes are to be taken to her husband or to strangers. In my long years of contact with Western culture, I have often wondered about the ado people make over decorations and table arrangements and the like. But although we do not sit at tables, our foods are decorated beautifully so as to make them look very palatable indeed. To dish rice, a woman puts the hot rice in a bowl, wets a spoon with water and presses it lightly to make it stick together. It is then turned upside down on a plate to look like a hemisphere. The rice crust, brown in appearance and flavorful in taste, is placed on the side of the rice. Most men in the nation like to see their rice crust, and many a man has sent back his dinner to his wife because there was no rice crust. The sauces we have described above are placed either separately or over the rice.

There are numerous other dishes like *kumalikpondo,* known on the coast as "palm butter soup." Usually, when the palm nut is young and fresh, it is deseeded and after straining the roughness out of the water, this water is placed into a pot, where it boils with fish, meat, or chicken. Sometimes the bones are removed out of the broth before putting them into the palm oil water. It is then cooked until it makes a thick gravy. Pepper, and plenty of it, and salt are added. This is then placed over the rice as described for other sauces or eaten with boiled cassava. After going to Monrovia, I learned that people there gave the Kru people the credit for this particular dish. These various vegetable sauces that accompany rice dishes are all generally called by the term "palaver-sauce." Cut potato leaves, pounded cassava leaves in a mortar, and cut okra, each prepared like the vegetables described above, are very popular palaver sauces.

Apart from rice, a secondary staple is *fufu* prepared from fermented fresh and grated cassava. It is placed under water and a powdered starch develops. The water is then poured away and the fine starch remains. This starch is then rolled into balls and cooked with a little water, constantly stirred to produce a gooey consistency. This is served with many of the sauces described above. When it is dried, it gives what is known as "farina" and is flaky and this is served as a sort of cereal. It can also be soaked in water and eaten with honey or sugar.

There is also *diba,* a dish made from manioc, which is peeled, sliced into tiny cubes, and dried. After that it is powdered, sifted, and boiled in a little water, as one would make pudding. This is also eaten with one of the described sauces and others. A great cassava dish, and one that I personally did not like, is *dombai.* It is made by boiling the cassava and stamping it in a mortar until it looks like a thick pudding. It is then eaten with sauces above described, especially palm butter soup. I always had difficulty in swallowing this food.

The eddoes, yams (cultivated and wild), sweet potatoes, and other foods are notable among my people. The eddoes scratch one's mouth, if one should ever attempt to eat them raw. But all of these are eaten roasted in the ashes, especially for morning meals. The potatoes are often fried and consumed that way. Of course they can also be boiled. The eddoe-leaves also give a tasty vegetable dish, as do their stems. Sometimes the stems are boiled into a sort of vegetable soup. Cassava, sweet potatoes, and eddoes, usually make big dishes during the rainy season of the year when food supplies become low. Many times they are fresh, while at other times, they are processed by flaking and drying in the sun, and then stored in attics for consumption in the rainy season.

Paw-paws also grow in abundance here. When ripe and yellow, we eat them as fruit. When green, they are cooked with meat and fish and eaten with rice as vegetables. There are also peanuts, which are not only used to produce oils, but also for making *gendelein,* which is a type of bread made out of ground and roasted rice and roasted peanuts pounded together. Some people add pepper to this mixture, others sugar. The peanut butter is also used to cook peanut soup for eating with rice.

The palm tree, as we have seen, plays an important role in our lives. It is this tree that gives us oils of various types. It also supplies us with raffia for making mats, for bags, baskets, hats, blinds, and even sandals for shoes. This same palm gives us the palm wine, which foreigners have loved so much. After the palm tree is hewn down, a hole is made on the side. This hole is covered with leaves of the palm, and soon, there accumulates a type of milk. At first, this is mild and on the first day can be given to children. But the longer it stays, the stronger it becomes through fermentation, tasting like champagne, and only adults can drink it. After a time, the hole inside is so foul and fermented and it gives no more milk. Then worms gather in it. These worms grow to the size of a small carrot and are creamy looking, with reddish brown heads. These worms, *sos* as my people call them,[7] are gathered, heads removed, and after salting and peppering them, they are placed in a hot skillet and fried in their own oil. They then become so crispy that they sometimes taste like either fried ham or chicken. I told you that you might want to turn up your nose at this. But please remember you are dealing with other people.

In case you did turn up your nose, here is something that may help you to turn it down again. When I was quite a child, Ma Sedia, after a trip to Europe with father, told me that people in France ate frog legs. I thought it was nasty, for had I not seen frogs devouring flies? Had not these same flies sat on the people's sores and on other unclean things? A friend in Switzerland later told me that if I tried them, I would enjoy eating frog legs. This eventually happened in the home of the parents of a friend, Herr and Frau Kuenzli-Bauer. On Good Friday, 1936, they made me taste frog legs and I liked them, and subsequently found myself actually ordering frog legs when in Europe.

On this fascinating and strange trip that you have taken to the restaurants of the Vai country, I am not forgetting that you are born and bred in another world. Hence, I must not close this menu, without placing some fruit, and what might possibly serve as dessert on the "carte de jour." We have of course many varieties of fruit. Most of them are known to you. There are several types of bananas. The red banana, the ordinary banana as you know them, and the plantain. In the mornings, you will find plantains roasted in ashes, fried or boiled, dished out to you. During the day, not with your meals, mind you, you will have occasions to eat as many of the other types of bananas. You receive oranges, pineapples, melons, paw-paws, mango-plums, and other delicacies dished out to you as snacks. You can also get roasted peanuts in between meals.

Then, if you want some citrus fruit, there are oranges in abundance. Some of you can pick from the trees yourself and eat them between meals. Others are stored in attics and a fire made under them, making their skins very dark and hard. But the juice has become concentrated and as sweet as honey. In case you want to chew on something hard, there is also the sugarcane.

For those of you who are accustomed to taking your morning coffee as soon as you wake up in the morning, I am afraid, you cannot be accommodated. You see, in the first place, although my people get up very early in the morning, people usually, except growing children, do not eat until they have done some work. Even then, no coffee is served as a beverage until someone has been out in the rains and becomes wet, and fearing to catch cold, he might take a cup of coffee to keep warm.

Although we could not include all the Vai dishes, you have eaten enough for one day. Besides, the waiters would like to clear the tables.

Notes

1. Cf. J. Büttikofer, *Reisebilder Aus Liberia* (Leiden: E. J. Brill, 1890), Chapter 2.
2. ["Uncle" and "Aunt." *Eds.*]
3. [This is the same custom for the neighboring Mende. *Eds.*]
4. During the course of writing this autobiography, word has come to me that Habibu died in 1940.
5. The same sad news came about Mina, also occurring in the same year.
6. In those days, domestic slavery existed in the Vai country. But it was abolished in 1930–31. [It was a system of dependence with rights and privileges, very different from the plantation slavery of the Americas. *Eds.*]
7. [The Mende call them *gbawei*. *Eds.*]

CHAPTER 5

ON BEAUTY AND ASPECTS OF VAI SOCIAL ORGANIZATION

Each American book I have picked up speaks of the jet-black African with his wiry short hair and his protruding mouth and very flat nose. But we are not of one complexion or type among my people—and this is the only vital point I am trying to drive at in this connection. We range from the very dark to the lightest brown. Our noses also range from as flat as an ironing board to the curves of a bow or the ridges of a mountain. While we may differ widely in complexion, almost all of us have woolly hair. What people think is beautiful is known by what they praise or admire. There are songs and praises for very dark and smooth skin. One often hears the expression *"A kpolee zene a gbon"* (her skin is black until it is glossy).

But skin complexion is not the criterion for beauty; there are many elements in beauty. I have noticed that the criteria that typify a person as being beautiful or ugly differ with various cultures and groups of people. So, for example, my people can stand long hours praising the *kankpoti,* or rings or cuts in the neck of an individual, while people here, especially the women, run to the masseur and have it massaged away, calling the rings "wrinkles" and believing they portray old age. So people can misunderstand other cultures because they have different values. In a course on psychology, where diseases were being discussed, I heard a professor say that people suffering from strabismus or crossed eye are likely to be sensitive about it, because people might laugh at them. But that could only be true where strabismus is considered a disease. People with slanting eyes among my people are considered special or pretty. A person answering that description and having a quality that people seek out certainly need not be sensitive about it.

Although nature can bestow much beauty on an individual, attraction depends on how much he or she does to bring out this beauty. It seems to be with all people and it is particularly reflected in dress and hairstyles among the women. With regard to hairstyle, the Vai woman is very creative and revolutionary. Dressing hair is done by all women in the community. They do their hair mutually and one rarely ever does one's own hair. It is a long and laborious procedure. One has to lie or sit so long and undergo the combing of the hair. I went through it as a child.

One style of dressing hair among the women of my home I shall call the diamond braids. The hair is parted and braided into small diamonds, especially when it is very short. I have only seen girls and children of Blacks use this style in the south [United States] among the rural people. Simple and old as this style is, I often wondered that it got here when these people left Africa. Another style that has come and gone and returned again, even in my generation, is parting the hair into tiny plaits and braiding it from front to back.

Other fashions have been to braid the hair over something stiff or even over a piece of cloth. This is what we called the *jojo*. But braiding the hair is not enough. Just as nowadays, when women wear flowers and the like in their hair, Vai women also add different decorations. I remember several of them. Some were the bones in a feather, around which a gold edge had been made—real gold. For, with them this was as good as wearing a necklace. The head then was covered with the bandana, but the golden edges of the feather pins stuck out. This was for important festive occasions. For common use, a long wooden pin served the purpose. Since the styles are so elaborate, it took several days, even a week sometimes to put them up. The Vai woman puts up with the procedure and takes great care to ensure the style lasts long, even if she has to sleep on her face.

Since America is a country where cosmetics are widely used, I think it would be interesting to see what your African sisters do to make them appeal to their husbands. While men are mostly engaged in this here, it is a close preserve and monopoly of women only, among the Vai. Our cosmetics are not easy to make. It takes several days, even weeks, to prepare a crème or other oil mixtures. Here is one which I saw my mother, and later Mama Jassa, preparing. The grease around the kidney of the cow, sheep, or goat is taken, cut into very tiny cubes, and placed into a bottle and tightly stopped. Several days later, the juice of some aromatic plant is squeezed into it. Again it is tightly stopped up. Sometimes palm kernel or coconut oil is added, and the whole mixture is placed in the sun every day to allow the grease to melt thoroughly. After several other days, cinnamon and other sweet smelling seeds are added. Every day, when the sun is not very hot, the bottle is placed in the sun. This procedure is continued until all the ingredients have become one, and, several months later, the people may then start using it. White clay, found on the shores of streams and swamps, which is often used for whitewashing houses and huts, is also sometimes applied.

Since the impact of Western culture, perfumes like Kolnisch Wasser (4711) and Florida Water are added to the ingredients. All this mixture amounts to a crème. The fact is that my people strive to have a shining and glittering skin, while you strive here to take the shine and gloss away from your faces by using powder. For us, powder is often used on children or for girls in the traditional school. The crème that Vai women use is very effective and lasts all day. I remember in this connection, that since my arrival in this country, Rev. W. L. Turner,[1] superintendent of the Hunstville District of the Methodist Church, who was father's guest in the Vai country in 1922 or 1923, at a time when 15 other Vai rulers and father were celebrating the fiftieth anniversary of my grandmother's ascension to her throne, asked me what it was that the Vai women use that after shaking hands with you, you can smell the perfume on your hands for days. I asked him why he didn't find it out when he was there. He said that the men did not know, and that the women would not tell.

It seems that from time immemorial, African women have been using rouge and lipstick. But not in the way others have been using it. That is to say, we have the habit of using colors that would blend with our complexions. For example, I remember that the adult women wore dark blue and black lipsticks and eyebrow pencils. Sometimes, even charcoal is used on the lips, in case the person involved happens to be very dark. I was therefore thoroughly bewildered on my arrival here to find dark women wearing the reddest of reds on their lips. They just looked too red and funny to me.

Another way in which women attempt to make themselves appealing is to take care of their teeth at all times. To us, having bad teeth is as bad as being ill. We usually use charcoal, ashes, and rattan for polishing the teeth. Since the preservation of the teeth is of great importance, it is considered quite decent to brush your teeth in public. The little sticks, when freshly picked daily contain juice and are used only once, and people can be seen brushing all the time. They chew on them as often as people here chew on chewing gum.

On matters of sanitation, I saw no one in our town who did not take a bath, morning, noon, or night. Of course we do not have the comforts of this great America, in having beautiful bathtubs, but buckets full of water were used in the *kuuwu*.

A powerful society of compulsory male membership called the *Pɔɛɛ* (*Pɔlɔ*, Anglicized to Poro) was founded from time immemorial to curtail the authority of the monarchs who had absolute power. Poro means "law."[2] It is a generic term in the whole area. Foreigners call these "secret societies" or "sacred societies" because they are never able to obtain much information on the organizations.[3] According to my father, "the secret societies of the tribe or grove schools are zealous custodians of spiritual and cultural wealth. The introduction of these cultures into modern African society through the medium of our educational system, there to be conserved as Africa's share of contribution to modern civilization, is the task and duty of the African scholar."[4]

The Poro has two main divisions, which in turn are further divided. These are the youth organizations and the adult organizations. The Poro for youth is a training school, designed to prepare youths for adult responsibilities in the community. Boys usually join between the ages of seven and about nineteen and the training takes place in a forest clearing, which the Vai call *Beli-fila*. This Beli-forest is a permanent location in each area, and is one that is usually not far from the main capital. Every district has its permanent Beli-forest. Because the schools are not held in town, you people of Western culture have given it names like "bush school" and "grove school."

This society is where the authority of the monarch ends and it is headed by the *dazo* (a person endowed with wisdom and mysterious powers). This person is respected highly by even the king, elders of the nation, and, practically worshipped, admired, and honored by the youths of his days. The camp grounds upon which the forest stands is the director's official possession; even the king cannot enter therein without special permission from him.

The training period varies with the nations involved. Our neighbors, the Gola, for example, held their Poro sessions for about four to eight years. The Krim of Sierra Leone held theirs for three years to approximately five, and the Vai and Mende for about two to three years. Nowadays, since most people want to attend Europeanized schools, these years are reduced among many of the groups. The Vai and Mende have a term of about eighteen months, the Krim about two years, while the Gola have their terms fixed for about two to three years.[5]

During the training, boys learn to construct houses and huts, which is a man's job in the community. They learn the art of farming, acquire knowledge of all the arts and crafts of the nation necessary for survival, iron smelting, smithery, tool-making, herbal medicines, and they study African dances. Story-telling and dramatization, the study of wild animals and their habits, are all part of the curriculum. Most important, they are also taught chivalry and the art of war, courage, public-spiritedness, reverence for those in authority and elders, and obedience to the law, history, and traditions of the organization and the nation as a whole.

During all the years in training, the boys are thought of as dead, or caught by a big ghost. After training, they are supposed to be reborn and restored to life again with a great traditional ceremony. During the period the boys are in the school, they are not allowed to visit the towns or see their relatives. The Poro boy has now enjoyed his days in the institution and all who have come out of it usually express the pride of having been initiated just as people look back on their schooldays in Western culture. When the boys are about to come out, the king, who during the whole training period has only been allowed to visit the school as a private individual, visits them and he sends his representatives in a formal manner to meet the dazo and give the boys a sort of examination. The celebration to welcome the new adults is one of the greatest kinds of celebrations that can take place among the Vai. A special pavilion is usually erected in the king's compound, and decorated with the greatest of pomp and splendor.

Now the formal presentation of the forest to the king and elders takes place in an all-male ceremony. The dazo makes a short speech, after which the king and other elders also make formal responses thanking him. The dazo then kneels down before the king sitting in his chair of state, with the boys kneeling alongside of him. The dazo places the palm of his right hand on the right knee of the king and makes a formal statement somewhat like this: "I at all times pledge loyalty to you and my country and I am hereby returning your boys and your forest." Great rejoicing and shouting takes place, after which drumming begins. The parents, friends, and relatives of the boys, as well as well-wishers, from far and near, have assembled by this time in the town to witness their arrival there, because all of the preceding ceremonies take place outside the town.

During this stage, however, they are not yet allowed to speak to them or come near them because the boys are still clad in clay and Poro clothing and the ceremonial washing has not yet taken place. The boys are now lined up on the outskirts of the town, each holding a staff in his hand. When the signal of drums gives echo, they suddenly break loose and amid voices, shouting and yelling, divide themselves, not consciously of course, into the various parts of the town. In doing this, they gaze ferociously into all parts of the town for booties seizing animals left on the loose and demonstrating their skills in killing them.

They then proceed to the river and wash off the clay and put on new clothes. They are now led to the bush by a route different from the one they used when they first entered the town. They then march into the town quietly with the accompaniment of a gentle guitar, and are led to the pavilion amid shouting, applause, and rejoicing of friends and relatives. The elders as well as their friends and relatives come to greet them. They are reborn, and since this is the first day of rebirth, they are babies and are not allowed to do anything for themselves, even feeding themselves. They are provided with servants who do everything for them. The boys are kept in this pavilion for about five or six days, and during all this time, people are feasting and rejoicing. While they are in the hall, they are considered privileged characters. They can order the best of everything that is to be had there, and usually get it. After this, they are returned to their families and homes and are now considered eligible to take their places along with the other adults of the community.

The female counterpart society for women is the *Sande* (sometimes also called *Bondo*) society into which I was initiated, and which I know more intimately. One day Mama Jassa, fearing that my father would take me from her, arranged for my initiation, so that I would be able to take my rightful and permanent position among my people again, even if it should be after a separation of long years. So, although neither in age nor in other ways was I eligible to join the Sande, plans went ahead.

Sande is the proper name in Vai and Mende for this institution for females. It convenes on the outskirts of town. This is probably the case because the scope of teaching does not require too much space as the Poro. A large building or several smaller buildings are erected, called "Bondo," which means privacy, and fenced in with giant forest wood, and no uninitiated person may enter its compound. It is especially forbidden for any man to be found around. If this happens, he is fined heavily or sometimes even punished with a life sentence.

The leader or director of the women's society is called *Sowo* in Mende or *Zo* (short for *Zowo*) in Vai. There are two kinds of Zo. One is the dancing Zo, a masquerade whose duty it is to appear on festive occasions and represent and preside over the functions and ceremonies given in connection with the institution as a whole, in case dances learned in the institution are to be presented. This costume consists of raffia, which has been dyed black. The head of the figure is carved out of wood and also dyed black. It represents, by the way, the head and face of a dead person. The reason for this is we believe that our illustrious ancestors, who left us the bush, should be represented in all we do, and should likewise be in our ceremonies in spirit. Western missionaries gave the name "devil" to this and all other African masquerades to undermine the institution. The dancing Zo, then, is a figure only. The real Zo, the Sande director, is a person, who as in the Poro, gains her position by heredity.

Next to the Zo are three other positions, the *Ligba* or the assistant Zo, the *Kpakpao* or active assistant to the Zo, and finally, the *Mambaie*, a sort of matron of the institution. She supervises the cooking, washing, and other domestic affairs. The first girl to be initiated into the Sande is called *Kelema*, or *Keema* in Mende, meaning one who assembles or calls the others together. Each girl entering receives a new name given in accordance with her talents.

Learning arts and crafts is the first part of the curriculum. It is, for example, a woman's job to spin cotton into yarn, while men do the weaving. The girls may learn this in the Sande. It is a woman's job to cook, which she also learns in the Sande. She is further instructed in singing, dancing, fishing, and making nets for fishing. She learns about herbs, and their names and uses, especially for ailments of women. She is instructed in taking care of babies, how to make cosmetics, and most importantly, how to care for her future husband. In short, the Sande teaches a girl everything she needs to know to become a well-bred and functional woman in the community.

Like the Poro, the Sande ends similarly with great feasting and shouting and rejoicing. Nowadays, girls may be sent to their parents without demonstration of their arts. In olden days, they had to demonstrate over several days what they had learned in the Sande. Apart from covering their skins with white clay like the boys and wearing a little horn around their necks filled with a little red seed or berry, the girls wear no particular uniforms while in the Sande. Around their wrists and waists they usually wear the *Sande-julu*, or beads. These beads are strung around with raffia fiber.

As already intimated, an emergency session of the Sande was called on my account. This is the second time, I am told, in the whole history of the Vai people that this had ever been done. The first time was when a British slave trader by the name of Charles Rogers wanted to marry Jafoi, a daughter of one of the Massaquoi kings, around the middle of the eighteenth century. It was not time for the Sande to convene, and Rogers, having to live on his ship, needed his wife to go with him. Incidentally, this is the marriage that split the Massaquois into two houses. Jafoi had one son for Rogers, whose descendants became the Kpakas, from *kpakai* meaning chair in Vai and Mende.[6]

I rather enjoyed the days in the Sande although I remained there only a very short period. The bathing places, story hours, and herb and mushroom hunts were some of the most fascinating moments. A special part of the curriculum that I enjoyed most, and perhaps therefore excelled in, was the dances. They were several and intricate. It was there that I was given the Sande name *Kibi*, which means swift like lightning. There are in both the Poro and the Sande, other measures in this process of preparation for life that are not necessary to relate in detail. One of these is the measures taken for sanitary and other considerations.[7]

Thus, the societies that shape and model our lives are not wrapped in mysteries, as anthropologists and other writers hitherto have led us to believe; it is just that the writers do not understand what happens and how they function. Much can be gained from the training given by these organizations. It is to be regretted that the traditional system of government, the *Sawa Beli,* has taken the natural road to a gradual death in the nineteenth and twentieth centuries. This is due to the introduction of another system of government into the areas where it is strongest.

By the way, the "bush schools" are common to all areas in West Africa. But the Vai take credit for the founding of the Sawa Beli. It was the Vai, the worthy descendants of the Great Kamala, who brought it about. From them, the other neighbors, such as the Krim, the Gola, the Mende, the Sherbro, and many such adjacent neighbors have patterned their organizations after it.[8] There is so much more that can be said about these organizations, but this account must remain a fragment, to give you an idea of how my people regulate their lives. Of course, there are other organizations in other societies that have had their share in the shaping and modeling of the lives of the African. They too are worth knowing and introducing to other peoples in the world, that is to say, they would be vital to form civilization for all people.

Usually, after a Vai girl leaves the Sande, marriage comes about quite naturally. Marriage customs and courtships differ widely in various parts of Africa, but this narrative deals with the particular customs among the Vai and the Mende. Also, it must be remembered that Islam has influenced these customs. Courtship, as practiced in Western society, is very different, where a man wishing to marry a girl will approach the girl first and later the parents, but sometimes just the woman's consent is enough.

Although marriage only takes place after the girl has been initiated into the Sande, several arrangements are made with the parents long before this. Sometimes parents promise their children to each other. Or a promise is made between families or between two nations. In any event, such a promise is more binding than any marriage license I have seen in Europe or America, where the divorce rate is so high.

If a king or chief sees a virgin whom he wishes to marry, there are three main procedures that he must follow. First, he does what is called *julu-kili* (tying the rope), implying that the woman (or child in many or most cases), is engaged to someone and is not free for anyone else to try for her hand. This does not actually mean tying a rope to a person. It is a symbolic expression.[9] A *tindu*, or messenger, usually a respected female member of the family, is sent with full powers to negotiate for the hand of the girl. Gifts are presented to the parents of the girl and acceptance means agreement or consent has been given. The same goes for a nation promising a bride to another nation for political reasons.

The second stage in courtship is *ndiamobila* (holding friendship). The proposed husband may now show kindness to the girl, talk to her, or give her presents. If done before the tying of the rope, it is usually looked upon with suspicion. The proposed husband is also expected to share the expenses of the bride when she joins the Sande in case she is not already a member.

On graduation from the Sande, the girls spend three days in a hall and the tindu brings another present. During this period also great feasting takes place; people from all over the country reunite to commemorate several events in one. One of these is to accept the girls into the fold of adulthood. For some girls, of course, the first stage takes place during this time, since there is no law that girls must be engaged before going into the Sande. But in case the two initial stages have been made before this period, the final stage is reached. The tindu brings the last gifts. But this time, not only does the proposed husband give gifts to the parents, but also to the Zo. The other responsible women of the Sande are also presented with gifts. Even the dancing Zo receives gifts. All of this gift-giving depends strictly on the station or means of the husband.

For the actual marriage ceremony, the tindu brings the kola. For Westerners, the kola nut is something you know and use for medicinal purposes or in your coke drinks. For us, it has a tremendous symbolic value and takes a great place in the shaping of a marriage union. The messenger now gives, with the final presents that anthropologists call "bride wealth," a bundle of kola nuts, skillfully tied in selected leaves. Although this bundle of kola is presented to the parents, it is intended for the girl. She unties the bundle, which may or may not contain other valuables such as money, jewelry, or other valuable items. The money in the third present (since its introduction into the area), varies in amount from about six to fifty pounds sterling. In the old days, the bride wealth consisted of cattle, African hand-woven cloth, gold, and silver. Wealthy and prominent people often used to include domestic slaves.[10]

After untying the kola nuts, the girl distributes them among the members of her family. All of this must be done in the presence of the tindu. She starts with her father and then mother and on to the other members of the family. After this, her father will ask her in the presence of the messenger a number of questions, to which she will respond in the affirmative: "Do you agree to our using up or disposing of these kola nuts? Is the man who sent these kola the one you love before all others? Do you agree to follow him at all times to *Jinnɛ*?[11] And give him no cause to disrespect us or neglect and abandon you?" Such is the performance of a marriage. Peculiarly enough, this is not been done in the presence of the intended husband, as this may cause the girl to be embarrassed and not answer honestly.

The preparation by the parents who accompany the girl include one wild fish preserved in water, domestic animals (cat, dog, etcetera), earth taken from the girl's home, and any common plant that grows in her home. In the case of a royal bride, she will be given male and female servants to wait on her in marriage. She will then be escorted by relatives and a great crowd of servants to her husband's hometown or abode. The items—land, animal, plant—signify that the bride has a right to everything at home, and therefore should have the same right in the home of her husband.

The girl leaves with great pomp, accompanied by relatives, drummers, and dancers. They are met on arrival in the husband's home by another party of drummers and dancers. Finally, the husband's family arrive. After great feasting, rejoicing, and other demonstrations the husband and wife meet formally as the bride is presented. The husband is expected to keep his wife more or less for good. Separations can be made for a period of six weeks, but the parents must always pledge themselves to send their daughter back. These customs however are changing because of the impact of foreign influences including Islam and Christianity.

The above marriage customs go for young girls. The marriage of a widow differs slightly. In case the husband dies, his widow receives the kola personally, from a male member of the husband's family, one of course who is eligible to marry her. If she accepts, then she has consented to the marriage. If not, others will try until she accepts. In case an outsider should try, and she does accept him, he must pay back a part of the "bride wealth" that the husband's family paid.

The life we led in the Vai country was thrilling. My playmates consisted mainly of Mama Jassa's grandchildren and great grandchildren. There were about forty or fifty of them. Of course I didn't know all of them or did not have a chance to play with many of them. They were in many cases much older. An interesting thing with children is that they usually play the games and events of the happenings of the day, whether these are wars, marriages, or whatever else is taking place in the lives of the adults. I remember once when the Poro ended and the boys were brought to Njagbacca for a ceremony. Mother Kula had brought me, among other things, some beautiful head-cloths and some chains tied together in two bundles for the waist. These were pure silver bundles, with bracelets and earrings, and chains or necklaces, to match. It was quite good then, when I arrived in Njagbacca and found the feast in full swing. I was able to dress fully and look on.

This feast at Njagbacca was remarkable for the fact that it gave us children something to imitate. There were two boys who danced remarkably well. They are the ones of whom it could be said that they danced like lightning. Their Poro names were *Kpanbii* and *Ngongobeke*. They were said to have been Gola. When they danced and swung around, you could hardly see their bodies, only the costumes they wore and their movements. After the feast was over, some of the other grandchildren of Mama Jassa were constantly imitating these boys and applying the names of the dancing boys to themselves. Although these were dances for boys,

I attempted learning them from what the grandchildren or rather my nephews had been able to catch.

There were not many girls in Njagbacca around my age. So, I had to play with boys. As a matter of fact, the only girls there for me to play with were Vanja, a Gola girl who was there for that purpose, and Bini, Ngoh Hawa Sheriff's daughter. But Bini was younger than I and hardly could have afforded an appropriate playmate. Mama Jassa's grandchildren who were my playmates were the boys around my age, like Kolli Selleh Tamba (son of her daughter, Famata Sheriff). Kolli's nickname is Moli Jaalee, or the red Mohammedan. Varney Tammuzu's nickname is Moli Pisi, the small Mohammedan, because he had been a very puny baby. His mother, by the way, is Hawa Sheriff. Her other children are Bini (girl) —this is only a nickname and I don't know her real name—and Kula (a girl) who was never in Njagbacca while I was there.

The other grandsons of Mama Jassa who were in Njagbacca and formed part of my play circle were To Moli, Moli Namaa, and Njagbacca Moli. The latter three are sons of my sister Jeneba. Others were Mina's sons whose names I do not quite remember, except Tammu. Momolu Sandimanni, son of Bala Sandimanni, a nephew of father's, was part of the group. These boys really knew how to play. Of course I played with the few girls there, but following the boys in their play was much more fun.

The king of the whole gang was Koli, or Moli Jaalee. He was wild and there was no tree he could not climb. The boys usually made bows and arrows and played wars and the like. Of course all of these boys were not in Njagbacca at the same time, or when they were, they did not stay there for a long time. But when Moli Jaalee or Koli came, there was always trouble, because, although he was not the oldest in the group, everyone obeyed him. There was not much fun without him. My admiration of him must have had its beginning then.

In the plays, banana trees were cut down. Orange groves and branches climbed and ripe oranges, mangoes, and other fruits, ripe or green, found their way to the ground. On the outskirts of Njagbacca was a little monkey bridge leading to the farm and we took a great delight in crossing it, in spite of the dangers.

But our play did not consist of only these spoils and dangerous games. There were peaceful ones too. One which we played with the greatest of delight was the counting game. The object of the game was to ascertain who can speak fastest and count backwards:

Wulu le?	Where is Dog?
Wulu be sowo lo	Dog is in the hole
Mo londo le?	Where is one man?

Mo londo be wulu baa sowo lo	One man is with dog in the hole
Mo fela le?	Where are two men?
Mo fela be mo londo baa	Two men are with one man
Mo londo be wulu baa sowo lo	One man is with dog in the hole
Mo sakpa le?	Where are three men?
Mo sakpa be mo fela baa	Three men are with two men
Mo fela be mo londo baa	Two men are with one man
Mo londo be wulu baa sowo lo	One man is with dog in the hole
Mo naani le?	Where are four men?
Mo naani be mo sakpa baa	Four men are with three men
Mo sakpa be mo fela baa	Three men are with two men
Mo fela be mo londo baa	Two men are with one man
Mo londo be wulu baa sowo lo	One man is with dog in the hole
Mo soolu le?	Where are five men?
Mo soolu be mo naani baa	Five men are with four men
Mo naani be mo sakpa baa	Four men are with three men
Mo sakpa be mo fela baa	Three men are with two men
Mo fela be mo londo baa	Two men are with one man
Mo londo be wulu baa sowo lo	One man is with dog in the hole

As can be seen readily, the rhyme increases. The questioner asks and the group answers as a whole. The person who omits something or is left behind, has to forfeit. The game proceeds to ten, always counting forward. Between ten and twenty, it proceeds backward when answering.

Like all children, some of the games consisted of teasing each other. For instance, I was ever annoyed when the boys would take a stick and hold it in the palm of their hands and would recite a rhyme to the effect of the eating ability of the individual whose name is being called. They would walk around the court while doing this. If the stick falls, then that person eats very little. If it stays long in the hands, then the person eats a lot. What I much later found out is that the stick in the hands would be helped along a little when they got to the name of the person of whom they wanted to say eats very much. Bini and I were the ones who became very annoyed when it was said of us that we ate a great deal.

Mina's daughter, Zuli, had married after coming out of the Sande. Upon this we played marriage in imitation of the ceremony. In all of these games, Moli Jaalee was the king. One reason I am inserting this business of marriage is because when we played marriage, the boys would come and ask the king, who was father of everyone, whether or not they could marry this or that person. I remember that Moli Jaalee would never let me marry anyone. Instead, I was always designated to be the one to go as a girl in waiting. Both Moli Jaalee and I remembered this later on as a young man and young woman, when discussing some other matters vital to both of us.

Aside from having fun, many of our plays were wholesome sport. Since we lived on the Njagbacca Creek, one of these was bathing in the creek. At the source of the river, nobody bathed. This was almost at the back of our house. The town was situated on a hill, and in spite of the flood during the rainy season, our huts were never touched. There, at this mouth, we obtained water for drinking and home use. Further down the river, or rather creek, was the place where clothes were washed. People took their daily baths there as well. The source of the creek was shallow and one could almost walk across it. But further down, it was so wide and deep that a canoe was needed to go across. Crocodiles occasionally showed up, but we bathed there all the same.

On the other side of the Njagbacca Creek was the road leading to Kpassalo. But since there was no town directly on the other side of the stream, people who came from there had to yell for help in crossing, whereupon the canoe was taken across and they were brought to Njagbacca. We children, who usually bathed in the stream, heard these yells and were naughty enough to respond. The person across would say *"wo na Bioooooo,"* which translates as, "come and get me." We would usually respond, *"I ma woseke ya kinaoooo, faliye nu ma na idanda."* ("Don't make noise where you have to spend the night. The crocodiles might hear you"). We were often scolded, even punished for doing it, but nothing seemed to help. One day, my mother's brother Mbimba came to Kpassalo, to see their brother (cousin), Jaakoli, and was bringing some items from mother for me. He yelled for a crossing, and not recognizing his voice, we treated him the same way. When he was finally brought over, I had the shocking surprise of my life, to have aided in forcing my own uncle to stay across the river until almost dusk.

Another time, we played a prank with a baby we were really very fond of. When the women went to harvest on the farms, the children stayed behind under the supervision of an adult woman to take care of their needs and cook for them. One of the women had the habit of not giving us all that was due us, but took everything to her husband first. We never had enough to eat. The boys reported the matter to Mama Jassa, but she did nothing. The boys therefore took the baby and hid it on the outskirts of the town. There is nothing so awful as a mother in terror. She searched for her baby in vain. I was almost at the point of telling where the baby was, when the boys finally obtained the promise from her that she would in future give us all the food that had been left for us.

Traveling was an important passion in the life of the African. This fact is in a way difficult to understand, when we stop to consider the difficulties involved in trying to get from one place to the other. Our traveling in those days was by canoes, in case we had to cross rivers, in hammocks, or simply by the wheels given us by nature. Yet, in spite of these facts, we travel as much as Americans, who are people constantly on the move. It is therefore not surprising to hear that during the short period I was with Mama Jassa, I traveled extensively through the Vai country.

I went to spend a short time with my sister, Jeneba Sheriff. Mama Jassa, on hearing that father had married, had a suspicion that he would soon be coming for me. She told me one day that we were to go on a trip. Of course, before this trip, my sister Hawa Massaquoi, had taken me to her home in Pala where she was married to Chief Varney Papa.

This visit to Sister Hawa was very enjoyable. Varney Papa had many of the colonial type houses known already in other parts of the Vai country. He made a great deal of money by trading with Europeans and with the Bassa people. Pala is one of the most beautiful Vai towns that I have ever visited. In the center of the town were coconut groves, with houses at the end of each. Pala had the physical surroundings of a seat of government. The square had the coconut groves, and surrounding them were a courthouse, guesthouses, and several bungalows. In one of these lived my sister. Around the same square was a large kitchen, where all the women of Varney Papa did their cooking.

It was in Pala that I saw a person in the stocks called "block," for the first time. The block is a stick into which holes are cut out, and a person's foot or feet are stuck in. A chain is tied into it and the person drags one foot while holding the chain. This is one way of being punished for a criminal offense. Sometimes men even punish their wives that way when they believe that adultery has been committed. This is how criminals are punished, not locked up in jails and prisons as in the West.

Before Mama Jassa and I took the trip to some of her daughters, I visited Kpaasalo to see my Uncle Jaakoli, who was, among other things, a Muslim priest. His wife, Maangei, held an important position in the Sande. In fact, she was the assistant director of the district. Sando, Mama Jassa's baby daughter, was married to a chief in Gbawolokolo. Since this town is not quite a day's walk from Njagbacca, Sando often came and got me to spend days with her.

Mama Jassa and I decided to visit some shrines in the Vai country. One of these, I remember, was in the town of Sulima, where the holy crocodile was. There are many legends on both the Sierra Leonean and Liberian sides of Vai country. One legend claims that an ancestor once got angry and jumped into the river. Another legend is that someone had a dream in which the king was to sacrifice the best person he had, in order to prevent canoes from capsizing in the rough water. So, the best the Vai king had was his son who was duly sacrificed to the river. And, curiously enough, for a long time, several centuries now as a matter of fact, no canoe has been reported capsized there. This son is supposed to have turned into a crocodile, which guides the waters and prevents us from harm, so we are introduced to the holy crocodile.

Mama Jassa took me there to the side of the water. And, holding me in her arms, she and the people called aloud: *"Maada naooo!"* meaning "come grandfather." And, this call had not been long before we could see the splashing of the waters and there was "grandfather." He came, and approaching Mama Jassa, came nearer and nearer, and finally smelled my feet. My heart nearly stopped beating. *Mamada*[12] ran into the water and came back several times, standing near Mama Jassa while she was holding me in her arms. He went to a tree to which a white hen had been tied, took the fowl, and devoured it entirely before all of us. Before each act of Mamada, something was said, but I was in too much terror to understand. Mamada was then given a bottle of gin or whiskey, which he also drank in front of us. But all of this may not seem real to you at all.

While visitors from elsewhere were terrified by Mamada, the people in the town nearby were not afraid of him. Not only did he answer to calls for a presentation for his descendants, he often crawls on land and creeps around the town. Mamada must be very old indeed. My reason for saying this is that father often told us how, when he was a boy, Mamada would come around the waters of Cape Mount where he was in school, and how he would climb on his back and swim to some other part of the water, much to the horror of the missionaries at St. John's School, which he was attending at the time.

Mama Jassa took me to many other shrines in the Vai country. Among them was the tomb of the inventor of the Vai script, one of the few indigenous writing systems in sub-Saharan Africa. A spiritual chief of the Vai, Dualo Bukele had been very sensitive and an unusual boy in his childhood with a great vision. He was apprenticed to an Islamic priest, who had treated him with all the severity of a trainer. When the priest traveled, he left Dualo in the charge of a colleague, who then reported his misdemeanors in writing, which was placed in a Koran and given to Dualo to take to his master. Upon his arrival, his master could tell him everything he had done in his absence and accordingly punish him for his misdeeds. This left a great impression on the boy who thought writing must be a great thing.

When he grew up, he never gave up the idea of a writing system for the preservation of documents of our people as well as for personal and commercial purposes. Strange, how often something that is on our minds also haunts us in our dreams. This was just what happened to Dualo. He dreamed and saw the hand of a great spirit. This supernatural Being, whom he was not able to see, spoke to him and told him that he had come to designate him as the one who might show his people a system of writing. This hand wrote signs in the sand with their meanings. When Dualo awoke, he was surprised to find that he remembered a dozen or so of the signs. He called the elders of the nation together and told them his dream, demonstrating to them their meanings.

This writing was at first in crude form. But before Dualo's death, a few other characters were added. Since his death, many Vai scholars have worked on the script and have developed and added to it considerably (see figures 5.1 and 5.2). My own father, if you will pardon the somewhat subjective way of treating the matter, compiled the script and published it in journals. Before him, Clark, a German, the missionary Koelle (who visited the area in the late 1840s), Maurice Delafossse, Sir Harry Johnston, Büttikofer, and many others had made the script known to the Western world, but in its incomplete form. Lately, while father was

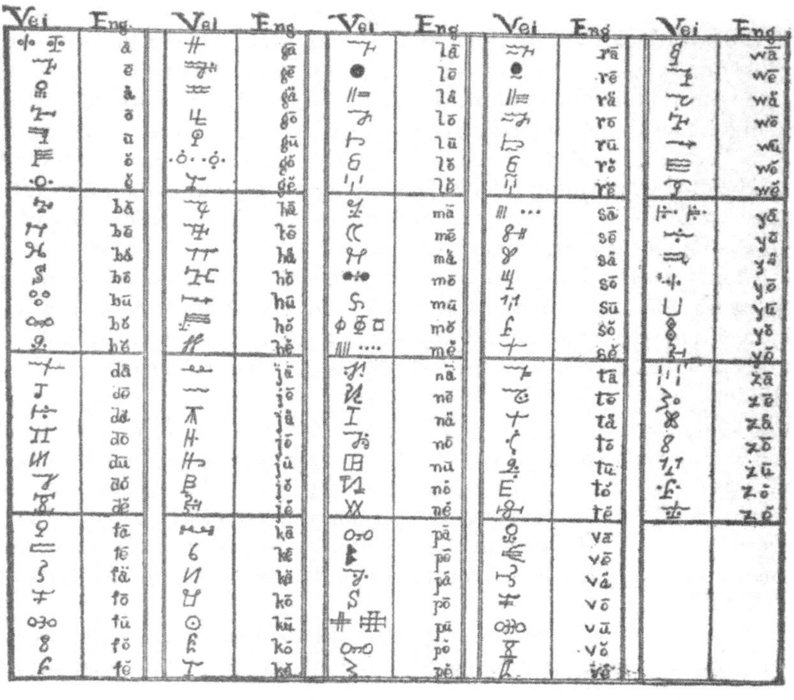

Figure 5.1   Vai script character chart by Momolu Massaquoi, 1899

guest lecturer at Hamburg University, he added to the script through a system whereby words that are not strictly Vai, or even African, can be written using this script. The script is syllabic writing. His student Dr. August Klingenheben, now director of the Seminar für Afrikanische Sprachen, Hamburg University, has had these published.[13]

I tried at one time to have father show me the method of systematically adding to the script, but although I was able to see what he did, I was not able to understand the method clearly. That is something that he just had to take with him to the grave. It was perhaps intended that each generation should strive to make their own contribution, and not ride on the backs of the parents.

Near Jondu, then, where a Vai man now has a coffee plantation, lies the remains of the great Dualo Bukele of the Vai, who left us a heritage of which every Vai is justly proud. No wonder that Mama Jassa should

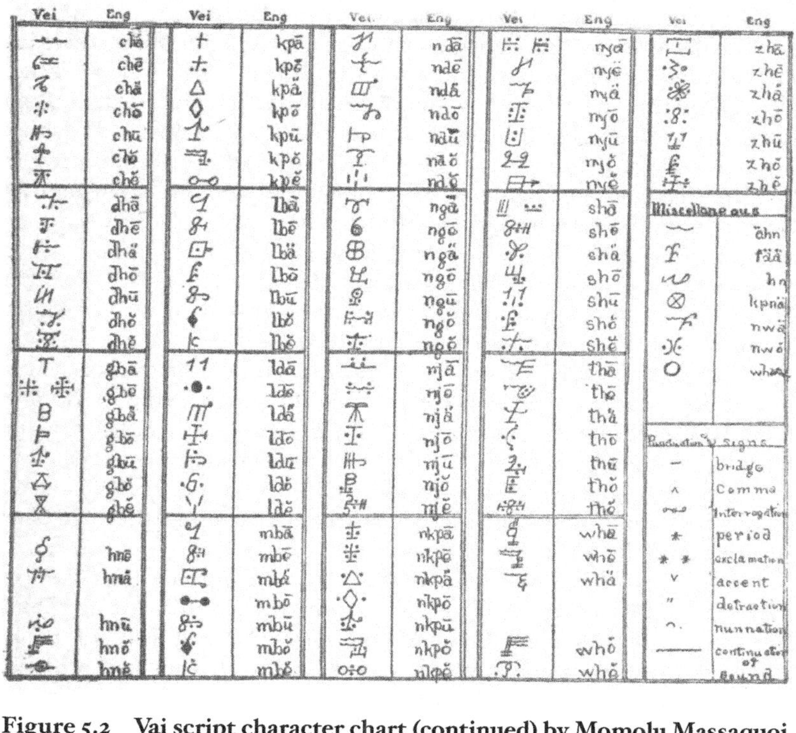

Figure 5.2   Vai script character chart (continued) by Momolu Massaquoi, 1899

have taken me to the resting place of this wonderful man. Of course we visited schools, which the Vai people had established for the teaching of the script and other documents. One such school is situated in Jondu. No Vai is considered learned, or no one is considered knowing Vai, until he or she has passed through these schools, either by examination or direct attendance.

Mama Jassa and I spent some time with her daughter Hawa Sheriff, whose husband's home is really in Tienimanni. Tienimanni was sandy and the surrounding soil depleted, so the inhabitants first opened a place called Tibo, which had virgin lands around, first for farming purposes, but at the time of our visit was gradually becoming more and more a place for residence. Mama Jassa left me in Tibo with sister Hawa and proceeded to Gbunaaja, where sister Famata and her husband were living at the time, although they originally had their home in Jondu. All of the towns I am mentioning here are in that section of the Vai country usually known as the Gawula District.

In Gbunaaja I took ill. I would be sick for a day or two and would be up for a day or two. This continued, until one day, while I was watching the pots boil early in the morning I saw three boys arrive. When Mother Jassa called their names, I knew they were my brothers Jawa (Jalawa) and Ibrahim (Abraham or Boima), as well as the son of a Vai chief whose name was Siafa. Father was in the interior and had heard that we were in Gbunaaja, and, not being able to come to us and not knowing that we were about to return to Jondu (we would have been there but for my indisposition), had sent the boys with a message to Mama Jassa. I was so happy to see my brothers that I stared at them for a long time. Mother Massa had spoken a great deal of them, as had Mama Jassa and Mama Soko, so I knew them at least by description.

Jawa was the eldest of my two brothers. He was attending school in Monrovia and we had never met. Ibrahim was attending school in Freetown, and Siafa, my Vai cousin who had been given to father to raise, was older than both of them. The boys left before sunset as they had to return to Bomboja, which was nearly a two-hour walk from Gbunaaja before dusk. Since they had come very early that morning, they had been able to spend the whole day with us.

I do not remember how long we stayed on at Gbunaaja after the visit of the boys. But a few days later, we left for Jondu, still visiting Mama Massa's daughter, Famata. Of all Mama Jassa's children, Famata speaks the most beautiful English you have ever heard. Father had sent her to the mission school, and later to Annie Walsh Memorial Secondary School for Girls in Freetown. While in Freetown she met her future husband who was attending the Sierra Leone Grammar School there. Not caring very much for "civilized life," she had returned home and even readopted African ways of dress and manners. Her husband, although living in the interior, wears European dress.

We spent several days in Jondu and many of the female members of the family around that section came together. Father had remarried in Monrovia, and was expected to be in Jondu to present his wife to his family. Father's wife this time was the former Miss Rachel E. T. Johnson, great grand-daughter of one of the founders of the Republic of Liberia, and grand-daughter of the first Liberian-born president, Hilary Richard Wright Johnson, and her father was Brigadier General Gabriel Monroe Johnson.[14]

Several days after our arrival in Jondu, father, his wife, and his entourage arrived there. I had the most exciting experience of my life, when my new mother, being presented to us, gave all of us a "kiss" as did her mother and her friends. This experience was exciting because I had never seen kissing. Not knowing what that meant, I asked Mama Jassa for days before she explained that it was called *dadondaa*, meaning mouth stuck to mouth, which made no sense to me. She did not say it was an expression of joy and affection. I guess you Americans, who believe in kisses, must be thinking that we are missing all the fun in life.

I cannot complete the travels in the Vai country without paying some tribute to my ego. As a child, I conformed to all the conceptions of beauty there. My sisters, Hawas (both Massaquoi and Sheriff), Jeneba, Sando, and the rest, made an exhibition of me—even Mama Jassa did. No place did we visit without our hearing the question: "Whose beautiful child is that?" and they proudly replied, "Momolu IV...and her mother is the Bali woman...do you remember the quiet girl who was his wife in the Gallinas?" But on later visits, I expected the compliments in vain as no one asked the question any more.

During the last days in Jondu, I took seriously ill. Mama Jassa and the rest of the family then hurried on to Njagbacca with me. There, it was discovered that I had developed the measles and also that I had worms. I don't know exactly what herbs Mama Jassa used to treat me, but I remember she gave me roots of herbs to drink. These roots were boiled and tasted very acidic. Habibu had a new hut where banana leaves were spread on the floor for me to rest. Since I had a very high temperature, the cool banana leaves were meant to reduce it. The leaves withered due to the heat from my body so fast that they had to be replaced often. Perhaps this is one way of drawing fever out of a person's body in my culture.

While convalescing at Njagbacca, I was taken outdoors one day and introduced to my brother Nathaniel Vaali or Varney Massaquoi, whom

I had never met as he was attending school in Freetown. On the way to Jondu, he stumped his toe and developed a sore. Mama Jassa and Mama Soko washed the sore as the poor boy screamed "Mercy!" He spoke no Vai, only Mende and Creole. As I did not understand any English, I asked Mama Jassa, who "Mercier" was and why he would call him. I offered to go and fetch him for my brother, if that would ease his agony.

Since I had to deal with the meeting between me and another brother, I quite forgot to mention how my father's new wife, Rachel Johnson, my mother, became a family member. Although we had already met her in Jondu, her general acceptance into the Vai family did not take place until the group came to Njagbacca, Grandmother Sandimanni's old abode. Of course she had been introduced to many Vai leaders in many places, but for this purpose, paramount chiefs and other leaders had come to Njagbacca to witness the occasion. Of course all the leaders of the various female organizations of the country as well as the female leaders of the various families were represented.

Rachel Johnson was then formally initiated into the Sande, and a great dancing and rejoicing took place. She had become a Vai and had to have a Vai name. Thus, she was given the name Sedia, after Mama Jassa, whose full name is Jassa Sedia, and who at the time was the oldest living member of the family. The name was conferred upon her on this formal occasion by Mama Jassa herself, and by Grandmother Bee, who was the only living sister of Grandmother Sandimanni. All over the Vai country, she is not known by any name other than Ma Sedia, even to this day.

My mother, father, and the traveling entourage left for the Teewoh district to introduce Ma Sedia there. It seemed my father's plan was to take me with him to Monrovia, when they returned from Teewoh. Everyone around me seemed to know something of the plan but me. In the following days, my Uncle Jaakoli, having been informed by Mama Jassa, came bringing me gifts and to find out whether I had any message to send to mother, as he thought he might be visiting them soon.

Not only did Uncle Jaakoli's visit appear suspicious, but Mama Jassa began acting queer. I would catch her crying at times. Moreover, she began lecturing me that times were changing and that people needed a foreign education in order to be able to get along in our country. She expected me to go and come back with the best that the Europeans had to offer. I was to return soon and take care of her in a new way as no other daughter of hers had done. She added that those who failed to acquire Western education would later become the servants and slaves of those who did. She talked about the new era every day. She pointed out to me that the *puumo* (European/Westerner) was corrupt. One had to be very careful and choose the good things that they have to offer.

But her regrets over my having to depart did not end with lecturing. All my favorite dishes were prepared. Once when we were expecting guests, and I did not feel that the chicken she was about to kill would be enough for all of us, she killed a large one instead and stood there with a switch and made me eat all of it, so as to kill my appetite for fowl for all times.

Not only Mama Jassa, but all other female members of my family as well tried to impress on me forever the Vai moral and social conduct and behavior. Mama Soko, Mama Bee, all of my sisters…they were all trying to show me the proper way. But while the grownup female members of the family were lecturing me, the boys, their sons, were teasing me. Some said that people in Monrovia only eat on flat plates and with forks, the food not enough to cover the palm of one's hands. They also told me that I would not be allowed to take a daily bath in Monrovia, where I would be given only a glass of water in the morning, with which I could only wash my face. My nephews also told me that I would no longer be able to use rattan or ashes to brush my teeth and will only get used sticks to use for months making my teeth decay and fall off to be replaced by dead people's teeth! They said that over there people bought sticks that had been made in faraway places, and that probably had been sold and used by other people before being sent there. This stick I was to use for months to brush my teeth. Eventually, all my teeth would decay and fall off, and then the teeth of dead people would be substituted in place of my own.

With these horrifying and disgusting stories, I made up my mind not to go with father when he returned. I told Mama Jassa, who promised to see what she could do. When father and Ma Sedia returned from the Teewoh district, father did not dare face Mama Jassa to ask for me to go. So, Ma Sedia who could not speak Vai came with my sister Famata Sheriff to interpret for Mama Jassa who did not speak English. I was not asleep, but was already in bed and as quiet as a mouse. When Ma Sedia asked Mama Jassa to let me have the opportunity of attending school in Monrovia, she responded that she had tried to convince me but I did not wish to go. I felt very happy, but suddenly, I was utterly flabbergasted when I heard Mama Jassa tell Famata to say that she was growing very old and feeble and that I needed a younger and more vigorous person to look after me. She was therefore giving her permission for me to go. The perspiration at this point ran down my back and all over my head and face.

Feeling betrayed, the only course left for me to take was to carry out a little plan that I had formulated in my mind, and kept it a secret all to myself. I had heard someone say that if you wished to hide, you should go into the shrubberies and bushes, then hold your index finger in your mouth, and nobody would discover you. When the time of our departure came, and I saw people loading the boats, I quickly ran and hid between the cassava patches. And, to my great surprise, the old saying worked like a miracle. The boys who were to place me into the boat looked everywhere. Mama Jassa looked and everyone called, but I could not be found. Men and women of Njagbacca, children, my brothers, father, everyone called and looked. They looked for what seemed like hours to me. Suddenly, they pretended to have given up the search and gone. Someone who stayed called out to me to come out because the party had gone. I came out, but hardly had I made my appearance, than one of the men grabbed me and took me to the boat, while I kicked and struggled in his arms. I could see Mama Jassa still as she attempted to keep pace with the man carrying me, calling out to me and asking me not to feel sad that she would soon be sending for me or coming to see me. I can still picture her standing near the shore as the boat carried me away, slowly but surely... farewell, Mama Jassa!

Notes

1. [Walter Lee Turner served as the dean of the Stokes Bible School in Monrovia in the late 1920s. *Eds.*]
2. [The Rev. Max Gorvie who was a member says that it means very, very old, ancient. See Gorvie, *Old and New in Sierra Leone* (London: United Society for Christian Literature, 1945). *Eds.*]
3. [A few Europeans, even government officials, were able to acquire membership. *Eds.*]
4. "Commencement Address by Momolu Massaquoi," p. 15.
5. [Today the session can last for as little as one week. *Eds.*]
6. [The Rogers in question was likely a son of Zachary Rogers, agent of the Royal African Company in the Sherbro in the late seventeenth century (see C. Fyfe, *A History of Sierra Leone,* London: Oxford University Press, 1962, p. 10); For a more detailed account of Rogers/Kpaka, see Adam Jones, "White Roots: Written and Oral Testimony on the First Mr Rogers," *History in Africa*, Vol. 10 (1983), pp. 151–162. *Eds.*]
7. [An allusion to clitoridectomy, the practice of removing the clitoris of a girl as part of her initiation, variously called today female genital mutilation (FGM), female genital cutting (FGC), or circumcision. The justification of sanitation or cleanliness derives from Islamic practice but not Islamic law. Hence several Islamic societies have abolished it. *Eds.*]
8. I am deeply indebted to my brother S. Ciaka Massaquoi, for constantly furnishing me with information that I have needed while writing this autobiography for clarification of things I do not clearly remember, since my association with the subject matter was mostly during my infancy. Especially, almost all the materials on the male divisions were furnished by him.

9. [Among the Mende at least, a bracelet like a rope is actually tied around the wrist of the young girl, and represents the engagement ring of the West. Once people see it, they must look elsewhere. *Eds.*]

10. This was before the abolition of domestic slavery that existed in the area before 1930.

11. Place of confinement due to some dreadful or incurable disease, sometimes a village, sometimes a single hut. The person or patient placed there is allowed to have no communication save with his or her doctor. The wife during such a time is expected to remain faithful to her husband. Any misconduct on her part tends to react on the patient, even hinder his cure. This is a popular belief. This statement corresponds to your "for better or worse" in the church marriage vows.

12. [Great grandfather. *Eds.*]

13. For evidence of Momolu Massaquoi's first compilation of the Vai script, see: "The Vai People and Their Syllabic Writing," *Journal of the African Society*, Vol. 10 (1911), pp. 459–466. [Actually, Massaquoi's first of several Vai script publications was "The Vey Language," *Spirit of Missions*, Vol. 64 (1899), pp. 577–579. The missionary philologist S. W. Koelle, who Momolu Massaquoi actually met on the streets of London in the early twentieth century, visited the script inventor, Bukele, and recorded his story, in Vai country, in 1849. See Konrad Tuchscherer and P. E. H. Hair, "Cherokee and West Africa: Examining the Origins of the Vai Script," *History in Africa*, Vol. 29 (2002), pp. 427–486. *Eds.*]

14. [Gabriel M. Johnson was a general in the Liberian army, the mayor of Monrovia, and the cousin-in-law of Liberian president Charles Dunbar Burgess King. Johnson was also the Universal Negro Improvement Association's "Potentate" in Liberia, a topic discussed later by Fatima Massaquoi. *Eds.*]

CHAPTER 6

LIFE IN MONROVIA

Our trip was pleasant, exciting, and full of novelties. I would have enjoyed it much more had my thoughts not lingered constantly on Mama Jassa. I kept wondering what she was likely to be doing at such and such a time, and who would take my place with her reminding her of the various items she would have on the calendar for the day. Meanwhile, my brothers and I were slowly becoming acquainted.

We streamed down the Njagbacca Creek in may-gig-boats, surf boats, and canoes to the bar and then to the Piso Lake, which led us to Bendu where we were received by Chief Tie and his brother Fewe. Bendu is a beautiful modern Vai town. Vai traditions relate that when they first settled in the area, there was scarcity of water. The only body of water near enough was the Atlantic Ocean at Cape Mount. Doves visited them, coming from the direction of Cape Mount. They fed these doves. In appreciation of what they did for the doves, one of the doves dug a wide and deep hole. This hole later developed into the great and beautiful lake known in Vai as *Piso*, meaning dove hole but in Liberian geography books known as "Fisherman Lake."

Our house in Bendu was beautiful. It was built in a cone-like shape. It also had several large rooms on both wings of the building. Father and my mother and some of the other females on the trip had their quarters on one side of the wing, while I had a room on the other side with friends of Ma Sedia whom she had invited. Father had much work to do in Bendu, especially in the settlement of disputes, some of which had been decided in Vai courts but appealed to the *manja* or king, for at the time his was the last word in Vai law. Although we stayed several days in Bendu, we did not see much of the manja. But we, the children, had enough time to amuse ourselves, bathing all day long in the Piso, and on clear days we had the special joy of looking over and seeing Cape Mount.

It was in Bendu that I had the pleasure of meeting Kula, Mama Jassa's granddaughter, who had been given away to be brought up here. This is a general custom in this area because people believe that at times strangers are in a better position to bring up the child. Not being so closely related to them, they would be likely to see their faults and correct them more quickly than would their own parents. In the case of our giving out children to be brought up in Westernized families, this has happened because of the changing tide in African life. This is hence not a practice peculiar to the Vai alone, but applies to many of the other nationalities around.

I rather liked Kula, because she bore a tie between Mama Jassa and me. She appeared plump while I was skinny at the time. Kula came to play with me daily, and we quickly became good friends. Oh, how I wished at that moment that she could have gone to Monrovia with us! Father must have guessed my thoughts, for he asked the lady who was taking care of Kula to allow her to go to Monrovia and be put into school there with me. But this was difficult to do, because the lady had been Kula's aunt on her father's side and she did not wish to give her consent to this without first consulting her father. Since there was not enough time left for us to get this consent, the idea of her going with us was dropped.

When the time came to depart, the men in charge of the boats came one by one to pick up Ma Sedia, the ladies, and the others who were wearing shoes. Up to this point I had thought that this was only my father's privilege. I began envying them and wished I could be taken up too. Just then, one of the men came and wanted to take me into the boat, but my father said, "leave that child and pick up the grown people," which made me inwardly furious. I later asked my father why, and he explained that those people had on shoes, and could not walk in the water to climb into the boats without ruining their shoes.

On that sunny morning then, we must have spent about three hours on the Piso and then on foot to Jondu. Of course the younger children in the group did not walk all the way; we were taken into the hammock with either father or Ma Sedia when we got tired. Through dense forests, shrubs, crossing rivers, creeks, well-built roads, bad roads, narrow paths, and monkey bridges, we made our way forward. The Poro was in session in the Gawula district of the Vai country, so the women and the children had to announce their presence. Father's nephew, Mr. Kimba, who had been in school in Sierra Leone and had not had a chance to become initiated, was picked up by the Poro. This showed me that even people who had great influence like father, could not surpass the Poro. This further heightened my respect for the organization.

The rest of the trip went on without further incident, and we finally approached the Lofa River, crossed over and reached the beach on the shores of the Atlantic Ocean. We walked a whole day before we reached another river and after riding downstream, we were finally in sight of

Monrovia. I had heard a great deal about Monrovia and my bosom was full of excitement as I saw how beautiful the city was at night.

The foundation of Liberia, a Negro Republic on the West Coast of Africa during the early part of the last century, is known to all. It is likewise known that Monrovia is the capital of this republic, and that the city was named after US president Monroe. It must therefore not be surprising that in Monrovia live those people who believe in the great ideology of democracy.[1] The African name for this place was *Dulu-Kɔlɔ*, from *Dulu* (river), and *Kɔlɔ* (under; below), in Vai, Kpelle, and other languages. The name is usually contracted to *Duu-kɔɔ*, which is written in Liberia as Ducor.

As we approached the city that night, I saw that all the houses were lit so bright that as we made the turn around Vai town, it seemed as though we were lying at the foot of a lighted mountain. All of this was indeed quite a treat for me. If I had previously admired the moon and stars at night, which now seemed too far away, these lights appeared near enough to touch. My wish was to one day be in the position to bring Mama Jassa and mother to all the places that I had visited with my brothers, father, and Ma Sedia. They too, then, could see the bright man-made stars. We landed at "Massaquoi-wharf" and walking through narrow paths reached our home. It was Sunday, because the next morning I saw washing hanging out in every yard I could see. I was later to find out that the weekly washing in those days was done on Mondays.

There were many friends and relatives at the house to greet my parents. They were invited to have dinner with my parents but we the children could not eat with them. Kona (who later became Alice Johnson) and I sat in the passage room of the house on two chairs, while my brothers and the other boys sat on the floor on beautiful leaf-green linoleums with yellow flower designs. All of a sudden Angeline, Mama Sedia's youngest sister, came for a chair. I could not understand what she wanted. She pulled the chairs we sat on, bringing about a fight between us that very night. Father, however, heard the noise and came out and scolded me.

After dinner, Cousin Boima Sandimanni told me that father had agreed for him to take me to his house to spend the night with his daughter Titi. We came back home the next day, yet we were almost always together, for she lived with us on Ashmum Street until we left for Germany. In Monrovia there are many houses of corrugated iron sheets either on the roofs or as siding. Otherwise, many houses were weather boarded, and still others were built of cement or brick. Most of the houses I saw had two or more storeys, while in Vai country they were mainly one-story homes. The furniture was usually imported from America or Europe, and in very few cases do we have African-made furnishings.

Our home on Ashmum Street is built on eight or ten large cemented pillars. When people came from the interior the basement was screened very tastefully to accommodate them. At other times, it was simply a basement and was used on washing and ironing days, and for storing things like cages. We children had a great deal of fun in it. It provided an excellent abode for doll homes and for the baking of cakes, which Angeline, Titi, and many of the children in the neighborhood and I delighted in.

From the front of the house, our home could be entered by two stairways at each end of the piazza that almost surrounded the house. Inside was a waiting room where we sat on the night of our arrival in Monrovia, and a parlor that had blue velvet furniture with a beautiful red Persian carpet. The entrance doors to the parlor had red water-glass designing at the upper half. There were also beautiful and delicate display cases with trinkets and rare porcelains. In the parlor was a three-legged table, a chandelier around which were posted pictures of the family and friends, two or three rockers, also in velvet, and a piano. The other walls had chairs and a sofa. I loved this room. Perhaps that is why I remember it so well. But it was least used. It was locked and opened only on Sunday nights for visitors or evening devotionals. There were various other rooms but the bedrooms were upstairs, while the attic was remodeled to include some bedrooms as well as storage for trunks. Father had an office up there with many books.

Our family, all who ate out of the same plates, was huge. We came from many groups and ethnicities. Father had been settling disputes for government prior to permanently residing in Monrovia and had made valuable friendships with Kpelle chiefs and others who chose him to bring up their children. Vai and Mende were dominant in the house, and to be sure the boys coming from other ethnicities, usually one or two, all learned to speak Vai or Mende. Some of us learned their languages too. The languages spoken in the house included Vai, Mende, Kru, Gbandi, Gizi (Kissi), Gola, Buzi (Lorma), Dey, and others. Woe unto him who did not try to understand the languages of the others. There were altogether 26 boys, including my brothers and an unstable number of girls since they were never able to stay for any length of time.

No wonder the family was dubbed "the little mission." When one entered our dining hall there would usually be one plate after the other lined up on a very long table, just as at a mission school. Whenever the roll was called there was no end to the Massaquoi name, for almost everyone in the house became a Massaquoi. In my family circle there was no difference between the boys my father was bringing up and my real brothers. As a matter of fact, one of my brothers would often get along better with one of the other boys than he would with his biological brother.

Also in our home were the sons and daughters of one of father's deceased cousins. He and his wife had died during the flu epidemic of 1918.² This was perhaps a compliment paid back, because father used to live with them whenever he visited Monrovia.

My brothers in the house began school at the opening of the various sessions, and Titi and I had a dreadful time while they were away. The house was very quiet after they left. The boys had their study periods and we could not disturb them. Since father never wanted you to sit around the house doing nothing, one of my brothers was designated to teach us our ABCs (the alphabet) and to read. Nat was my tutor, and Ibrahim was Titi's tutor. Momolu Sandimanni also tutored one of the boys in the house. All tutoring had to be in English, not Vai. Father set a prize for the person who could read the primer first and spell the words in them. The group, tutor and student, would be rewarded.

Our family circle and life was fascinating in many other ways. On Sundays, in the evenings, the parlor would open and we would all gather and sing, with Ma Sedia playing the piano. The first hymn that I learned in this way was "Bless be the Tie that Binds," which father said was a hymn he learned while he was a student at Central Tennessee College which later became Walden University in Nashville, Tennessee. Not only did we sing hymns, but we sang folk songs as well, this being done on one other day in the week.

When Ma was playing the song "My Darling Clementine," and came to "thou art dead and gone forever," I understood the group to be singing *"A mu li; jei lɔ gbilima,"* which in Mende means "let us go because it is getting cloudy." Nobody ever stops other people's singing just to get the right text as the joy of singing with others was what mattered. No wonder a poet said, *"Dort, wo man singen hoert, kann man sich getrost niedersetzen, dort koennen keine boesen Menschen wohnen."*³

In the process of learning English as well as entertaining ourselves as best we could, there were many factors entering the picture. Ma Sedia wanted to learn Vai and she had learned a great deal from father. But as father was away in his office all day, she had Titi and me teaching her. She would tell us the names of things around the house in English and we would give her the Vai equivalent. This form of teaching did not last long because I learned English so rapidly.

Aside from the activities that Ma wanted me to participate in, and aside from all that I learned from her, there was my ever-present ardent craving for folk stories. Everyone who has heard me dramatize folk stories here in America should really not wonder. Everywhere I went in my childhood I always found someone who knew some stories and who would indulge me—my mother, Mama Jassa, and others. In Monrovia, my next sources supplied Western, not African, stories.

We children sat down every evening, shortly before dusk and dinner time, on the long steps in front of the house. My brother Jawa had come back to live with us, and he told us stories. Before that, Ibrahim and George did this, since Ali did not have the patience. Although they had a mine of stories, they did not have the power of drama, exaggeration, and coloring as did Jawa. Ibrahim had an everlasting craving for meat and to get him to tell a story, Titi and I promised to let him have all our meat portions. My brother George, on the other hand, told the stories free of charge. However, whenever we ate with my parents, it was very difficult to honor our promise to Ibrahim for his stories. But since we wore aprons, we would steal appropriate moments when father or Ma was not looking, to slip pieces of meat, fish, or fowl into the pockets of our aprons. We continued this act until the mice began eating up the sides of our aprons.

With the arrival of Jawa back to the family, a different era began. He undertook teaching me how to count: first by ones, then by twos, then by fives, and finally by tens. Ma Sedia had tried to teach me how to tell time, but she contented herself by telling me the difference between the long and the short- hands. She would send me upstairs to look at the clock, then return and tell her the position of the hands. Jawa now showed Titi and me how to tell time. For teaching us, Jawa did not demand meat portions as his younger brother had done. But occasionally he had us beg father for two cents, which he used to buy peanuts with.

My greatest joy was when Jawa told the story of Cinderella, and he had to tell it over and over again. When I heard the story, I began regretting my position and everything about me in my life. I was very proud that I had been born the daughter of Momolu IV. Now, I wanted to be poor. If I didn't become absolutely poor and mistreated, there would come no "Prince Charming." I dreamed of myself as Cinderella, but I could never be poor in those dreams. I began worrying. Each time I heard the story, another angle appealed to me. Of course, the Prince Charming in mind could not be an ordinary one. For me, he had to meet certain requirements.

Although I admire beauty, I didn't want my Prince Charming to be at all handsome. He was not to be on a horse. He was to be the best in throwing the bow and arrow, and his art and skill with the sword and spear, as well as fencing, must surpass that of all men. He must be thoroughly versed in the art of warfare. He was to be black like ebony and straight in bearing like a stick. He must possess muscles so strong that no living human being could bend his arms once he stretched them out. On winning wars, he was to be serious, with few words, and then I would come and play the sassaa for him, which again would bring him back to higher possibilities in his pursuits. After each war, the lullabies I would sing to him would be the only things that would make him fall asleep. I didn't want to meet him in the ballroom, but on the battlefield, where he had won the battle, finding me as a prisoner about to be led to slavery. The only war indemnity he was to ask from his enemies would be me. In this way I finally was able to settle in my mind, the problem of a "poor girl."

There was another problem that presented itself in the matter of becoming a Cinderella. If in Bendu I had admired the helplessness of people in shoes when they had to be carried on the backs of the men to the boats, in Monrovia I now had a dream to not wear shoes, for I had found out that shoes made people's feet and toes shrink together into very ugly shapes. When Titi and I were sure my parents would not be attending church, we would stop on the pavement of the store of the late Mr. Wilmot Dennis on Broad Street, take off our shoes and stockings, and leave them in front of the store until our return from Sunday school or church. Yes, Shelley was right, "Each child has its fairy godmother in its own soul."

In those early days of my childhood there seemed to be a difference between those Liberians who were descendants of the people who founded the commonwealth of Liberia and those who were generally described as "native," or rather as persons of indigenous heritage. Prior to father and his contemporaries joining government, not many people belonging to the latter group occupied positions of importance in the republic. I am not at all making an attempt in this narrative to go into that phase of life in Liberia, because I firmly believe that things in this respect will adjust themselves and are rapidly progressing toward a good solution with each passing generation. And, perhaps before not too long, there will be absolutely no difference, and we will all be just Liberians. After all, my father was able to become wedded to the descendant of one of the first founders, Elijah Johnson, whose motto, "Here we are and here we will remain," stands in our history as a symbol of independence and search for freedom. Johnson's eternal words, "The Love of Liberty brought us here," are used on the coat of arms of the state. That many prominent Liberians out of the pioneering group have married and are being married to the same class of what is usually termed as "native" points to the future disappearance of all such differences.[4]

In those days, the government had many tensions and disputes with the interior people, the "natives," and my father was responsible for settling many of those. His settling down in Monrovia meant that he held positions in the government there. All this aside, he was still considered as the ruling head of his own people, and had a hand in the shaping of the affairs of the others. He had a great reputation among them and settled their internal disputes besides the ones they had with the government. If the basement of our house was decorated and arranged, you were likely to awaken one fine morning and see chiefs of many nationalities coming out of the rooms. Sometimes, these rooms were prepared upstairs. But that house, with only 13 rooms apart from the attic room, could not possibly house all of us when you have an army of guests.

These guests, or rulers of the various nations, came to settle disputes. We enjoyed the sight of seeing people of various nationalities speaking a confusion of tongues, with only father there who understood and could converse with all of them. In his contacts with them he had learned all their languages. Thus, he has taken over 17 African languages with him to the grave.

During the whole period that I was connected with Monrovia, and prior to going to Germany, father held the following positions: secretary to the president, secretary of war (acting), and secretary of the interior. These positions, as everyone who has connections with government affairs knows, carry social responsibilities as well, such as celebrations and parties. Thus, every once in a while, the place was scrubbed, decorated, and we children enjoyed watching from somewhere or the other, people streaming in to celebrate some event or occasion. The first of such celebrations was not a governmental one though. It was the wedding anniversary of father to Ma Sedia.

At the time the celebration was taking place, I did not know what was going on. Relatives living across the Montserrado River in Vai Town cooked what was usually termed "country chop," consisting of most of the delicious African dishes I described previously. Anybody who was anybody had been invited, among them government officials, foreign and local merchants, missionaries, and preachers. Cows, goats, chicken, and other animals and certain parts and portions had been given to the relatives in Vai Town to be cooked for the anniversary. Grandmother Johnson and her friends, also versed in the culinary arts, cooked as well. I have never seen so much food in all my life. All the doors of the lower house were open, and one decorated table extended into another, and all over the piazza on the lower floor of the house. People would come, eat, congratulate my parents, and then go. After this, others would come and do the same. Titi and I watched this spectacle from the upper piazza, laughing and commenting on the various individuals, their gaits, hair, and the like.

It was not always for gay celebrations, feasts, picnics, and such occasions that father became important. As is generally known, in many ways we have a type of minority group problem among the two segments of our population. This being the case, people like father and others, exponents of the indigenous population who had advantages, naturally got together to discuss the issues of the day. There were meetings in which the forthcoming elections and various candidates were discussed, and what they as a whole group thought such and such a candidate would do for the native welfare. Not only this, they had to take stock, pointing out how many of them had achieved or contributed to the progress made in Liberia. The topics of the day discussed were about rights and what could be achieved in the future.

I am not boasting or trying to stir up something about the situation, such as it is. I am a Liberian, and proud of it. Besides, I personally believe that our conflicts will resolve themselves in due time, as is happening gradually. We have administrations in which the individual officials are shortsighted and selfish, but at the same time there are increasingly more individuals who realize that we Liberians, natives or Americo-Liberians, are all needed to make our country a better place to live. We have increasingly adopted the philosophy of Voltaire: "I do not agree with what you say, but I will defend with my life, your right to say it." This is the real principle to which any democracy can pledge itself, and Liberia is striving toward that goal daily.

During my first stay in Monrovia, something else happened that impressed me greatly, and made my respect for father's authority rise over the top. It was when the frontier force revolted. I did not know of course what it was all about, but I remember that many people, especially women and children, came flocking into the house. Father walked out, and after speaking in Vai, Mende, and other languages of the men who made up the force, they quietly laid down their guns on the ground. To me, who had always admired bravery, this was something. While everyone came to the house for safety and staying inside, my brothers and I were on the piazza watching the whole scene.

It was during the stay at Monrovia that I had the accident with my hands.[5] Uncle Lamini, father's youngest brother, was a physician and was teaching at the Muhlenburg Mission on the St. Paul River under the auspices of the Lutheran Church of America. I was first treated in Monrovia by both the German and French doctors. After that, Uncle Lamini Massaquoi and his beloved wife, Aunt Ketura Massaquoi, who were living near the school, asked father to send me there for further treatment. This, they thought, might allow me to recuperate as well as give Uncle Lamini a chance to see what he could do for me.

While I was at Muhlenburg, uncle performed two main operations on my hands. Between these operations, I spent about three exciting months at Muhlenburg. The Muhlenburg Mission School had two main divisions, one for boys and one for girls. Jemina, my cousin, was the only girl attending school with the boys, since the family had to live on the side with the school for boys. There were chiefly Gola children who attended the school. Our house, which to this day is called "Massaquoi

House," because it was built by my uncle and aunt, has now been left to the school. Jemina went to school in the mornings but was home during the afternoon hours to play with me. The school was about 15 minutes walk from the house, and I looked forward to her coming.

Besides Jemina, there were many other relatives attending school at the mission. There were my brothers Siaka and Bey, whom you will remember from earlier. They were staying with Uncle Lamini for training. There was also Faikai, a nephew of father's and Uncle Lamini, along with many other boys. The boys all called Uncle Lamini "Little Papa," and father "Big Papa." Behind Uncle Lamini's back they had a nickname for him, which was "Gbuen." The boys loved, respected, and obeyed him. He was rather strict. Perhaps that is why they gave him his nickname.

As much as I enjoyed my stay in Muhlenburg, it had to come to an end. One Saturday, my second oldest brother, Jaiah, arrived suddenly toward dusk, saying among other things that father had sent him to look me up. I have not discussed my brother Jaiah very much here—well the truth is that I hardly knew him at the time. He and my brother next to him, Mannah, had come from Freetown, where they had been in school, shortly before my departure to Muhlenburg, and I had not had much time to get acquainted with him.

I went and asked my brother again and again whether father had sent a whole boat, with crew, just to get me; I could hardly believe it! He had been so strict that you would have thought he didn't care much about anybody—I mean his children. But, when you think of all the good things he did for your welfare, you would never entertain such an idea in the least. I was to go to Monrovia and spend Christmas with the family. This must have been a week or so before the event for it was not long after our return to Monrovia that I was told that we were having Christmas. My heart burst with pride when I thought of father caring enough to send for me in this manner. It was on a Monday morning that we joined the boat, the "Vaikai,"[6] a little steamboat which father owned and used for his business and for traveling purposes of the family.

This was my first Christmas in Monrovia, not my first on earth, but the first I was to know anything about. You must bear in mind that Christmas is not a Vai holiday and thus I had had no occasion before to become acquainted with it. The girls at the house planned a "country cook" for the occasion. They flattered me by telling me that this cook had been arranged in honor of my returning home.

At a country cook in those days, the girls and boys who arrived would go to the piazza of our home. Then the hostess or little ladies giving the party would appear. After taking your hats, you would be led to the yard where games were played and plays enacted. No "country" games were played, but rather those games that were brought back to Africa from America. On that occasion I was "going down to Georgia," before I knew that there was a Georgia, besides the Georgia in Liberia. English songs had their place too. We sang "Queen Annie, Queen Annie, Sitting in the Sun," "London Bridge is Falling Down," and "Little Sallie Walker." Of course we also jumped rope and had other such amusements.

The thing that I could see that was very "country" about such parties, aside from the food of course, was the fact that most of it, by fair weather, took place out of doors, as all native social gatherings usually are. Also there were large quantities of food to be served to the guests. Often children would eat out of the same dish, while guests may or may not have been sitting at a table while being served. Whether the party was country or not, it served its purpose. We had a grand time of it, and, at dusk, each guest went away with shining and telling eyes of joy.

On Christmas Day, father organized a large picnic on Bailey Mbelema, not far from Monrovia. When one hears about such a farm as it existed in those days, one might think first of the farm as a means of contributing to family income. But in those days this was not the case at all. It was fashionable for people of certain standing to have a country farm and home, and my parents were probably "keeping up with the Joneses." The picnic took place at this farm and I remember our traveling there early that Christmas morning in a boat.

The picnic was memorable in many respects. We children played on the swings under large trees, ate, and drank in the open all day. I learned my first "civilized" dance, too. Up to this point I knew none of the dances that had been performed in Monrovia. I had only watched them from afar. A girlfriend showed me the "sixteen steps," danced to typical Liberian songs, full of rhythm and harmony. On April 10, 1918, the German submarine came and bombarded the French cable at Monrovia. The song sung to the music to which the dance was performed was in connection with this event. And, if I remember it correctly, it began thus: "O German Submarine, Aba; Come to bombard Monrovia, Aba..."

Another thing I had learned through the events of the day was about the First World War. I had not known anything at all about the war. Mamma Jassa or no one else in my previous environment had ever mentioned the war to me. It was on the day of the picnic that I learned to admire father's display of the spear and sword. People had assembled during the later afternoon, and drummers had come. He swiftly changed into his African robe, and to the beat of the *fanga*[7] (drum) he began the dance. Oh, how I wished I had been a man! The skill he exhibited in throwing that implement was marvelous. The rounds and turns it made and the swing of his garments were all sights of beauty and admiration.

The one thing that interested us children foremost about the farm was the fact that the land was sandy and, everywhere you looked there were pineapples. Titi and I ate pineapples and returned with our mouths all sore. For a long time, after our short visit to the farm, I could not bear the sight of a pineapple. On the farm were two houses where two of my mothers had moved. These were Mother Beendu and Mother Zo, who I mention because they would take care of Titi and me whenever we were sent there for a break, especially the older woman of the two, Mother Zo, who claimed some sort of relationship to Mother Massa. Coming from such a large family, I cannot possibly remember how everyone is related. She had been willed to father by an uncle, the chief of Jennywunde, as his "goat's head." But, since father was married in another fashion, she just stayed a year or so. She claimed she liked Monrovia and us the children. I think she left when we were about to leave for Germany and I have never heard of her since.

Along with mothers Beendu and Zo were many workers on the farm who were responsible for its upkeep. These men arranged fishing and swimming parties for us, since the river was a little way off, and we were not allowed to go bathing by ourselves, especially when my brothers were absent. The farm provided enough for the consumption of those living there and taking care of it. In those days, the rest of the family only used it for recreational purposes. After leaving us at the farm, on the day of the picnic, father and Ma Sedia visited us on weekends. I was very happy to see them. Father was a very good shot, and he shot game, pigeons, and other birds, the English names of which I do not know. On one occasion he shot so many birds and animals that we had meat for a whole week after they left. This splendid time of running about naked or clothed, whichever we chose, came to an end one weekend when father came and said that as schools were reopening we were to return to Monrovia with him and Ma Sedia.

We left Mothers Zo and Beendu with broken hearts, to return to Monrovia and make preparations to attend school. Thus ended the first phase of life for me, in Monrovia. With this phase, I had gained a little glimpse of Western civilization, and perhaps thereby a little understanding of some of the things I dreaded to face in "civilization."

Notes

1. [It is common knowledge that democracy in Liberia was just a sham as it excluded the "natives" of the interior most of the time. One of the most scathing criticisms is from Tuan Wreh, *The Love of Liberty*… (London: C Hurst, 1976). *Eds.*]
2. [A reference to Sandy S. Roberts and wife Ida C. Roberts. *Eds.*]
3. ["There where one hears singing, can one confidently sit down, there cannot live evil people." *Eds.*]

4. [President William Tubman (r. 1944–1971) made "unification" the cornerstone of his policy for the interior. But progress was not as fast as the sanguine expectations of Fatima Massaquoi, and this partly accounted for the bloody events of 1980 in which President Tolbert and his cabinet were murdered in a coup led by "natives". *Eds.*]

5. [Discussed in the Introduction. *Eds.*]

6. ["Vai man." *Eds.*]

7. [A small talking drum played holding it under the arm. *Eds.*]

CHAPTER 7

SCHOOL BEGINS AT
JULIE C. EMERY HALL

T he days following our return from Mbelema were very dreary indeed, with father and Ma Sedia pondering over what school we should attend, and discussing the pros and cons of various schools. Finally Julia C. Emery Hall,[1] under the auspices of the Protestant Episcopal Church, became the choice. The school was located at Bromley, and offered the advantage that the matron of the girls was our relation (cousin). So was a teacher there (a cousin of Ma Sedia's), and many of our cousins attended it. But after hearing horrible stories about the school from my brothers Ali and Ibrahim, we decided we were not going to school. Not even father's assurances allayed our fears.

Then one night, Mr. Johnny Carr, who ran the John Payne, a steam boat that traveled from Monrovia and White Plains on the St. Paul River, came to our house because father wanted to arrange for him to take us to school. When he heard the boys teasing us, he said that he passed by the school all the time and the girls seemed to him as being happy. He said that he would give us a shilling each if we went and would bring us back to Monrovia free of charge if ever we felt unhappy and came to his boat and told him so. This gave us the confidence to go.

The school required us to bring the following items: one white dress, one blue dress, one pink dress, two sheets, two pillow cases, one quilt, two pairs of stockings, a pair of shoes, a plate, a knife, a fork, and two serviettes each. These and many other items were prepared for us to take to Bromley as both Ma Sedia and father were anxious to make the schooling as appealing as possible to us.

We also decided that we would leave on a Saturday. We must have started school in the month of February or March when schools begin their new terms in Liberia. I am not certain of the year, perhaps about 1920. I do not know exactly how to describe our feeling of having to leave for school. Our cousin, Ellen Johnson, who was really a Vai but was being brought up by a family in Monrovia, came to bid father farewell; her pending trip to Bromley was not her first for she had attended school there for many years. We found out that she too was planning to leave the following morning. Father asked her to keep an eye on us, and write him. She asked us about our problems and was able to console us greatly. By the way, she died during the first vacation after our first term in the institution.

After breakfast on that eventful morning of our departure for school, Ma Sedia called us upstairs to get the boxes that she had packed for us. These were boxes containing tin cracker, cans with farina, fried crabs wrapped in paper, and fried herrings. Another box included carbolic soap, sardines, salmon, and crackers. We were thus fully equipped for school. We then bade Ma Sedia farewell, because she was not in a position to accompany us to the wharf where father was awaiting us. She gave us sixpence a-piece to buy whatever we liked when we got to Bromley. At the wharf was Mr. Johnny Carr who said he had been anxiously expecting his two special passengers. Father kissed the three of us goodbye, and left with the boys.

Our eyes filled with tears as they walked off, and the John Payne steamed slowly up the Montserrado River. Ellen told us some of the exciting events that usually take place at the school, how we should treat the people there, and keep certain standards to show the best behavior of a Vai girl, and to be the best in our various classes. We were to report any problems and hide nothing from her.

Along the way we made a stop and Mr. Carr came to see us. He gave Titi and me the shilling each as previously promised, and also returned our fares that father had given him, which was another shilling each. With what Ma Sedia gave us, we were each two-and-a-half shillings rich. We had never had that much money. Up to this date we had only about a cent or two given us to use in collections at church or Sunday school. Of course we had no idea what we were going to do with all of this money, but it further gave us a sense of security when we thought of any future hardships facing us.

About ten miles up the St. Paul River from Monrovia was our final stop. The school building stood on the left, majestic and towering as if to compete with the skies. At the sight of the school building, the steamer seemed to slow down, as if she were deliberately doing so out of respect, respect for those women who seem to have refused their share of the riches of the world, to bury themselves in a castle of isolation, thus devoting themselves to remaking African girls, seeking the removal of superstition and ignorance among mankind. They demonstrate thereby their absolute distaste for selfishness and greed by striving to break in these girls who attend, and help them attain the hard knowledge of self, thereby enabling them to render serviceable lives, the greatest of all virtues. This is the way in which they see fit to carry the flame of the religion within their hearts. They do this because they know that there is no approach to the Great Creator without duty to fellowman, and on the other hand, no true service to a neighbor can be performed unless it is done for the Maker of all things small and great.

There were two dormitories, one on each wing of the building. Out of the windows of these buildings, girls' heads were sticking out. This, I later learned, was forbidden, and we were punished again and again, when a teacher happened to be on the boat and complained about it. The day we landed was no different; the girls looked, commented, and talked. From below, we heard girls express their joy over the return of Ellen to school. Then, behold some new students! These comments were about our clothes, from head to foot. We had not been careful enough to wear our best, but we did not know that the girls would pay attention to clothing. We told Ellen what we heard and asked what she had thought of our clothing. Of course she thought we were perfect.

We walked up to Julia C. Emery Hall, named after a famous woman in the Protestant Episcopal Church, who, by the way, died in 1922 — I remember when news of her death reached us at the school. We went to the principal's office. She rose to meet us and told me that she knew father long before I was born. She said that she met him in Philadelphia when she was taking a course in nurses' training. Her name was Mrs. Mary Elizabeth Moort,[2] called "Godmother" or "Godma" Moort by all the girls. She had our trunks opened and checked before they were taken upstairs. We were then turned over to one of the older girls, who was to lead us to the other girls, in whose activities we were to participate.

On Saturday afternoons, the girls went to collect wood in the little woods nearby. When we had reached the woods, the big girl who was supervising the wood gathering told me that I should become her friend. She was good looking with very sleepy eyes. Her name was Fannie Valentine, who later became Mrs. Speer. I agreed, and another phase of life began.

We returned with bundles of wood for cooking at the mission station. Almost immediately, the bell rang for supper. We were lined up two-by-two, from the smallest in height at the front, to the tallest at the back and we marched to the dining hall. The teacher who accompanied the girls to the dining room and supervised their eating was Mrs. Danielette Innis. When we reached the dining room, each new student was shown her table and seat. There were six tables altogether, and Titi and I were seated at the sixth table. The first two tables were the privileged tables in those days. These girls received food in large dishes, from which they could serve themselves. At these two tables also, there were about ten or twelve persons only, while there were more at the others. The food for the other girls was dished out into the plates, and, the further down the line we got, the smaller were the portions. Although we were requested to bring knives, forks, and spoons, we did not use them; we used what the mission had.

After dinner, the little girls, and those who were not working in the dining room clearing tables or washing dishes, usually went to the front yard to play. Ellen sent for us, wanting us to meet "Ma Esther." She was a young Kru lady who had been at the mission a long time—hence the girls called her "Ma Esther." There were only a few girls who called her simply "Esther," among them Ellen. Ma Esther spoke beautiful Vai as she had lived in Cape Mount before. She told me that she liked me very much and wanted me to become her friend. I made the mistake of not telling her that Fannie Valentine had already asked me to be her friend. The point is I didn't know that a person couldn't have two friends. If you did, this other friend has to be the sort of play-relative, but not a friend.

After playing a little while, the first bell rang for the evening devotionals, and we ran in to wash our hands to proceed to the schoolroom. The schoolroom was very large and on the right wing of the building. This room had six rows of desks, and each row had seven seats, and in each seat two girls could be accommodated. Thus, eighty-four girls could be accommodated this way. I received a seat in the fifth row. Again, the rows proceeded according to sizes. These seats became smaller and smaller, the further down the rows reached, from one to six.

The teachers sat on both sides of the principal or the person holding the devotionals in front. This person sat in front in the middle of the room. Some teachers sat on chairs at the side so as to keep order especially among little girls who were talking. When any teacher entered the room, all the girls would stand up and greet the teacher. When the principal entered, all the girls rose with a "Good Evening Godma." All this discipline impressed me greatly. I found myself loving Bromley immensely.

By the time of the second bell everyone had to be inside. Godma Moort would then call the roll with every girl present answering to her name. If anyone came in after the bell, she had to remain standing. On that very first evening, something happened that is not only characteristic of Bromley, but of missions in general. I was quite surprised when Godma called the roll and gave me the name "Louise" instead of my usual Fatima. I never intended being called by any other name than that of the great Queen Sandimanni and I simply did not answer. She repeated it, and I did not answer. She looked to the seat that I had been assigned and marked me present anyway. Titi on the other hand was given the name "Lulu," and she responded to it. Godma Moort, though, did not give me this name. She had written Ma Sedia to ask her to suggest some Christian names for us and she sent this name of her deceased sister for me.

After the devotionals, I went to Godma Moort and told her that "Louise" was not my name. I told her that I bore the name of the Vai Queen, my grandmother, and since I wanted to be like her the name had to remain. The next morning Godma Moort called me in and told me that I must now bear a "Christian name," but that she would call me "Fatima" until she heard from my father. I wonder sometimes why missionaries change African names even though I know that the names are difficult for them to spell and pronounce. But still having to have a "Christian name" is something very difficult for me to reconcile with facts about names in general. In my opinion it is not the name that makes the Christian, just as it is not the name of the building that makes the church; it is the people gathered there.

Father, in his youth, had received the name Albert Thompson (sometimes Momolu Thompson).[3] In his adulthood, he changed his name back to Momolu Massaquoi. Whether Momolu Massaquoi or Albert Thompson, I have never seen a greater Christian. Perhaps realizing this, he must have written Godma Moort that I should not be called "Louise," since I did not wish to bear this name. And nobody ever called me by that name at the mission ever again.

After calling the roll, Godmother called out the number of the hymn to be sung, and after that, the Psalm for the day was read out of the "Book of Common Prayers." We then sang another hymn, and with everyone kneeling, Godma prayed for the peace that had come to the world, for the advancement of the newly arrived girls, and that the torn universe would be spared from misery. After this she said "take your places girls," whereby the girls replied, "Goodnight Godma, goodnight teachers."

The last three rows of girls—fourth, fifth, and sixth—lined up, and Miss Ellen Johnson, one of the teachers and a relative of Ma Sedia's, led us upstairs to the small girls' dormitory. She gave orders and everyone knelt down. We prayed for the teachers, everyone who supported the school, our mothers, fathers, and the world. This ended with the singing of the well known "Now I Lay Me Down to Sleep." We were then given orders to stand up again, and if we did not talk immediately after rising, we were dismissed, at which we would say, "Good night Miss Johnson."

Bromley is a place on a hill by the St. Paul River, about ten miles from Monrovia. The spot on which the school is situated is called Bromley Station, and the house in which we lived, Julia C. Emery Hall. It was with this house that all the activities and the life of the school were concerned.[4] The hall or school building was a two-story cement or brick building, with an attic and a basement. In the basement were the chapel, laundry, bathrooms, and kitchen. The first floor was the schoolroom, but also had the principal's office and rooms for the principal and the teachers. On the second floor was the large girls' dormitory.

The outside of the schoolroom is beautiful. The building is of red brick. In front of it was a flat, large, and broad cemented pavement with many steps. Two lions are found on either side of the stairway leading to the center of the house from the front. They seemed to be reposing and had the words marked on the front under their claws: "Watch." These lions seem to be veritably watching that no harm comes to the girls who have come here to taste of the fountain of knowledge. Mr. Scott, a Grebo, was the sculptor of these statues, and he was also assistant pastor of the chapel.[5]

All around the building were large yards. There, chiefly at the front, were beautiful trees and flowers of all kinds. Not far away and to the left of the large edifice stood a small wooden house in which Mr. Scott had lived before moving to a town nearby, Clay-Ashland. The house was inhabited by another member of the faculty whose husband was also in the employ of the school.[6] On both sides of the grounds was land for farming purposes and a forest in which we had gathered wood on the day of our arrival at school.

Although Bromley was officially open, there were no actual classes during the time of our arrival. Students kept pouring in all week including other family members. The following Monday, after all these arrivals, class work began. Almost all of the relatives and friends had attended schools in Monrovia or somewhere else for three or more years. Hence, they knew how they would be classified. Titi and I had previously been sent to the Trinity Parish Day School, but did not even spend a month there; we just played around instead of going to school. We had no idea how we would be classified. Of course our brothers had taught us to read, but this was all the great learning we had had so far.

That Monday, Godma Moort called the roll and each girl whose classification was not certain was called to her desk, on which she had various readers. We would read a short passage and she would direct you to the various classes assembled in groups, all over the large school room. After I had been called and read for a few seconds, she told me to go to the class under the stairway, which was the third grade. Titi was sent to the second grade. We had both expected to be sent to the first grade, so these classifications on the whole we thought were not bad at all. Many of the girls who expected to be classified higher were sent to lower grades.

Our third grade teacher was Miss Nettie Meyers. She was wearing a black and white dress, and it was said that she was in mourning. Tall, slender, as if she would break into two when you looked at her, Miss Meyers, I thought, was the best teacher at the school. She was a missionary from America and was colored. She and Godma Moort were the only two teachers at the school who were not Liberians. Miss Meyers, who later became Godma Meyers for me after my baptism, was generally known to be the strictest person in the school. Reflecting upon her character and qualifications today, I don't think there was a better teacher who had the welfare of the girls more at heart than she did. And I am deeply indebted to her for all she imparted to me.

When I arrived at the class she was distributing books to the girls. She would ask each girl her name and would write it into the book and hand it to that person. She would then ask the girls to say "thank you." I could read the resentment in the faces of the girls. Being so strict, no one wanted to be in her class. So much about her had been spoken about during the time we were waiting for school to begin that everyone expected to have a fight with her soon, me included, but I dropped it.

Miss Meyers must have noticed that I was sympathetic toward her, for she asked me my name and told me to come to see her after class. When I went to see her that afternoon, she wanted me to tell her if I had been to school before and where. I told her that I attended the Parish Day School a few times but I was afraid of being in the third grade since I had not been in the other grades. She laughed heartily and told me that I am just the person for the third grade, and said "we will see that you do as well as anyone else."

Miss Ellen Johnson was a graduate of Bromley, and she was well accomplished in music. It was she who taught the primer, first, and second grades. A little later in the year, however, a Miss Scott from Bassa, taught the primer and first grades, leaving Miss Johnson to teach only the second grade. As already mentioned, Miss Meyers taught the third grade, Mrs. Danilette Innis the fourth, and Godma Moort, the fifth and sixth grades. Aside from these classroom teachers, there were other teachers at Bromley. Mrs. M. Gibson was matron in general and Cousin Annie her assistant. Later, Mrs. Gibson left and Annie Dixon became matron, until a Mrs. Yancy from Cape Palmas was able to take over. During my first year, we had a special craft and sewing teacher, but Godma Meyers took this on later.

The lead subject at Bromley as in all mission schools was the Bible. Godma Meyers assigned the third grade several Psalms to learn by heart and recite every day. Some of the books of the Bible were easy to understand, and the religion of the Bible poured into our hearts like the seasonal rains pour into the sand, and there, in the words of Rousseau, "struck us with admiration." Bromley had opened for me a new world, and I became fervent with a new ideal. With all my previous fancies, I now had another: to become a missionary, one who could hear "Divine Voices," and follow their instructions.

I firmly developed the notion that everyone around me was a sinner, and that they needed me to convert them. If I went to church and heard the preacher or minister describing those who were doomed for the fire, I could count numerous people who would fit into that category. I returned home after the close of school, reciting Bible verses to everyone, and acted as if they had never heard of Christ—even my own father. One day, father said to my brothers, "leave her alone; one more term at Bromley, and the whole world would be filled with sinners, as far as my daughter is concerned."

One of the most important courses was Reading-Spelling. On the very first day we were assigned to read the first pages of our first story in the book. There were several stories, but we also read and memorized many poems, and I have remembered the ones I loved very well, even to this day, despite the fact that they are in English, and there was a period in my life when I had completely forgotten all the English I knew. When reciting, we stood up, our backs to the wall, and facing outdoors. Of course each girl had a chair, and we would sit on them, in brief moments when we were changing books.

Godma Meyers, not wanting to embarrass the numerous older girls in the class, had arranged the class positions according to height. But, noticing that the larger girls tended not to study, she began a competition scheme. She had the girls who could not spell the words and define them punished by giving their place to those next to them, who could spell the words and give their meanings. This was something very exciting and fascinating for me. It seems as if this was the very moment I had eagerly expected, and one day everyone misspelled "candle" and when my turn came, I spelled it correctly and defined it as "wax with a wick in the center for making light." I was now at the head of the class.

The news of my going to the head of the class spread through the school like a wildfire. Godma Meyers called me after school and asked me sarcastically whether I still wanted to be put back into the second or first grade, but I didn't reply. We learned some history in the lower grades, as Godma Moort would write down the names of the presidents of Liberia with the dates of their administrations. She would call up various individuals to come to the front and recite the names on festive occasions or for the entertainment of visitors. Arithmetic in the third grade consisted of addition, subtraction, multiplication, short division, and later, long division. My great dislike for mathematics was not at all noticeable while I was at the mission. I learned what was required just as rapidly and as well as anyone else.

All of these courses could not be instructed without our learning to write. All of the girls knew how to write when we entered the third grade. Although my brother had taught me how to read, I had never tried to write before going to the mission. So, once or twice a week, Miss Meyers taught us how to write. It was a very arduous task indeed. The other girls were given slates with words. When she would get to me, she had me begin with the making of the slopes for "m" and "n." Gradually we proceeded to others, until I could finally write.

Geography was taught from the third grade upward. We learned definitions of isthmus, peninsula, continent, and the like. Although I usually knew my definitions, the lessons in geography in those days were not as fascinating to me as a year or so later. The beginning of this love and interest in geography came when a Miss Lomax, who had taught at Bromley before my days, came to visit the school. She had previously taught at the house of Bethany, while my father was the principal at the sister school, St. John's Mission in Cape Mount. At the time of her visit to Bromley, she was stationed at another school in Sinoe. The girls who had been long in the school always spoke about how mean and strict Miss Lomax had been. I was therefore greatly annoyed at Godmas Moort and Meyers for selecting me to go and meet her.

After I had been introduced to Miss Lomax, she remarked, "So, Momo IV has you for a daughter, eh?" She kept repeating this, and later on in the conversation remarked, "Your father and I used to be such good friends while we were both teaching at Cape Mount; did he speak of me to you?" Miss Lomax then continued telling the two missionaries and me about father's life as principal of St. John's mission, and later as king of the Gallinas, and how she had visited him there, and how much he had meant to the church and mission work in general. She told of father's training received through missionary efforts, and the places he had spoken of in America, Europe, and other places. This was so stimulating for me that from that day onward, I was definitely interested in geography, for now it had meaning.

School life did not consist only of classroom activities. Bromley conformed to the purpose of an institution, which is to model character to meet the needs of life. We were a diverse group with differences that assembled together to become one in the climbing of the ladder of knowledge. Kru, Mende, Kpelle, Gola, Americo-Liberian, Grebo, Vai, and many other groups were among us. We did not understand each others' languages, but this was eliminated, for we quickly learned the alien foreign language, English. For some of us, the gay print color dresses and other types of dresses replaced our little vanjas or beaded aprons. Our feet, with shoes placed on them, no longer needed to be abused by treading directly on the sand or stones, which had been heated by the sun or wet by the rain. Instead of listening to the shuffle of flopping wings of the cock—the best timekeeper of nature—the bell did this duty. This same bell regulated the whole day, dividing it into periods for specific activities: prayers, school, dinner, breakfast, baths, time to sleep. The bell rings all day long.

On the average day at Bromley, we arose about 5:30 in the mornings. After making our beds, we combed our hair, dressed, and then washed our faces, while the big girls were allowed to bathe. After this, each girl went about her daily morning chores, which were changed monthly. All the work at the mission was done by the girls—cleaning the kitchen, ringing the bell, sweeping everywhere. Six girls were in charge of the dining hall and three for each dormitory. On Saturdays, there were girls chosen to clean laundry, scrub steps, with other girls appointed to do the weekly baking of bread, clearing of papers from the front and backyards, and looking after the flowers.

During my stay at Bromley, the only duties I was ever assigned, along with some of the other small girls, were the cleaning of the front yard and looking after the flowers. There were girls assigned to assist each of the teachers with their rooms, too, taking their meals to them and cleaning their rooms. In those days, only the matron had her meals in the dining hall where the girls were eating, the rest of the teachers took their meals in their rooms.

About seven o'clock in the morning, the bell rang for early morning devotionals, similar to the evenings, and lasted about half an hour. The girls responsible for cooking for the month and those assigned to the dining room were excused. The rest of us remained and were called up one by one for inspection of our clothes, nails, hair, and general tidiness. Then the first bell rang for breakfast, at which we had to line up. With the second bell, we marched to the dining hall and had our breakfast. The half hour or so following the breakfast was used by those in charge of the dining hall to tidy up and for washing dishes. The rest of the girls used this time for last minute studying.

After this, classwork began and lasted until noon when the big bell in the tower rang, and all the girls again assembled for the noon devotionals. We were then dismissed for lunch after which we again assembled around one o'clock for another devotional, followed by courses in sewing and crafts until four, which all the girls had to participate in. On Fridays and Saturdays, there were no courses in sewing and crafts, so we did our weekly laundry. We would then have our recitals and physical exercises. This program varied often. On Saturdays, we were left to do what we liked, after completing the morning chores.

Our study periods at the mission that lasted from about 7:30 to 9:30 were an interesting as well as an important phase of our lives. Girls from the third grade upward had to study during the study period. Nobody could be in a class of Godma Meyers and not have time to do her lessons. As there were not enough books to go round, we had to study in pairs. Victoria Johnson and I studied all of our lessons together. The teachers were usually too anxious to help.

At the end of the school year, there were great ceremonies attended by the trustees of the school. We sang and gave performances, and demonstrated what we had learnt. In the upper three grades, examinations were held. During my first year, my class recited the twenty-first chapter of the book of Revelation and gave various numbers. The trustees asked us various questions on this chapter and on the life of the boy Samuel, which we had studied. Anybody in the class, who heard the questions, could answer them. Sometimes, the answers to the questions had been made out and we had to study them. One question ran thus: "What does Samuel mean?" The chorus of the class replied, "Asked of the Lord."

In the upper classes, arithmetic problems were solved. I remember once having such a problem to work out while in the fifth grade. This was done on a large blackboard, and the trustees would see whether we were able to work them. As these people only remained at Bromley about half of a day, there was never time enough to examine everyone, so the teachers usually called the students that they wanted. I don't believe that they intended for these exercises to be our real examinations, since they gave examinations before the trustees came up.

The girls of my class who were eligible were all promoted to the fourth grade except Clara Davis and I. But later on in the term, we skipped the fourth grade and were promoted to the fifth. I could not understand all this. I later learned that father had refused my being promoted so fast. He stood, as I even remember from the first years in Germany, in constant fear of my becoming confused or unable to adjust through these fast promotions and changes.

Life at Bromley had its pleasant and unpleasant sides. There were many minor forms of punishment at the school. One such was making those who had not studied stand in the middle of the floor, or stand during devotionals. Sometimes, when a person entered late, they had to remain standing during the whole devotional services. Sometimes girls were made to stand on one foot, either on the floor or on a bench. The old ways of corporal punishments were of course prevalent. This consisted in giving the girls who persistently failed to do their lessons, lashes with switches for every question missed, on their hands. Godma Meyers whipped you on the legs or somewhere else, but I don't remember her giving lashes on the hands.

I succeeded in avoiding punishment most of the time except on very few occasions when I joined others to go on a food hunt. Sarah Coleman, Victoria Johnson, Rachel Richards, Iola Cooper, Florence Tolbert, Kate Cooper, Danielette Johnson, Titi, and many other girls and I had heard that in a little half town not far from the mission was a man who sold fish and good manioc. The food situation at the time was particularly bad, so we decided to go and see. We were quite surprised when on our return we found that all the bath partitions were out of the laundry already. We were called and locked in the store room, which I dreaded.

The following week, we had to stand during all of the devotional services, also something that I found horrible and degrading. I pleaded with Godma Meyers to speak to Godma Moort on our behalf. She refused to do so, telling me not to always follow the crowd, since all on my own I had always managed to keep out of mischief. I learnt my lesson and there never was a next punishment for me. But there was a more horrible punishment meted out at the school.

One bright morning, Godma Moort called a roll of girls who were to remain in the schoolroom. Later I saw them with wooden boards on the front of their chests held by a cord around their necks. I was not so much concerned about what caused the punishment, but its psychological impression on all of us. The boards were marked in black ink: "untidy," "very untidy," and "untidiness." The girls who wore these signs had to stand during the devotionals and did not eat with the rest of us but had their meals afterward. I dreaded these boards and always wondered how those girls wearing them felt. I was very fortunate that it didn't happen to me.

There were numerous other deeds for which we were punished, such as cracking and eating palm kernels or using bad language. Many of the girls at the mission also tended to steal. They would take minor things from each other. For this reason, our clothes were kept in a clothes room, and we could change our clothing on Wednesday and Saturday afternoons. On Sundays, before church, the clothes room containing the trunks was opened for about an hour, in which time we could collect our clothes for church. On Mondays, the Sunday clothes would be put back. In spite of all these precautions, things still went missing. Of course, when the culprit was discovered, she was severely punished.

Since poems and songs tell the sentiments of the day, we tended to laugh at the ones who had been caught stealing. Thus, the following refrain, which we would repeat when possible thieves pass by, came into its own:

> Step my lady step,
> Shoes don't cost but one pound ten,
> So step my lady step.
> She goes to Monrovia and steps like a lady,
> Comes to Bromley and steals like a cat.
> So step my lady step.

When there was no shortage of foods, the following was our daily menu. Twice daily, mornings and evenings, we had fried scorched herrings with rice. Sometimes, we had codfish or smoked fish in the evenings, instead of the scorched herrings. On Mondays and Saturdays, we had boiled rice with raw palm oil and salt. We searched around the school for pepper, mashed it, and smuggled it to the table. For drink, we were served a cup of goose wine—water. Sometimes, and this was very seldom indeed, we had fried fresh fish on Sunday mornings. Thursday and Sunday dinners were our big times when we were served rice and beans with salted pigs' feet (or some type of salted meat).

For the lunch meals, we often had biscuits, which they called "hardtacks." Each girl received two of these unsweetened biscuits with a lump or two of sugar. When there was flour, bread was baked on Saturdays, and we had bread for lunch on Sundays, also with a lump or two of sugar or syrup. Often when I read of well-balanced meals and vitamins, I wonder how we survived on those menus. Apart from our occasional sweet potato greens, there were never any leafy vegetables, salads, or the like.

It is no wonder, then, that we found ourselves always hungry and searching for food. But I must pause here and admire the missionaries, because for the most part, they too had the same food that we had, except in cases where they would receive packages from home. It must have been harder on them, perhaps, since they had lived longer and been accustomed to a different diet. But they managed to survive. The girls too received food augmentations from their families that came in packages and we all managed to survive.

Life at Bromley was highly regulated as can be readily seen. In the hallways hung signs, "it is forbidden to speak loudly in the hall," or forbidden to do this, that, or the other. Even the wall of the schoolroom reminded us that we had gone to Bromley for a purpose, with the framed words on the wall, "I can and I will." In the beginning, I did not understand but later figured out that I can and will attain a goal at Bromley, that I can and will make something of my life, that I can and will become a good Christian. The purpose of Bromley and its regulations pierced through you at every corner, wherever you turned. But in spite of all the strict discipline, we had our fun with friends and played like normal children anywhere.

Notes

1. [Founded 1905. *Eds.*]
2. [Mrs. Elizabeth Moort was an African American missionary whose husband, the Rev. Dr. Paulus Moort, served as the rector of the Trinity Church in Monrovia. He played an important role in the founding of the school. Mrs. Moort leased land to Marcus Garvey's Universal Negro Improvement Association (UNIA) for a farm—the arrangement having

been made by Gabriel Johnson, the "Potentate" and Ma Sedia's father.
See M. B. Akpan, "Liberia and the Universal Negro Improvement
Association: Background to the Abortion of Garvey's Scheme for
African Colonization," *Journal of African History*, Vol. 14, No. 1 (1973),
pp. 116–117. *Eds.*]

3. [Momolu Massaquoi experienced this name change as a boy attending St.
John's Academic and Industrial School in Cape Mount in the early 1880s,
at which time he also converted to Christianity. The name Thompson was
probably derived from "James Thompson," who served as vice president
of Liberia while Massaquoi was at St. John's. Massaquoi later dropped the
name. *Eds.*]

4. There are small dormitories and houses now, instead of the one large
house of my days.

5. [Daniel Scott is known in Liberian history as a mystic and explorer who
discovered the rich iron deposits of Bomi in the late 1920s, two decades
before mining operations began in the area. *Eds.*]

6. The arrangement of the school buildings, grounds, and everything pertaining to it might be different today. I have pointed out one chief
change—that of the chapel and girls dormitory. There may be other
changes, which I might not know of, since I have not been there for over
a period of years. Everything I have written here pertains to my time and
that of my contemporaries.

CHAPTER 8

MORE ON LIFE AT THE
MISSION SCHOOL

Fun and life outside of the classroom depended, as I can remember, on the friends one had, their status, and relatives. The way you were thought of went hand-in-hand with your friends. I am thankful that I had a lot of relatives and friends at Bromley, and I was protected by them. Bromley at the time was a melting pot as we were from almost every group of the population of Liberia: Kru, Grebo, Kpelle, Gola, Bassa, and others, commonly referred to as "natives." Then there were Americo-Liberians as well as a group known as Congo (pronounced Kɔŋgɔ). These Americo-Liberians and Congos came mainly from the settlements around the St. Paul River, and seemed to have been in a definite cultural lag. The sociologist will tell us what happens when you place people of various nationalities and cultures together; it means conflict, tension, and domination. While this is generally not expected perhaps among schoolgirls, it happened to be the case there. When I reflect, I notice that although we played peacefully together, we tended to group and form our associations reflecting our ethnicities.

To top this melting pot situation, the girls felt that the teachers tended to be partial to the light-skinned girls from the upper-class Liberian families. In short, the school reflected all of the problems that existed among the adult population of the country. I understand this situation much better today, since visiting America, and seeing that a person's color has something to do with his chances of advancement—I mean color within the same group—which has become so vital in the thinking of the American Negro.

One day while at the mission, a girl who got angry with a group of us called us "uncivilized country things." I had certainly heard this before and was waiting for an opportunity to reply. This was my chance. My answer ran thus: "I might be uncivilized and country, but I have a heritage. I am not one of those who had to wait to come to school to learn to read and write. If I had never come to Bromley, I would have done this, by learning the Vai script. Furthermore, what you are calling your 'civilization' was something copied and borrowed while in slavery. It was the imitation of other people. Yes, I am proud to be uncivilized and country." Well, perhaps this was enough. Many of the other girls standing around pulled me away, and from that day onward, nobody dared use the word "country" anywhere around me.

Regarding the teachers, many of the girls felt that they favored certain groups and classes and gave them the lighter work of the school to accomplish. Personally, I had no problem or complaint, in spite of the fact that I was neither light-skinned nor Americo-Liberian. These factors are what I am referring to as status. I had friends among all segments of the girls in the school and had no difficulties with groups, especially those meant to search for food and fun.

In time, many of our relatives left, so Titi and I and our friends were left alone at Bromley. During this time, all packages came to us directly and I had more to share with my friends in this respect. The packages from the Vai Development Company (VDC), a firm that father established, came to us directly. This made us feel secure with regard to food. Victoria's father also had a business and she received frequent packages, so that our trip to the bell tower to share food became a daily routine. Aside from the pleasure of having our lunch in the tower, it was a beautiful thing to stand in the middle aisle of the building directly under the big bell and look into the surroundings of the school. On clear days, we could distinctly recognize Monrovia. It was during this period in Bromley that the girls gave me the nickname "Development," because of the VDC and because of my general progress in the school.

I had many friends among small and big girls. I think today that the reason many of the older girls bothered with me was due to the fact that I had several older brothers. In fact many of them and my brothers were passing notes to one another at the time. None of those youthful romances lasted. They are all married today. However, the fact remains that this made me quite popular at Bromley. Victoria sometime later told me that she believes the reason I had been popular at Bromley with everyone was that I had been very friendly and quiet. Well, whatever was the cause of my pleasant stay in Bromley, I am deeply grateful for having been there, and I often find myself observing the moments fleeing away from me, pleading with them to linger, because of their beauty.

During the period before Easter, Godma Moort would write songs and poems on the blackboard, and every evening we were taught the music of the songs. Sometimes, individual groups too would be selected for readings, solos, duets, and the like for the Easter season. The Sunday before Easter, Palm Sunday, is a great day at the mission. It is this day that usually brought those of us attending the school into the fold of the Christian world, and make us members of the great family of the universal brotherhood of man, a keystone of Christianity, as no other religion seems to convey.

During the first Palm Sunday spent at Bromley, schoolchildren who had not been baptized were sought out and messages sent to their parents or guardians about their Christian names, godparents, and the like. On that memorable day, Titi, Victoria Johnson, Danliette Johnson, and many of the older girls and I became Christians. Godmas Meyers and Moort became my sponsors in this undertaking, along with Bishop Gardiner, Uncle Lamini, and Uncle Waller.[1] The latter could only become my godfather by proxy, since he was in America while I in Liberia.

During the week that ensued, Holy Week, we had church services everyday, and reviewed the songs for the Easter ceremonies. It was all great fun. Our parents, Ma Sedia and father, came for the baptism carrying new clothes, having been told what type of outfit we wanted for Easter, as well as a box of food for the week following Easter.

It was grand to rise with the sun and go to the early Easter services in the chapel, which a week earlier had been decorated with palms, and now, with flowers and other shrubberies. That Easter afternoon we had a special program. We sang songs, which sent one's spirit crying for the beauty of nature, in a much deeper way than the Psalmists have ever been able to demonstrate. The yearning for nature was evident through the melodies of the birds and the beaming glitter of the buttercups and daisies. The spirit of Easter was there as it always is everywhere.

I played an important part in all these ceremonies. I was with the group that had to recite the portion of Matthew 28 early that morning. The evening ended this very joyful day for us and we looked forward to a week of relaxation and activities and plays. There were no classes following the week of Easter at the mission. Usually, though, no one went home. A tradition at the mission had been for the students to arrange various programs, which were usually presented on the last evening following Friday after Easter. In between, the girls arranged cooking and playing parties. We could invite teachers and older girls to this. The girls had told us of the custom, and that is why we had asked for the food when father came to visit.

This box with the Easter outfits and food arrived on the Saturday before Easter. Of course we had already made our plans for our parties. Victoria, Kate, Ida, Danielette, and the whole gang had gotten together pots, salmon, sardines, and their cans, meats, dried fish, rice, palm oil, cookies, and everything that was there for a grand week of cooking. The other girls in the group had of course received their own packages, and we had something good on the menu every day. As I write this, I can see the various girls, with smoke and tears in their eyes from the fire, preparing various types of foods. I can hear all the quarrels and fights we had. For, as with children everywhere, these activities did not proceed without fights. Victoria and Kate would always fight, no matter what. But they would make up in no time, and when we cook on Saturday afternoons they would be together again. Now, as grownups, they are the best of friends.

There was another member of the group who was also always ready to fight, my own niece Titi. She had the reputation of being fussy. She fought with anyone who crossed her path. She fought me at times. But she was good when you really knew her. I remember how remorseful she was when we settled a quarrel.

At the time I was at the mission, the missionaries faced the great problem of where the girls who had faced a change of cultural environment were to spend their vacations. Some of the girls were from pure African homes, and the missionaries feared they would join African institutions like the Sande, which they considered as heathen. I knew the case of a girl who was not permitted to return after she had joined the Sande. If they understood what really happens there, they would know it does not prevent a person from becoming a good Christian. The point here is that vacation time meant a great problem to the mission. Nobody could leave unless the parents sent for them or some host family was found for them. For this reason, many of the girls usually had to remain at the mission during the vacations.

During that first term at Bromley, my cousins and I had anxiously looked forward to our mid-term vacations in July. We were all quite ready—nine of us—to climb into the Vaikai, when it appeared one day with my brothers, Jaiah, Ali, Jawa, and others, bearing a letter from father to take us home. Nobody can imagine the joy a child feels when coming home on vacation after the first term at school. Since my cousins Isa and Annie were old inmates of Bromley, they were busy telling our parents what we had achieved at the mission. But more than this, we were anxious to show what progress we had made and all the wonderful things we had learned. In our minds our parents knew not the least of these things, and we ached for an opportunity to demonstrate all the knowledge we had acquired, which seemed supernatural, magical, and above human ability.

My brother Jaiah founded the Boy Scouts in Liberia.[2] That year he had to turn his position over to Ali, since Jaiah was now too old for it and was then eligible for the regular army. My older cousins and Ma Sedia were busy cutting out kerchiefs and hemming them for the Scouts, and we were made to stitch up the hems. Apart from our sewing the scout kerchiefs there were many other activities. Many of my young female cousins had their friends whom they entertained. Although we of the younger group could not participate in the dances and other social gatherings they had, we were never bored for we stood outside, watching them and making comments.

I remember in this connection that Ma Sedia's brother, Uncle Hilary Johnson, had returned from school in America and brought with him some American dances. The very next morning after watching such dances, we would turn on the gramophone and have one of our cousins, and my brother Jaiah, who indulged us somewhat in this respect, show us the dances they had done the evening before. Jaiah was very much a man in those days and definitely a choice of the ladies. So was my brother Al-Haj. Thus, we learned to dance early. There were also wrestling matches, fights, and drills of all kinds my brothers engaged in. So also were swimming matches in the river, but the girls were forbidden to swim with the boys.

Father himself was always very humorous, a thing that I was only just beginning to realize. There is nothing he would not do for a good joke or a good laugh. He was constantly telling anecdotes, out of which one could learn a great deal. I guess that is why people loved to be around him. When my brother Ali (commonly called Nat), was about 12 or 13 he wrote a letter to a girl who was very much his senior in years, saying that he would like to marry her. The letter was beautiful. Unfortunately, the poor chap must have forgotten to send the letter to the lady in question and left the letter in the pocket of his clothing, which was put in the laundry.

The letter was shown to my father who called the poor boy and the rest of the household together and announced that "Nat" wanted to marry, and so we were to prepare him to get married. He made a full orchestration of the wedding that my poor brother began begging, *"O, papa, make I no marry,"* whereupon father replied, *"entee wo na say wo na be in love."*³ Upon hearing this, Titi and I began crying and begging that Ali should not have to marry.

The big boys only laughed. Father then had the whole party go across the street to our friend and neighbor, the late Mrs. Johanna Coleman, widow of the late president Coleman of Liberia.⁴ We were to have a bridal party and ask for her blessings. Mrs. Coleman was sitting on her front porch, when she saw us thus attired, she yelled over to father: "O, my, Momo, what are you up to with these children now?" Ali replied, *"He said I go marry, I no want marry. Mrs. Coleman, tell am please, make I no marry."* Mrs. Coleman laughed and returned to the house with us and supposedly begged father not to make Ali marry, whereupon Ali promised not to write false promises to girls. On that day, Ali was saved from marrying.

One of our vacations was not spent with my parents. Father and Ma Sedia had a belated honeymoon during a business trip to Europe. My various cousins—Mary Dent, Woki, and others—had gone to live with relatives and friends. Titi and I were still at Bromley at the time, so that year Grandma Johnson invited us to spend the vacations with her and the family. This was nothing unusual because we had frequently spent nights at the house. Since cousins Isa and Margret had also been left to spend their vacations there, we felt quite at home.

Ma Sedia and father returned from Europe during our vacations. We had expected them for Christmas, but they did not arrive until January. We had made all sorts of preparations to receive them. I made a necktie for my father during one of my crochet classes at Bromley. It was wine red in color with a white cross in the center. Ibrahim teased me saying that father would not wear such a tie. Father, of course, pretended he was most happy to have the tie and wore it for a few minutes, but I never saw him wear it again. I thought it was not elegant enough, but two years later, when my brother Ibrahim followed us to Germany, I saw him with the tie. Then I understood why my father had not worn the tie.

The night my parents returned, Ma Sedia asked me to come and spend the night with her in her room. She knew that I had a very good memory and she wanted to catch up on the events of the town. I lay in bed with her, telling her who had died, who had married, what people wore, what they ate, and even the manner in which they cried. I begged her to tell me about the children in France, Holland, Greece, and other places they had visited, as the geography of the world and customs of other peoples were beginning to take active shape in my mind. It was this night, by the way, that she told me of eating frog legs in France and other stories of adventure. She gave an account of the great Negro tenor who had appeared and sung for King George and Queen Mary of England, Mr. Roland Hayes.[5]

When Ma Sedia and father were about to visit Europe, we had asked them to bring various gifts for us on their return. I had asked for a music book since only those with their own books took the course at Bromley. On a stopover in Freetown, my father's younger brother, Uncle Jaiah, whom father had sent to school there, gave them one such book, *Smallwoods*, to bring for me. I practiced all the pieces in the book so that I would know them when my parents returned. I had been told also that Uncle Jaiah would be returning home to settle down, and I wanted him to see that his niece had used his gift wisely.

I was now anxiously waiting for an opportunity at the piano to show what I had learned. Cousin Ellen Johnson, my teacher, had great patience in helping me with the music. The morning after my parents arrived, I went downstairs and asked them to stay upstairs and listen for something. I then went and played a few of the melodious little pieces in the book. Uncle Jaiah heard it too and they were amazed to see me play because previously I had attempted to play but only with my elbows, my hands being sore. Now I was playing with my hands.[6]

But waiting to play was not the only reason I had wished for the day to dawn. Ma Sedia told me she had brought us some dresses. There was a red dress with embroidery on it and a beige one with an embroidered butterfly. I could not wait for Sunday to come for me to parade the dresses, since at that age, your parents usually decided when and where they should be worn. I remember counting the days, and it seemed Sunday would never come. When Sunday came we stepped out to show our new dresses. There were other things that our parents had brought from Europe. Father called me in and gave me a harp, which so absorbed me that even the new apparel became secondary to this gift. I also received a doll that I loved very much, which I named Grace Hawa. Alice-Marie Johnson, the daughter of the American minister to Liberia, played with my doll in my absence. When I returned home again to Monrovia, Grace Hawa was one-legged. I told my parents that I didn't want the doll anymore and in my heart I wept bitterly.

Having participated in a spelling match at Bromley and gone to the head of the class for correct definitions, it would perhaps surprise whoever is reading this to know that I often fell short on definitions. One day Alice-Marie Johnson was invited by father to come to the house. After we played for a while, she asked for her "souvenir." I wondered to myself what it was. I went around the house asking my brothers what a "souvenir" was, which Jaiah explained to me. I went to father and he gave me a small elephant tusk, telling me to "decorate" it. Alice-Marie was happy with her "souvenir." Sadly, I never saw Alice-Marie again, for a few months later we left for Germany.

I don't know the chronology of the events I am about to describe—I mean whether they took place in the order that I am relating them. On one occasion, father allowed me to leave the mission and return home for our first-of-December celebration. This is one of our Liberian holidays, commonly referred to as Matilda Newport Day. It was on that day that Matilda Newport is reported to have saved the colony of the early settlers from invasions of warring indigenes, by the simple process of placing the fire from her pipe into the cannon, which frightened them away.[7]

Meanwhile, the John Payne had perished during a voyage to Cape Mount. Grandpa Gabriel Johnson, Mr. Joe Dennis, and father constructed or bought a steamboat, which was named the "Rachel-Agnes," in honor of Ma Sedia (Rachel), and Agnes, Mr. Dennis's only daughter.[8] This steamer was now making the runs that the John Payne made. Father and the Millers came to fetch me, and as soon as the steamer arrived, I rushed down to see if father was on it, and some of my friends accompanied me to the boat.

I went to father and whispered into his ears, and he gave me a shilling. The secret was that I had a new girlfriend, Nina Wea, a Kru girl, and since I was not going to be there to spend the first of December, I wanted some money so she could buy some sugarcane from the neighboring village. This was the first time I had ever thought of asking for money. Mrs. Miller was so touched by my loyalty that she reached into her purse and gave me two shillings, which I distributed to the girls standing by, giving them two cents apiece, which enabled them to buy sugarcane too. Mr. and Mrs. Miller, by the way, were from Liverpool in England. I believe that Mr. Miller was a business associate of the VDC, but I am not too sure about this. Their younger daughter, Catherine, and I became good playmates. The older daughter, Melvina, who was also with them, was an active Girl Scout in England. Together we steamed down the St. Paul and had a glorious trip to Monrovia.

Upon arrival, Ma Sedia took me upstairs and asked me to close my eyes. When I opened them, there in front of me was the most beautiful dress, which I was to wear for the holiday. It was pink silk with white stripes and large red roses were embroidered on it.

School closed for Christmas shortly after my return. We went home, at which time father was appointed by President King to go to Germany as Liberian consul general.[9] He took the opportunity to assure me that there would be another Grace Hawa soon after our arrival in Germany.

Many Americans know of the consecration of Bishop Theophilus Momolu Gardiner, a cousin of father's, but in Vai custom, they were brothers.[10] They were the children of two sisters. Bishop Gardiner and his family came to Monrovia from their residence in Harper, Cape Palmas, Liberia, on their way to a conference at Cape Mount. This event took place in January. I got along very well with his daughters, and he asked father to leave me with them in Cape Palmas when they went to Germany. But I heard father say he was certain that neither he nor Ma was thinking of leaving me behind. He said that going to Germany was an opportunity to have some work done on my hands, which in another four years or so I would need.

While I had gone on a short visit to the interior, Godma Moort and Ma Esther had written to say that I had to come to bid them farewell. I could see the reasons why they wanted me back. While in the fifth grade the previous year, Godma Moort had hardly taught any European geography. Now, this was being stressed. Everything proceeded at the mission as if I were not leaving. I took my usual courses and participated in the life of the mission as usual.

Once again, the week after Easter approached, and we were to give a program. I was chosen as mistress of ceremonies for the occasion. On Easter proper we had all of our activities at the school for boys — Montgomery Hall in Clay-Ashland. I did a reading for the program and sang with the choir.

The week following Easter, I went about finding talents for our little program. I had never planned a program before and was quite worried as to how I was going to do it. Here is something which I came across a couple of years after we went to Germany — my first speech, a welcome address, delivered as mistress of ceremonies: "Dear teachers and friends, girls of Julia C. Emery, and all others who are not on our program... We have invited you here tonight to listen to our program. We do not wish you to criticize us and we do not want to bother you with a lengthy program. Please sympathize with us for our mistakes, will you not?"

Easter fell on April 16, 1922, and the Saturday following Easter — the day after the program — father wrote Godma Moort to allow me to leave that Monday in order to be in Monrovia. That Saturday after evening devotions we learned about the sad demise of Julia C. Emery. Godma Moort told the girls that I would be leaving the school on Monday to go abroad, and that the girls should not make the parting hard for me. She said they should instead be happy that I was going on to get schooling and to have my hands cured. She said that those who think they would miss me should show their loyalty and love by taking my place by behaving as I had done. During her speech, she could not control her tears. I was touched because I never thought she cared as much for me as Godma Meyers and the rest of the teachers. Besides, I had only seen her shed tears once, the previous October, when one of the students, Lauren Andrew, passed away. Her tears were genuine and she later called me and had a long talk with me, giving me advice.

The time had come to bid Bromley adieu. The Sunday before I was to leave we had no church services because the pastor could not make it that day. That night, after devotionals, Godma Moort asked me if I would like to say something to the girls. I told them that although I was leaving, I would always be at Bromley in spirit. I then asked them to sing with me "Our Blest Redeemer, Ere He Breathed His Tender Last Farewell." After the song, I told the girls that I believed the Comforter will be with us to pray that I might be religious, and not follow the ungodly Germans. The latter comment echoed the teachings of our courses in which we learned about the German atrocities in the First World War — how the Germans had invaded Belgium and their treatment of the population and children there. I concluded that the girls should pray that I, their fellow Bromley sister, would become the greatest woman that Liberia had ever had.

On Monday, April 25, classes were dismissed because I was leaving. When I saw the Rachel-Agnes turn the corner, I rushed to the porch where Godma Moort was standing alone. I couldn't imagine where all of the girls were. I could see only a few of them, including Titi and Clara Davis. Before that, the girls were constantly around me, asking for the millions of things that African girls wish to have from abroad. I was to send dresses, pressing combs, fountain pens, and many other things once I had arrived in Germany.

Upon reaching Godma Moort I suddenly began to cry. She advised "do not cry, the best of friends have to part. Live a Christian life and remember Bromley expects you to become 'the greatest woman that Liberia has ever had.'" When I arrived where the steamer anchored, the girls were assembled there, waving with palm leaves. I wonder how they knew. This was interesting because at the time there was no Vai girl at the mission to know that this was the sign of hope among the Vai. There were too many girls there for me to say farewell individually. Besides, the steamer had been waiting too long already, so one friend was shaking one of my hands, the other kissing me on the cheek, and still another touching and squeezing my arm. I looked for Titi to say goodbye to her. She was not to be found anywhere but finally I saw her up on the hill, standing all by herself looking quite sad. Finally, the steamer could wait no longer and moved off. The girls ran up and along the hill, keeping pace with the slowly moving steamer. I waved and the girls waved, and last messages were given, to which I only said yes, even though I did not understand. We slowly turned the corner of the river, and the chapter of my life at the mission school, where I had learned reading and less arithmetic, came to a close.

Notes

1. Waller is an American Negro who became a friend of father at old Walden. I later met him in Germany, and he called on me on my arrival in America also. He lived and died in Brooklyn about 1939 or 1940, where he was a physician. [Owen Meredith Waller (1868–1939) was a founder of the NAACP and prior to his work as a medical doctor in NYC he served as rector of St. Luke's Protestant Episcopal Church in Washington, DC from 1896–1904. *Eds.*]
2. [Jaiah Massaquoi introduced the Boy Scouts in Liberia in 1916 after learning about the organization as a student in Freetown, Sierra Leone. Family friend Dr. Benjamin Payne, who had seen the Boy Scouts in the United States as a medical student, and served (1912–1930) as Liberia's secretary of public instruction, was the organization's first president. *Eds.*]
3. Spoken in Sierra Leone Creole, which my brothers spoke when excited. Father knew it and would speak it when the occasion demanded it. [The

standard transcription of this is: "Enti, una no say una de in love," meaning "It's true, you (plural) are in love." *Eds.*]

4. [William David Coleman (1842–1908) was born in Kentucky, USA, and
served as president of Liberia from 1896 to 1900. *Eds.*]

5. [Roland Hayes (1887–1976), who was one of the leading concert tenors in
the world from the 1920s through the 1940s, was a close family friend of
the Massaquois. Fatima Massaquoi lived with the Hayes family in Boston
in the 1940s. As a black musician, Hayes found audiences in Europe often
more supportive than those in America, and he performed not only traditional Negro spirituals but also the classical German genre known as
Lieder, performing the works of Brahms and Schubert. Be that as it may,
according to one scholar "the career of Roland Hayes, one of the first
classical performers from the United States to perform in Germany after
the First World War has been relatively unexplored to date" (Christine
Naumann, "African American Performers and Culture in Weimar
Germany," p. 104, in *Crosscurrents: African Americans, Africa, and Germany
in the Modern World*, ed. David McBride, Leroy Hopkins, and C. Aisha
Blackshire-Belay (Columbia, SC: Camden House, 1998). *Eds.*]

6. [Alluding here to her hand that had been severely injured in an accident.
Eds.]

7. [The holiday was abolished by the government of Samuel K. Doe in
1980 following the assassination of then president William R. Tolbert,
Jr., because it was thought adverse to promoting national integration
between settler and indigenous communities. According to the tradition
of the holiday, settler Matilda Newport played a central role in defeating
Dei peoples who attacked the colonial settlement of Cape Mesurado in
1821. *Eds.*]

8. [Joseph Samuel Dennis (1872–1933), who was at one time the Grand
Master of the Grand Lodge of Masons in Liberia. *Eds.*]

9. [Charles Dunbar Burgess King (1875–1961) was president of Liberia from
1920 to 1930. He was born in Freetown, Sierra Leone, where he attended
the CMS Grammar School. He later moved to Liberia with his parents,
and was educated at Liberia College and subsequently became politically
active. *Eds.*]

10. [Gardiner (1870–1941) was educated with Momolu Massaquoi at St. John's
Mission school. He was the first indigenous bishop of the Episcopal
Church in Liberia. *Eds.*]

CHAPTER 9

I BID FAREWELL TO LIBERIA

In 1920, C. D. B. King, running on the Whig Party ticket, was elected president of the Republic of Liberia, defeating the People's Party. A new era began in the history of Liberia with various political appointments. His cabinet and administration as a whole included many segments of the Liberian population who were now involved in shaping the destiny of the state. Father had been instrumental in acquiring native votes for the Whig Party, and as a result was given a responsible position in the new government as consul general to Germany.

Contrary to the numerous criticisms of King's administration, there was another side regarding the question of native rights, culture, and advancement, which I think was positive. Critics often forget that people have different cultural backgrounds, varied attitudes and different sentiments, and different religious beliefs and political structures, and sometimes even the interpretation of the very laws differs widely. The major task of nation building lies in uniting all these diverse elements into one culture, one political system, one educational system, one great family of religion, one nation, and one people. This must necessarily be a gradual process, with mistakes, even based on trial and error. For us, it is like a man taking a long journey over a very steep mountain carrying a large load and having to constantly adjust himself to the weight on his back. In this process, the strong should protect the rights of the weak and respect their cultures and beliefs.

During the administration of President King, there were more indigenous people in high government positions than in previous times. For the first time in our history, an indigene ran for the vice presidency of the nation.[1] It was during King's administration that for the first time a native became an associate justice of the Supreme Court of the Republic of Liberia.[2] He made contracts with both Europe and America, showing such tact that it became clearly evident to the world that Africans had a sense of diplomacy and commanded respect.

I learned something interesting in my conversations with returned American missionary, Rev. W. L. Turner, who during his sojourn in Liberia had become deeply interested in African languages and cultures.

President King asked Turner if he would be interested in working on a type of lingua franca for his people, which shows the interest he had in uniting his country. All of this is not being said in defense of the mistakes.

Despite the new policies and undertakings of the administration, father's appointment came as a great surprise to our people and gave me an occasion for jubilation. Although the appointment had actually been made in 1921, father asked for time to settle his affairs in Liberia and to obtain the formal consent of his people. I have often marveled about this. Father was looked upon by all Vai, many segments of the Mende population, and others as a great leader, without whom no issues of great importance could ever be settled. Yet, he never undertook anything without first obtaining the permission of his people.

Prior to the appointment as consul general to Germany, father had been secretary of the interior, acting secretary of war, secretary to President Howard, etcetera, in no chronological order. He wrote a note for some paper once, and Ma Sedia had me take it to his office, and that was how I knew he was secretary of the interior and what he was doing when he left the house every day. Well, all these positions had been in Liberia. This being the case, father had been able to find ample time to do other jobs on the side. You will perhaps understand this when you stop to think of the many mouths he had to feed, shelter, and clothe. All of these affairs could not simply be thrown aside for Germany.

I cannot discuss how father accomplished settling his affairs without marveling at his versatility. Sometimes, I wish this biography was about his life. When I reflect, I see him engaged in having additions made to the house, or building a new house in the yard, or supervising the construction of the wharf in Monrovia. He was on programs of various kinds, with orations and lectures, and was involved in discussions. He wrote treatises and authored articles on cultures and languages, and had an acumen for music and business.

When father founded the Vai Development Company (VDC), it was to get indigenes to sell their raw products (cash crops) to the European markets at better prices. In the interior, the company sold imported goods at wholesale prices, often on the barter system. All of this was a definite advantage to the people. A business like this required transportation. Father had become the agent in Monrovia for two West African steamship companies, a Danish line owed by Mr. Nissen of Copenhagen, as well as an Italian line. He had also been a representative for a British firm from Liverpool, and I believe his connections with Mr. Miller, whose wife I mentioned earlier, had something to do with this.

These were a lot of activities that needed to be taken care of. The management of the VDC was turned over to one of my elder brothers,

Al Haj, who showed a keen ability for business, having been involved in export business since his return from school in Freetown, Sierra Leone. The VDC had branches in various sections of the country. The steamer companies needed to be notified about changes regarding agents before father could go to Germany. They, in turn, had to make sure their interests were secure. All of these arrangements would take months.

There were other issues too. My father had been the leader of the Vai, so issues with the people needed to be settled before we could leave Liberia for the Reich. There were family issues as well. Jaia and Ibrahim were to be left with Rev. and Mrs. Turner, the former teaching the Bible at the Stokes Theological Seminary in Monrovia. Other siblings were placed with responsible family members.

As late as the end of 1921 or the beginning of 1922, prior to my farewell visit to Bromley, I had no idea I would be going to Germany with my parents. I had no conception of what I was going to do when I got to Germany, or what Germany was going to mean to me. I had no dreams of becoming a great engineer as my brothers had, or becoming the best-dressed girl in Germany as my cousins thought they would become. I was completely unconcerned about the prospects of going to Germany and for this I have no explanation. In fact, I had welcomed whole heartedly Uncle Momolu's (Bishop Gardiner's) invitation to go to Cape Palmas with them. In all the arrangements father made regarding his responsibilities that I have narrated above, and others that I have not made, he showed real judgment and insight, and everyone was happy with the business arrangements or the new homes where the children were sent to live.

After all these matters were settled, we prepared to bid farewell to our homeland. When the Gardiners left around the middle of January, Ma Sedia and the baby had taken a trip to Cape Palmas. In the meanwhile, father visited the interior. I did not go with him but was able to take a short trip to the interior because I had to return to Bromley before leaving. My stay in the Vai country took on a new note at this time. I was nearly three years older than I had been when I left and now I was acquainted with another way of life. This gave me a keener sense of observation of things Vai than I had before. Since I had been sent, in particular, to bid Mama Jassa farewell, she did not miss the opportunity of accompanying me to the Gallinas again, my birthplace, as well as to other shrines in the Vai country.

Mama Jassa took me again to *Mamada*, the holy crocodile.[3] Upon our arrival, Mama Jassa's son, Minna, held me in his arms while she called "*Mamada na*" repeatedly.[4] With a force as if the waves would burst, the animal appeared. As usual, it marched to the family members and smelled various individuals, before snatching a white chicken tied to a tree, which it then ate. After this, it would take a bottle of gin and drink it before the very eyes of those present.

From there our travels continued through the Vai country, and there was no better guide to explain things than Mama Jassa. Her patience in this respect was boundless, and her love and devotion to me was without limits. I sometimes wish I had been a little older throughout all of my contacts with her.

In one of the places we visited, the Sande was in session. The girls came out on that day and performed their dances and held exhibitions of things they had learned in their year or so of training. In many of the towns we visited, father had just been there or was expected soon. Finally, in one town, our paths crossed. He was awaited to sanction various ordeals for crimes that had been committed. Our people, as many other people I have met, have their beliefs, both natural and supernatural. I have in the past years, both in Europe and America, made an attempt to collect folk superstitions and beliefs. I often wonder, after examining many of them, whether in many cases superstitions are not born in order to instill in people good practices. If such is the case, superstitions would have some good qualities.

There are of course superstitions among our people that cannot be brushed aside easily as not making sense. These are based on religious beliefs in many instances. Many of them have economic and spiritual qualities, like the ancient beliefs of the druids in mistletoe, or other people who believed in a saint medallion for luck. Our people, too, have objects that are omens of good and bad luck. These have religious origins. Let me take one such object as a sign of a good omen among my people. This is the *"Nomonia,"* which is a soapstone believed to have been carved by the ancient Africans and is believed to be as ancient as five thousand years BC.[5] The person who possesses one of these stones is usually believed to possess great authority, and each king tries to have one in his compound. The image is consulted when a person is about to take a long journey, or placed on the farm to guarantee luck for an abundant crop. There are only a few of these ancient stones left in the hinterland of our nation, and they are consulted during times of war. They are believed to be jealous. Indeed, the man who possesses one is great and lucky. When these stones are discovered during the farming of virgin land, a great festivity and celebration usually takes place.

There are also various "ordeals" left to us by our illustrious ancestors which we now use purely for detecting crime. Before we bring a man to court, we have to first know whether or not he is guilty. After the establishment of guilt or innocence, then the objective in the court is to determine the form of punishment. Finding the guilty party of a crime is therefore not the same as punishment. There are various kinds of ordeals, oaths, and methods used, and I have observed several.

One is the hot oil, iron, or metal ordeal. One or several iron rings are placed into boiling pot of oil. The suspect places his hands into the oil and brings out the rings. If the hands are burnt, then he is guilty; if not, then he is innocent. Another ordeal is by the *gbato* or whip. This system is usually applied in cases of petty theft. The small whip is placed in the hands of a small boy, after rubbing both his wrists as well as the end of the whip with medicinal water. The boy follows the instructions of the medicine man or doctor and goes around the people shaking his body. When he gets to the culprit, he involuntarily begins to whip him or her. This offender is then taken to court to ascertain his punishment. There is also the thorn system.[6] Each person swears that if he or she is guilty, the thorn should hurt him or her. The thorn is then pricked into the flesh or wrists of each suspect, and the one whose flesh swells or hurts is the guilty party. The guilty party is then taken to court. The sasswood ordeal is also important. A part of the sasswood, just above the root, is boiled in water. After cooling the water is given to the various suspects. The person who can drink the mixture without vomiting is not the guilty party. He who vomits after the drink is guilty, and goes to court for punishment.

There are other forms, which I don't think fall into the realm of ordeals but rather "oaths." I was unable to ascertain how the trial for confirmation of the *kpangba* (to plant, to make tight, to cement) proceeded, since it is done in great secrecy. It is to detect those with bad medicine that hurt people. Those guilty were put into the stocks. Those who confessed their guilt were told to bring their medicine, which was burnt and a great lightning following gave the assurance that the evil had been destroyed.

After traveling through my homeland, we returned to Njagbacca, where most of Mama Jassa's daughters had assembled to bid me farewell. Father was expected, as he had invited some African chiefs to celebrate the fiftieth anniversary of the ascension of grandmother to her throne. On this trip were several Liberians form Monrovia, American missionary Rev. Turner, and Mrs. Fannie R. Givens,[7] a lady from Louisville, Kentucky, who was to lay the wreath on the tomb and deliver the oration.

In Njagbacca, I once again had the opportunity of watching Mama Jassa pray. Once again her face turned to the East or *Telebe*, as she proclaimed her *"Allah Akbar"* ("God is great" in Islamic prayer) during the early mornings and evenings. I was now very eager to know what she was saying, so she read portions of her Koran to me and told me the meanings of what she read. All the time she was trying to convert me to Islam, and I was trying to tell her that she was a "sinner" in not believing in Jesus Christ and would be ultimately condemned. Although I was leaving her, I at least wanted to meet her in heaven, should I never see her again. All that I read, heard, and learned at the mission school was reflected in my attitudes to other religions and to Mama Jassa. She did not agree with me.

Mama Jassa told me that she did not see Africans having much of a place in Christianity, and that it belittled everything Africans have long believed in. The religion had many times destroyed the traditional organizations and societies, which were built and thought out by our forbearers. She wanted to see them grow, not destroyed. Her religion, she claimed, left her the alternative to foster her heritage. If Christianity was the only way to achieve heaven, then she said she would rather go to the other place where she would see grandmother and all the other people of ours who had known nothing about Christianity. She pointed out that I believed in a religion that would condemn you because you did not have a last chance, in case of sudden death, like in war. The religion I was defending, she said, would punish them unnecessarily.

There are many things that struck me about her argument. I had thought she knew nothing about Christianity, and hence had been trying to convert her, but now to my great astonishment, I found that she knew. Perhaps you are wondering at my having no arguments to put up against all that she said. Well, today, I certainly would have had arguments, abundant arguments. But how could I have any in those days? So, Mama Jassa talked and talked but it was all in vain. Although I put up no arguments, or rather knew none, I insisted that she and all the others were heathens and sinners.

Apart from learning portions of the Koran, Mama Jassa intensified her effort in teaching me the Vai Script or *Tombekpole*.[8] I did not, however, complete the learning of the script until later in Germany under the tutorship of my father and brothers. My separation from Mama Jassa and her family cannot be concluded without special reference to the anxiety she felt over my well-being. For this reason, she took me again, as mother had done before, to soothsayers. They told of long voyages and how I would live away from home more than I would live at home—these and many more things were correctly predicted.

While I was back in Monrovia, having arrived from the mission, waiting for the steamer for Germany, I met one of the most important members of my family. This was my sister Sie Massaquoi (nicknamed "Kobo"). Father had brought Kobo, who had been with an aunt in the interior, to place her in school in Monrovia while we went to Germany. Since our steamer did not come for nearly three weeks, I had the pleasure of at least getting to know my sister a little.

One day, Ma Sedia gave me a note and told me to take Kobo to a school teacher. I became quite important and proud that I now had someone of my own to train—at least so ran my thoughts. I went to school with Kobo and instead of only handing her the note, I said to the teacher that we would be leaving for Germany shortly, and that she should report on my little sister's progress and character. Kobo had just come and knew no English. She kept asking me in Vai what I had told the teacher.

It was quite strange to see our home broken up when I came from Bromley to await the steamer. The house had been rented out and the furniture sold. While visiting a lady, in order to give her a message from her daughter and sister at Bromley, I came across our piano. She asked me to play and I banged on it so long that at the moment it seemed like the greatest object in the world. Ibrahim was then living at the Stokes building where my brother Jaiah had taken a few rooms. Father left instructions for him to move in with the Turners when we left. He often came to Grandma Johnson's, where Kobo, Ma Sedia, baby Arthur, and I were living while awaiting the arrival of our steamer. Father was in the home of a cousin with most of the other boys who were to make the trip.

Since we were going away, I was told that I could not take any of my clothing. Much of it was given to Kobo, including my trunk, while the rest were sent back to Bromley for Titi. But I was very annoyed at the country I was going to where you can't wear clothes you have on hand, I thought. Ma Sedia thought I should take only the two dresses they had brought for me from Europe. I was then sent to Ma's friend, Mrs. Edith Worrel, who had sewed for us, to get one or two woolen dresses she made for me. My parents promised to purchase appropriate clothing upon our arrival in Germany.

Since the steamer did not come on 1st May but only on 21st May, my friends Angeline, Clara Cassell, and others had little parties for me. Also, just before we sailed, Mother Soko, Sister Hawa Massaquoi, and Mother Bangu had all come to bid us farewell, and due to the delay of the steamer, I once more enjoyed their company and listened to the numerous expectations they had of me.

At last the actual day of the departure came. It was on Sunday, 21st May. Ma Sedia had gone to church and was singing in the choir when someone told her that they had seen the flag hoisted. She rushed home to get Arthur and me ready. I had not gone to church because all of my things had been packed and taken to the steamer company. Ma rushed to the house with the news that the steamer was there. And then father appeared to get us.

When we reached the waterfront, everyone was standing around and waiting for me. When I finally got there, I jumped into the little steamboat that was to carry us to our ship. Voices of Cousin Isa, Kobo, Cousin Margaret, and numerous others came bidding us goodbye. I was busy looking across the river, thinking at that moment of my relatives in the hinterland. I wondered if I would ever again meet any of them alive. I thought of Mama Jassa's age. The steamer set out when it was discovered that Ma Sedia had forgotten our tickets. Collinette, Ma Sedia's sister, was running along the hill, keeping pace with the boat, and when she saw us returning, she ran and came near and Ma was able to tell her where to search for the tickets. She returned with the tickets before we could anchor. A short while thereafter, we found ourselves sitting in the launch that had stopped aside the big ocean-steamer, the SS *Wigbert*, a Woermann-Linie ship of Hamburg, Germany.[9] The steps were let down and we climbed up.

There was too much noise and confusion on the steamer. Sailors were dancing about, hoisting cranes while Kru men were loading and unloading the steamer. Our passports and tickets were being processed by the steamship authorities, and father was taking care of all of this. When all of this was over, people who had accompanied us to the steamer made for their boats and roared away. The *Wigbert* was nearly ready to move off, when I looked across the waves and saw something that almost looked like a large fish. It turned out to be a canoe bearing my brother Al-Haj. He had been away for the weekend and on his return had learned that we had left. He thought father would like to give last instructions, business ones, and he did.

It was dark by this time and I stood on deck, watching the lines that the *Wigbert* made, first moving slowly and eventually increasing tempo into the open sea. I must have stood for a long time on deck, because it was already the peak of dusk when I noticed that we were passing Cape Mount. My thoughts once more ran back to the folks in the interior living in that direction. Soon the dinner gong sounded and I was called to go and change. Seated at the table, I was hardly able to eat a thing—*"aber in der Fremde, habe ich ihr Bild mit mir getragen, was nur durch Vereinigung der Liebe möglich gewesen ist."*[10]

Our traveling party to Germany consisted of father, Ma Sedia, baby Arthur, my brother Nathaniel Varney, my brother George Fromoya, Mrs. Payne (wife of the late Dr. B. W. Payne, who had been secretary of education),[11] Mrs. Sarah Raynes Barclay (wife of a member of the House of Representatives), Major Anderson (an American Negro, who was connected in some way with the Liberian army),[12] and yours truly.

Everything on the ship was something new. In taking her course, the *Wigbert* offered a new melody, the echo of which could only be caught by a sensitive and imaginative soul. The *Wigbert* sailed smoothly, rolling slowly but surely along the South Atlantic Coast. In this rolling, her engine seemed to be singing a song, the bitter song of parting. With it went a form of accompaniment that seemed very much like the beating of a drum, which went like this: *trala danan, trala laden, traladanantralaladen* in a somewhat 5/4 fashion with the stress on the first and fourth beats. I went about the ship imitating the engine to my brothers and the baby just the same, to the annoyance of the former and to the mirth of the latter.

As pleasant as the trip could have been, our group from Liberia had some complaint with regard to the food, which had practically no taste. Ma Sedia and father had visited Europe several times and had tasted everything good at parties. On the other hand, we were all rice birds, and there was no rice on our menu probably contributing to our dissatisfaction. I remember how relieved the party was when one day I visited the kitchen and told the cook that I did not like his cooking because he had not cooked rice. He laughed and said that the German cooking was the very best that the world had, but that next time, rice would be included, too.

From that day onward, we had our rice. At first only enough of it was cooked for the baby and me, but when the waiters saw that my parents loved it too, they prepared enough for all. The *Wigbert*, by the way, was only a cargo boat, but was the best kind of boat one could take those days, which ran between Germany and Africa. The fares, although a cargo boat, were very high. Fifty pounds had been paid for father, forty-five for Ma, and perhaps the same for Mrs. Barclay and Mrs. Payne, with thirty for me. I don't remember what was paid for the boys. Later, around 1936, one could obtain much better accommodations. On regular passenger steamers, the fare was about thirty pounds for adults.

There were not many other passengers on the steamer, since she was mainly a cargo ship. Aside from our regular traveling party, there was the German consul general to Liberia, a Mr. Foerster, another man traveling from Angola to Portugal, and two other gentlemen, whose names I do not remember. Life on the *Wigbert* was monotonous; it was nothing like the life even on an ordinary cargo steamer of today. There was not one single music record on the steamer. There was nowhere to play. However, on our voyage, the only thing we had to look at when in the saloon of the *Wigbert* was the mileage map, to ascertain how long the monotony would last to some port.

One night, we beheld the lights at Dakar. That meant something to me. I associated Dakar with Dolo and Elizabeth, the two girls from Bromley who had written such beautiful letters of their experiences in the city. This had awakened in me a desire to write beautiful letters of faraway places so that Godma Moort could read them to the Bromley girls after the familiar "sit down" following evening devotionals. How very simple the ambitions of a child can sometimes be!

The next day, 25th May, brought us to Dakar where we were entertained by the governor. I don't remember much about Dakar, except the impression of the two different colors of the lighthouses. Our voyage continued and we saw no more land until the early morning of Monday, May 29th. On that day our steamer slowly dropped anchor at Las Palmas, in the Canary Islands. We went ashore and took a long ride as far into the mountains as possible and through the city. Las Palmas vividly reminded me of Cape Mount, while in later years it reminded me of Switzerland. But I did not stop to make too many comparisons because I was so overwhelmed by the beauty of the city. I said to Mrs. Sarah Barclay, who by this time had become Aunt Sarah to us, "If Las Palmas is this beautiful, Hamburg must be a Paradise." This remark was based on the fact that the wireless operator on the steamer, who had taken keen interest in taking me around, had told me that Hamburg was more beautiful than any city that we would see during the voyage. It was in Las Palmas that I boarded my first car. It was there too that I boarded the first lift.

But everything in Las Palmas did not end as pleasantly as it had begun. Namely, before we could end the mountain drive and visit the Liberian Consulate, we thought we'll stop at Quinn's English Hotel to rest and tidy up. It was there that baby Arthur became ill and every one of us thought we would surely lose him. I saw anxiety written on the faces of my parents. He had just learned how to talk, and I was having a lot of fun with him. We had motored fast and the draft from the mountains had been too severe for the baby, or so the doctor said. Arthur was given every care and, toward the late afternoon hours, we could only hope for recovery and returned to the steamer without calling on the Liberian consul general to the Canary Islands.

In the Canary Islands little boys came alongside the steamer and begged for money. This money was not given to them directly, but the coins would be thrown into the water and they would dive for them. I spent much of my money just to see them dive. My brother Jaiah had given me a one pound sterling gold coin, which I was to wear as a souvenir locket from him. So when I needed a shilling or sixpence to throw into the water, I went to father and asked him to change the coin for me.

On the following morning, 30th May, we were in Tenerife. The whole family did not go ashore, for Arthur had not fully recovered. Varney, father, and I went. There were beautiful mountains and valleys. The next morning found us in Madeira. As we did not have a long stopover in Madeira, only father went ashore to buy some fruit and other things for us.

At each port we reached, father would give me money to spend. I bought my first cherries in Las Palmas. I enjoyed the cherries because they left your gums and teeth dark with stains. My parents bought clothing for us on the trip but it was more expensive on the ship than at any of the ports. Also, the merchants who brought goods to the steamer would sell them very dear at first, but as the steamer was about to leave, the price would decrease by the hour or even minute.

After leaving Madeira, we resigned ourselves to ship-life again, for we were to travel five more days before reaching or seeing any more land in sight. With the resumption of normal life on the ship, I once again turned my attention to my newly found friend, the wireless operator. He told me that he would bring his children around to play with me upon our arrival. He was constantly telling me of Hamburg and what a glorious and clean city it was. He took me around the ship and showed me its operations, which meant nothing to me at all at the time.

The 4th of June brought us to Lisbon, Portugal. The sight of the town was beautiful: the portion of the city nearest to the water was hilly, while the town was overwhelmed with cathedrals. We took a ride around the town. The day was gloomy, although it was not raining, but that did not spoil the picturesque sight for me, as the parks were large and full of green shrubberies and flowers. We drove around the town and found people selling fruit in the Jewish quarters. But I was quite surprised to find the people in Portugal were different because in my mind, I had somehow pictured them as being as dark as Africans.

After a very delightful drive in Lisbon, we ended up at the Hotel Continental for lunch. We ordered fried fish, but again we were confronted with the unpleasantness of having something not quite palatable. The fish had been fried in oil, perhaps olive oil, but in Liberia we used palm oil. So, only Ma Sedia, father, and Major Anderson proved themselves good cosmopolitans in this respect. They ate the food while Aunt Sarah and I simply looked at them.

We were served salad, too, but in my mind this was "green leaves," that is, uncooked. Although we eat a great many things raw among my people, we had never consumed raw leaves that were meant for cattle. Something else was ordered, and again something else, but each time our fate was the same. Of course that was my taste only in those days. For now, nobody loves lettuce and foods cooked in or with olive oil more than I do.

When we left the hotel, I was surprised to see how many people were coming from church, from the big cathedrals we had seen earlier. I noticed that although those people had sold goods on Sunday, they nevertheless went to church. We returned to our ship late that afternoon after driving and seeing all that was open on Sundays.

As our ship made her way toward the sea, I thought that she was trying to keep pace with the trains, the first that I had ever seen, which were running on rails. I asked my two brothers which one they thought ran faster, a ship or a train. At first the ship had been faster, but soon the trains passed her, one by one. So this is how the ship is crawling, I thought. No wonder we cannot get to Hamburg! My brother Varney retorted that I should stop asking so many stupid questions all the time.

From Lisbon, we were back to our old life on the boat again. But this time it was not boring as my new friend, the wireless operator, had found new and exciting things to relate about Hamburg. Other people on the ship also interested me. Almost all the people on the steamer had been Germans and naturally everyone spoke the language, even at meals. But Germans meant practically nothing to me in those days. My seat at meals was directly opposite the German consul general to Liberia, Mr. Foerster, and I had to look at him whether I liked it or not. I could not understand anything he said, only *"ja, ja, ja,"* or *"nein, nein."* I could guess that he was saying "yes" and "no."

As our steamer entered the famous Bay of Biscay, I offered a prayer since missionaries and travelers had told us it was rough. I was nevertheless disappointed when we entered the bay and I saw no tables turned over and the ship did not even rock a little. In fact, we had a very smooth voyage all the way through. I had nothing to write to Clara Davis, from my Geography courses, who I had promised to write to about how the water would behave.

Notes

1. [Henry Too Wesley, from the Grebo ethnic group, who served as vice president in King's second term, from 1924 to 1928. *Eds.*]
2. [Thomas E. Beysolow, Fatima's uncle, who was appointed to the Supreme Court in 1924. *Eds.*]
3. [The story is recounted in chapter 5. *Eds.*]
4. ["Mamada come." *Eds.*]
5. [These steatite (soapstone) figures, known throughout Sierra Leone, Guinea, and Liberia and usually termed "nomoli" (nɔmɔli) probably date to a period between the fifteenth and seventeenth centuries AD. They were carved by the ancestors of related Mel-speaking peoples (sometimes described as forming a "Sape Confederation") who are thought to have been the original inhabitants of the area, such as the Temne, Baga, Kissi, and Sherbro-Bullom. The figures, therefore, are "found," not "made," by peoples like the Kissi, the Vai, and Mende, who occupy the territory today and who latterly incorporated the stones into their belief systems. Historical accounts of the region have contended that the displacement of the so-called Sape Confederation was a result of the Mani invasions of the mid-sixteenth century, at which time related Manding peoples became new occupants of the land. The Mani invasions are characterized by the Vai in the oral tradition relating to the trek of "Kamala the

Younger," discussed by Fatima Massaquoi earlier in this autobiography. For illustrations and basic information on the nomoli, see A. Tagliaferri and A. Hammacher, *Fabulous Ancestors: Stone Carvings from Sierra Leone and Guinea* (New York: Africana Publishing Co., 1974); also W. A. Hart and C. Fyfe, "The Stone Figures of the Upper Guinea Coast," *History in Africa*, Vol. 20 (1993). *Eds.*]

6. Nowadays a needle is used instead of a thorn.

7. [Fanny R. Hicks Givens (1872–1947) an artist and missionary for the Foreign Mission Board of the National Baptist Convention. *Eds.*]

8. [This alternative name for the Vai script is virtually unknown today among Vai script practitioners. The name refers to "Tombe" (section of Vai country associated with the emergence of the script) and "kpole" ("writing" or "book") *Eds.*]

9. [See also Hans Massaquoi, *Destined to Witness: Growing Up Black in Nazi Germany* (New York: HarperCollins, 1999), p. 5. *Eds.*]

10. ["but away from home I always bore her image with me, which was only possible through the bond of love." *Eds.*]

11. [Dr. Benjamin Payne (1875–1940) was a medical doctor trained in the United States. He served as secretary of public instruction from 1912 to 1930. *Eds.*]

12. [Major John Anderson was a US Army officer in charge of the Liberian Frontier Force from 1917 to 1922. *Eds.*]

CHAPTER 10

I ARRIVE IN GERMANY

Our last stop before Hamburg was Rotterdam, Holland. It was planned to visit Professor Johann Büttikofer and family—you will remember earlier that Büttikofer was a friend of my grandmother's who wrote of her in his *Reisebilder aus Liberia*.[1] Büttikofer knew father since the time father was an infant, and father and Ma Sedia had visited them before. This visit was also important to the family because Büttikofer was a friend of Ma Sedia's grandfather, the late Hilary R. Johnson, under whose administration he had visited Liberia. It was very interesting to make this visit and hear of the days of all the actions and deeds of the fathers who lived in the generation before us.

On the night of 10th June, our steamer pulled out of Rotterdam. It was then that we experienced the rough voyage that everyone had expected. The North Sea rocked the *Wigbert* to and fro and most of the grownups spent the following day in their cabins recovering. We finally arrived in Hamburg on the night of June 11th, but were unable to land as it was too late at night. On Monday morning, June 12th, we finally landed, and father attended to all the immigration issues.

We rode through the harbor sections of Hamburg to the Palast Hotel, which is situated on a street called the Jungfern Stieg, one of the most prominent and busy streets of the German city. The street offers one of the most splendid views that the eye can behold anywhere. We were accompanied to our suite, and there was somebody from home, who father greeted with a familiar "Sir Charles."[2] He had been appointed Liberian consul general to England, based in Liverpool, at the same time when father was appointed to Germany. That whole day people came calling. Mr. Feighery, a British merchant of Liverpool, who had known father both in Liberia and in the Gallinas country, called on us. It was, however, chiefly the Germans who had been doing business for over a generation or two with Liberia who came to welcome us.

The hotel was elegant, but I was bored to death. Father went out daily for business and to look for a place to live. Sometimes, Ma Sedia and Aunt Sarah went shopping, and I could at times go along, but other times remained at the hotel to be near the baby while he slept. My brothers felt too grownup to play or go out with me. Sometimes, while Arthur slept soundly, I would go downstairs and observe the life and traffic of the vestibule below. For anyone who knew Hamburg before World War II will agree with me about all the traffic and splendor as observed from the Palast Hotel. From there one could see the Alster, and this means everything to the city of Hamburg.

The Alster is one of the greatest beauties of the city—made up of several lakes flowing together, ordinarily referred to as *"das Alsterbecken"* in German. Most important of these are the *"Binnen und Aussenalster,"* which are partly artificial and partly natural. The Alster affords opportunities for swimming and regattas. From the window of the hotel suite or the porch, I watched elegantly dressed people and listened to the afternoon music played from afar. One of the most elegant café houses of the city, the "Alster-Pavillon," was within sight and there business people, diplomats, and people of the world often sat while listening to music and sipping a cup of coffee or chocolate.

I longed to visit the Pavillon, and one afternoon father returned early from his business and offered to take us to hear some music and spend the four o'clock coffee hour at the Pavillon. That first visit at the Pavillon, of which there were to be many more in the years ahead, was delightful. Ice cream and coffee were ordered, but more memorable for me were the music and people. The special attraction that day was a Russian singer, remarkable to me more for her glamor than her selection, though her motions and posture were perfect.

For suitable lodgings, father wanted a house and not an apartment, but he finally decided to take an apartment in the interim. Since Consul General Cooper was leaving for his post in Liverpool, he asked his landlady, Mrs. Carrie Kohler, to let us have her apartment at Schlüterstrasse 52, Hamburg postal code 13. It had about six rooms, a bath, kitchen, basement rooms, servant's quarters, and etcetera. The location was splendid, situated in the residential district of the city. There were several parks in the vicinity and several main streets had tramcars leading to the life of the city. This was also only about the same five minutes' walk to the main building of Hamburg University. It took only about another fifteen or twenty minutes walk to get to the park, which was the center for ice skating.

There were cinemas and opera houses, and a main post office. There was a city railroad station, the zoological garden behind the Dammtor station, and the botanical garden. Numerous places of amusement and culture were within five or ten minutes of our apartment. There was the Museum for Völkerkunde (folklore) almost at our backdoor. There was the Curio house, a famous building used for many forms of activities, and the Voegel Konservatorium. Most importantly there was the Alster, just a short walking distance from our home.

The apartment of the Schlüterstrasse was surrounded by beautiful trees blowing a cool breeze in the summer, something which must have been very refreshing and comfortable for the German people, but naturally not for us, who froze and felt chilly at each turn, despite the fact that it was summer. A German summer does not mean tropical heat.

Mrs. Kohler was a charming and energetic woman with three children, two boys, Hans and Dietrich, and a girl, Dorothy, in her early teens with whom I had to share the same room. Dorothy had just completed high school the previous Easter. The boys were both in boarding school, at the famous Plöner Gymnasium, whose most illustrious student was Otto von Bismarck. They were with us for only a few weeks in the summer. All three of the Kohler children were kind, charming in manners, as well as sociable. They were always anxious to help us. Mrs. Kohler too brought her numerous friends around, and was helpful in many ways. She was Ma Sedia's major source of information concerning German social life and ways. The Kohlers, for all practical purposes, were not landlords but friends.

Even Frau Kohler's cook, Fräulein Elizabeth, was very kind. She became our cook and was a very good one. She was healthy and imposing, and many a day I ran to her quarters to see how she prepared the various meals. Her home was the Rhineland, and, when we moved from Schlüterstrasse, she went back to her home. I was the only person in the family who heard from her until 1936. (I have a knack for keeping up with people throughout the years). The Kohlers, by the way, have all in the meanwhile migrated to America. First, Mrs. Kohler and Dorothy came over, then the two boys. I remember, in the early thirties, when the two boys went to the consulate one day, where I was working for father, to bid us farewell, but father was away on furlough in Liberia.

At Schlüterstrasse, father reserved one room for the work of the consulate. My brother Ali, who had spent his afternoons working and typing at the State Department when we were at home, knew how to do clerical work in general. During our first months in Germany, he was most useful in establishing the work of the consulate general. They worked all day and sometimes far into the nights, always with the typewriter clacking.

Ma Sedia and her best friend, Aunt Sarah, spent their days shopping and having fun in general. Two days after we moved in to Schlüterstrasse, a nurse was obtained for baby Arthur. The three of us took daily walks and were constantly together. This relieved Ma of the baby. The name of this first nurse of Arthur's was Kathie Warncke, who had been an assistant to a dentist before working for us. She was very nice.

I found time for new experiences and observations, such as at the parks, playing with sand or playing German circles with other children. This way I quickly learned to converse in German, almost fluently. The post office building had the central exchange for telephones in Hamburg, which fascinated me greatly. I had seen people call numbers, and in doing so, they got numbers through the operators working at the offices. I went to Fräulein Elizabeth, who had in the beginning been summoned to make the connections, when anyone in the house wanted to call a cab, or speak to other people whose numbers we had or whose acquaintance had been made. In this way, the number for the taxicab, or *"Autoruf,"* which I remember to this day, became known as *"Vulkan siebentausend..."* then came the answer, *"Autoruf". "Autoruf"... "bitte, ein Auto,"*[3] or *"ein Auto bitte, für Massaquoi, bei Kohler, Schlüterstrasse, zwei undfunfzig"... "So fort."* The difference in the numerals, which is the telephone language, was to avoid misunderstandings for *"zwei,"* which could be confused with *"drei"* very easily.

There were several numbers that I learned by heart. One was the number of the place where Mr. Karl Kuhrmann was living. He was a great friend of the family, having lived in Liberia for many years prior to the war, and even had a Vai daughter. He was then making some efforts to return to Cape Mount, where he had been very successful as a merchant. His landlady was Mrs. Luhmann, who had a son and a daughter. The daughter, Margot, was my interest as we were of the same age. She was already in school.

The Kuhrmann family and ours spent much time together, even though they lived in a villa situated on the opposite side of the Alster, on Schaeffer Strasse. Whenever we were invited there, the grownups and the boys would take their coffee in the dining room, while Margot and I were usually served on the sun porch, where we usually had the most delicious cakes with Schlagsahne und Torte[4] and some special chocolate as beverage to which I was quite partial. Among my most cherished memories are those of Mrs. Luhmann, Margot, and me playing among the beautiful flowers and fountain in their garden.

During these first months of my stay in Germany, I had fun with other friends. At the front end of the basement of our home was a fruit store, owned by Jews—the Mannsbach family. I went there about a day after our arrival at the Schlüterstrasse to buy some cherries, of which I had now learned to make earrings. It was difficult for me to make Mrs. Mannsbach understand what I wanted. She told me to wait until Ilse, her youngest daughter who worked at the telephone office, came home. Ilse went upstairs to see what I wanted since she spoke English, a preparation for her going to America. But it did not end with the purchase of cherries, for Ilse and Daniel, her brother, invited my brother and I on Saturdays and Sundays to go to the zoo, cafes, and etcetera. All of this bored my brothers and they were later left out. Ilse and I remained friends until she left for America, and later, within two years or so, the whole Mannsbach family left one by one.

It was during the time when we went out to have chocolate and listen to the afternoon music in the garden of the Dammtor Café that I noticed that people of color were quite a novelty in Germany. A lady left her table and came to touch my hair and to see how I would drink my chocolate. I wondered at this, but this was just the beginning.

As our circle of acquaintances grew larger and more diverse, the Bruces from Cameroon or Togoland[5] learnt about us. They had troupes and gave performances all over Europe. Regina Bruce, the oldest of the Bruce daughters, came to see us, and enquired if we knew anything of her folks. Her father, mother, and brothers had disappeared during the war on one of their performance tours. She had last heard from them when they were in Russia.

The troupes of the Bruce family must have been in Europe for a very long time as Regina and her sisters—Lisa and Annie—were born there. All the three sisters received good training in the schools of Hamburg and were very smart. When Regina found out that I was in the family, she asked us to go and visit her *"Kinderheim,"*[6] which was located on the outskirts of the city of Hamburg. There, at the Borstelchaussee 199 was a German nurse who owned a boarding home for children from kindergarten age to 14 years. Regina later asked father for me to stay there. Father did not want me away from home since there had been rapid changes in my life but agreed to let me take German with her or play there, in order to help. My parents also bought some of her crafts, which were very well made. I don't think I would have loved staying there anyway since all the children had to go to bed at six o'clock, in broad daylight during the summer months, something I consider one of the worst punishments I could be given.

At 1.30 p.m. I usually took the tramcar 13 and rode to the end station, a little village called Borstel. This village by the way was a big place for making movies in these days. Upon my arrival there, at 2 p.m. sharp, some of the bigger girls from the Heim would be there to walk to the Kinderheim with me until I learned the way. Supposedly, I was learning German. But all the German I learned in these days was more from associations than from lessons that I took. We played from the time I arrived there until my departure. If there was a visitor at the Heim, all the children would be called together to entertain that person. Aside from learning German, I enrolled for all of the crafts classes that the other children took.

It was in this Kinderheim that I learned my first German song. There was a girl there, called Mariechen Sagner, who had the loveliest mezzo soprano voice. One day, a lady from Switzerland was expected to visit, and we were to learn songs to entertain her. I was able to learn one of the songs, although I didn't know what it meant at all. However, the refrain, *"da hat er garnicht übel, garnicht übel dran getan,"*[7] is about all of the songs that I remember today. To be sure I did not sing the text in that way, but *"da hat er garnicht übel, garnicht übel gangantan..."* With the association at the Kinderheim, my days became complete because I spent the morning hours with Kathie and the baby in the parks, and left the house right after lunch to go to the Kinderheim. I cannot complete the story of this Kinderheim without mentioning Schwester Hann, Regina's partner, who had taught her and with whom she stood in perfect harmony, in spite of the difference of race.

We had friends among the neighbors. Two sisters, Jewish girls, Leoni and Ilse Silberberg, mother British and father Jew, were added to my list of friends. Leoni was in school, but Ilse joined us in the park daily. Ilse was quite surprised one day when a girl in the park and I quarreled; she pulled me away and asked me not to play with that girl anymore. It was while we were playing baking cakes one day that a girl looked at me for a very long time and then asked, "Did your mother beat on your nose to make it flat?" I said, "No, but did your mother pull your nose when you were a baby to make it so sharp that you have to stick it into things that do not concern you?" Well, perhaps I might have forgotten the incident, but for Katie Warncke who related the incident to Mrs. Kohler and Mrs. Warncke on various occasions. While Ilse had feared that this girl and I might fight, Kathie took out her handkerchief and laughed herself red.

Major Anderson had in the meanwhile left for America soon after our arrival in Hamburg. Mrs. Payne was in the hospital, and we visited her at the Graumannsweg Klinik. One day I spent the whole day and night with Mrs. Payne for I had made friends with one of the nurses, who later became the head nurse, and later even the head nurse of the institution. She asked me to spend the night and I did. This woman, Schwester Elizabeth, took me around to the curious women so they could look at me. I resented this inwardly, but didn't know how to tell her to stop it.

The Graumannsweg Klinik was owned by a lady, Professor Vesseler, whose husband was also the director of the zoo.[8] Mrs. Payne's operation went successfully. She came out of the hospital late in July, but she must not have been out for more than a week or ten days, when one night she took a turn for the worse. Mrs. Payne complained and was taken back to the klinik, where she died a day or two later. The secretary of education, Hon. B.W. Payne, had her body shipped to Liberia, since that was her last request.

Since the one-room consulate in the apartment was not convenient, we moved to the Johnsalle villa, in the same general location at

Schlüterstrasse. We lived there longer than we did in any other house during our entire sojourn in Germany, and it is the dwelling I personally liked better than any other. It was nearer to the Alster in the first place, and was also within two or three minutes walking distance from the university, Moorweiden, and other places of interest.

The Johnsalle house belonged to a wealthy Jewish lady, a Frau Reis, who had died the previous May. Since her heirs could not come to immediate terms regarding the settlement of the house, Herr Kuhrmann persuaded the nephew administering the estate to let it to us. We got the house just as Frau Reis had left it. Even her housekeeper became ours. Fräulein Elizabeth could not move in with us, having been Frau Kohler's cook. The villa had fourteen rooms, servant's quarters in the basement, and an attic room, which my brothers took as their study. The front garden of the house had three lilac trees. Two of them were purple and the other white. The back garden too had lilac trees. In the middle of this garden was a large round flower bed. There were cherry, plum, apple, and pear trees.

Since a painter and his wife were occupying the third floor, we did not have immediate access to it, and therefore I did not have a room of my own and had to share with Aunt Sarah. She did not want to be by herself in a room; stories of war atrocities were still in her bones. Even at the hotel, in our joint room, she used to carefully place all the trunks in front of the windows and doors. We shared the guest room at Johnsallee until her departure. While it was Aunt Sarah who in the beginning had wanted me in the room with her, I found out that I was not at all ready to sleep in a room by myself. If I had previously not been afraid of ghosts, I now found myself being afraid of them.

The boys were responsible for this. My brother Ali had accompanied father while he made all the business arrangements for the house, and on his return had told me that Frau Reis did not wish Negroes to live in her home, so her ghost might haunt me. Besides, since I did not believe in the Talmud, which hung on all of the doors, she had them placed there for those who believed and could read it. I pretended that I did not believe him, but deep down in my heart I imagined seeing Frau Reis at night, standing beside my bed. As a result, I begged every night not to have to go to bed, before Aunt Sarah was herself ready to do so. Sometimes I succeeded in delaying by making father believe that I wanted to wait for him to talk to him before I went to bed. All of a sudden, I loved to comb and scratch his head at night while enjoying him telling of the days of old. In time, I learned that there was no Frau Reis anywhere around.

Meanwhile, as I did not go to bed early, or had sleepless nights thinking about Frau Reis, I could not get up early. We had moved to Johnsallee in September. The days had become shorter and shorter, with long and dark mornings. I found myself sleeping as late as it would be dark, which father did not like at all. He told the boys to only wait until Aunt Sarah left, and then he would make sure I stopped the habit.

But the boys did not have to wait until Aunt Sarah left, because father came home one day and with him was Fräulein Gertrude von Bobers, whom he introduced to me as my teacher. With the coming of the winter, he did not want me to continue going to the Kinderheim. I was to take private lessons at home. Of German British aristocratic stock, Fräulein von Bobers was born in England and attended school there until she was sixteen, although her native home was Hanover. She attended boarding school in Lausanne, Switzerland, and learned French, so she spoke German, French, and English equally well, and even a little Spanish. She was very good at playing tennis and swimming.

Miss Bobers asked me about courses and I told her that I would like to take history, and to learn to read and write German. But father asked her not to let me do much writing until after the operations on my hands. So, we read and recited a great deal in the beginning and wrote about once or twice a week. We began learning the history of England in English. I learnt about the Plantagenet kings, the life of the black prince, the Plague, William the Conqueror, Alfred the Great, and etcetera. But I was most keenly interested in the story of how Richard the Lionhearted was found, for we have a Vai legend similar to that, only with a ring, and not by a musical instrument. I proceeded telling her the story, which amused her very much. After studying certain periods in the history of England, she would bring corresponding periods in German history to study.

Fräulein von Bobers paid great attention to the genealogies of the various rulers, and she saw to it that I thoroughly understood the kinship between the various ruling houses and rulers of the two countries. Of the German rulers, I amused myself greatly in reading the minutest thing I could find about the life of Friedrich the Great and Friedrich Babarossa, due to my admiration for great warriors.

Aside from the history classes, we read about various birds of the various climatic zones, flowers, animals, and the like. The *"Gebrüder Grimm Märchen"* were my favorite companions. Fräulein von Bobers and I also discussed geography, but at this time the only thing I wanted to do in geography was to draw maps and color them. We did not only have a teacher-pupil relationship, as she became my confidante, companion, and friend. She was my guide and my ideal in many respects. She later moved to live on the third floor with us after it was vacated. I would go to her for advice on behavior and circumstances concerning life in general.

Fräulein von Bobers also became secretary to the Liberian Consulate General and remained in this position for nine years. She was well prepared for the job. She also translated the book *Soudan* from the French into English for father, who knew the Arabic version but wanted it in English. These were of course all separate jobs. With Fräulein von Bobers moving to live in the Johnsallee, my schedule for the day changed considerably. She had to be in the consulate at nine, so we both arose at six a.m. and had two hours of lessons by nine. For two days of the week we would have another class for two hours in the afternoon.

We had heard terrible stories of winter and were afraid of the experience that awaited us. Only Ma Sedia and father had experienced winter before. Alas, the dreaded time came. But it did not catch us unprepared or afraid—the expectations had been for the worst. We bought clothes, and heard the familiar phrase, "that garment will help you be ready for the winter." Everyone had a special garment that was his or her particular "ready for winter" outfit. There were many such outfits, especially for the baby and for me.

My particular "ready for winter outfit," which I had chosen for the picture we were to take to send home to the rest of the family, was a wool navy blue sailor suit with pleated flair skirt. I had high boots, a cap, and long leggings which went clear up to my knees. There were also two green and red woolen coats, along with my white ermine coat. The green and red were for school and everyday wear, and the other for invitations to special functions.

October 28 became a red-letter day on our calendar. It was Aunt Sarah's birthday and we had a birthday dinner. Father went for a walk and we waited for supper quite a while for him. Finally, we heard his voice calling us. We rushed out of doors and the ground was covered with snow; it looked as if hundreds of sacks of sugar had been spread on it. How beautiful, we thought. I suddenly discovered that I rather liked the snow, since with the snow on the ground it grew warmer than it had been previously. Father took each one of us newcomers to make acquaintance with the snow by rubbing our heads and noses into it with the remark, "Who is boss now?"

After we moved to the Johnsallee, each of us raced increasingly to use the phone. I had started the whole thing and now everyone was rushing to make their own calls. Everyone was trying to speak German. In the beginning, we noticed that our parents turned to us children whenever the maids or anyone spoke, looking for us to interpret for them. A lack of knowledge of this language had struck all of us keenly the night father's addition to the diplomatic corps had been written up in the papers. We were still in the Schlüterstrasse when Dorothy Kohler brought the paper into the living room and gave us a short resume of what it contained. We could see that the article was very long and that we did not have all of its contents, but father had it interpreted the next day by Mr. De Lopez, who we thought knew more German than we did.

Everyone was competing to speak better German than the others now. Ma Sedia and Aunt Sarah showed real progress among the adults. I guess you are wondering what became of our teacher, whom we began to call *"Nero bellt in der Nacht."*[9] His German was the worst, since he sat in his office all day and did not come in contact with the spoken language, although what he later learned to read and write was accurate.

Father and Ma Sedia often stood in keen competition. One day, we children decided to test them and decide the case once and for all. George gave the examination. Ma knew all the idiomatic expressions and could speak the language fluently for the oral test. "Nero" could write and spell, but he thought we were speaking Hindustan when we dictated something to him or spoke fast to him. So, we decided, to his great annoyance, that Ma was the better of the two. He accepted the fact that the children knew more German than he did, but he did not wish an adult to beat his time. Ali and I were considered the experts and were the judges on this test. Well, although it is not a part of our tradition for children to laugh at the parents, we often had great fun over the two of them, husband and wife.

Aunt Sarah had come to Germany for a pleasure trip. She and Ma Sedia had been the best of friends and thought about enjoying being abroad together. This meant that sooner or later she would have to leave us. All of us had grown very fond of her without any expecting that this would be the case. So, her leaving was very painful. She was beautiful and jovial, and participated fully in our home and social life. Since we were roommates, Aunt Sarah and I had grown close. Whenever she and my parents went somewhere, and the children were not allowed to go, I would wait in bed to be awakened by her pleasant voice to give me an account of what they ate, and what the people were like.

While Aunt Sarah was packing her things to leave us, I sat on the cedar chest at the foot of the bead watching her. She went downstairs to get some things and when she returned she saw me crying bitterly. She told me she would miss me very much and that she was going to ask father and mother to let my sister Sie-Kobo, who had been left at Grandma Johnson's place, to come to Germany. Sie was later named after Aunt Sarah and a cousin of Ma Sedia's, Miss Anna Cooper. When Kobo became Sarah Anna Sie Massaquoi (Sie being her Vai name) at her baptism, Aunt Sarah was her godmother. Aunt Sarah was kind and generous to me, and gave me the little things that my parents refused me.

The day before Aunt Sarah left we had a party, and all the lights of the Saal (the big dining room) were switched on. There were lights on the wall, and a beautiful crystal ceiling light also hung down from the middle of the ceiling. It was a beautiful spectacle. For ordinary purposes, we hardly used the room. When people called, one or the other lights was turned on, but never had I seen all of them on together. The little French divan, which was twisted in the middle so that one could sit on both sides, stood in one corner, with small chairs surrounding it on all sides. It was particularly beautiful—green in color with a sort of grayish border. In other corners of the room, there were leather sofas and chairs.

My parents had taken this opportunity to invite German officials and people interested in Liberia to the house. That first party was a big success. When the dinner and all the toasts were over, pictures were taken. Some of the people left by midnight, but those who knew us well remained for the dance. They danced long. Before everyone left, the children were dressed and called for an introduction. Father had told the people that I could do African dances very well. They asked me to dance. I went in and played the Saasaa—but dance? I was so ashamed to dance that I ran and hid.

Arthur and I had often danced around to entertain our guests, but that was when there had only been two or three people visiting us. Now I was to dance before all of these people, giving them a chance to laugh at me. The German social dances had been so different—different and funny. The man would take the lady in his arms, and they would fold their arms so that their elbows flopped together like the wings of a bird. They would then jump around the place while *"Komm in die Diele"*[10] was sung. How can the people who dance that way want to see me dance? But later, I enjoyed parties and dancing so much that I felt hurt and neglected whenever there was one and I was not allowed to attend. Well, the party was beautiful just the same, and the picture we took that night shows me with the saasaa, holding it in playing position.

That farewell party for Aunt Sarah was also to honor father's nephew, the Hon. James S. Wiles, who many years later returned to Germany as his successor to the post as consul general. He had been in Germany since the previous August and was also returning home on the same boat with Aunt Sarah. The following day, November 3rd, we bade farewell to Aunt Sarah, and they left by the S.S. Tshad, a new steamer that was making her maiden voyage to Africa.

That winter I saw some girls with whom I had played in the parks, going to the *"Eisbahn"*[11] to skate, and followed them. We had subzero temperatures and before I could return to the house I was frozen through. Everything was so cold that I went to the stove in the dining room and put some pieces of coal into it. I then took the poker and began poking into the stove. Suddenly there was an explosion, and my face was covered with smoke and burns. All of my hair burned off. I looked so bald that from that point on, I was ashamed to go out. The German winter made your hair stiff anyway, but the boys laughed so much that I had to hide and it seemed like an eternity before my hair grew again. After that experience I never tried to make a fire again. And, I got punished by my father for my misdemeanor.

Meanwhile, Arthur, spoiled by father immensely, lost his immunity. He did something wrong but this time father put him across his lap and gave him a good switching. That was on January 11 and we marked it on the calendar. It was also the day the French soldiers occupied the Rhineland.[12] I remember the day because I picked up the newspaper and for the first time discovered that I could really read German.

I took private lessons until it was spring again, and then we sought out the doctor for my hands. Professor Bernard Nocht, founder and director of the Institute for Tropical Diseases, had recommended an operation on my hands[13] to be performed by one of the leading surgeons, Dr. Kotzenburg. My father sensing that I dreaded it, arranged with Prof. Kotzenburg for me to have friendly visits with his little daughter. This made the thought of the operation much easier for me. When the day did come, it was not difficult at all for me.

I was taken to the Wunsch Klinik for the operation, which was successful—at least on one of the hands. I enjoyed being in the clinic, as Nurse Schwester Frieda, a red head from Prague, spoiled me. One day, after one of the electric massages, I went to sleep. My brother George, who always came to the clinic from work to see me, announced that he had a surprise for me. I was too sleepy to notice that he was serious. He told me that Jaiah was in the room. I thought he was teasing me and refused to open my eyes. But I heard Jaiah's voice! I lifted my hands and touched Jaiah, bouncing up so that one of the strings that the hand was sewn with broke, but I didn't notice this at all. Jaiah had arrived that afternoon and George picked him up from the ship. I need not tell you what Jaiah meant to me while I was a child and you can imagine my joy in seeing him.

Notes

1. [Johann Büttikofer, *Reisebilder aus Liberia,* 2 vols. (Leiden: E. J. Brill, 1890). By this time (June 1922), Büttikofer was 72 years old and curator of the Leiden Museum. His visit with Fatima Massaquoi's grandmother, Queen Sandimanni, had occurred 36 years earlier. *Eds.*]

2. [Charles Edward Cooper (1885–1951) was, along with Momolu Massaquoi, the earliest of Liberia's European-based consuls general, both appointments resulting from a law passed by President King in 1920. Cooper was consul general in Liverpool, but was charged with overseeing Hamburg until Massaquoi's arrival there. Cooper was known as a businessman and has the distinction of being one of Liberia's earliest novelists, with his

Love in Ebony (London: John Murray, 1932) written under the pseudonym of Varfellie Karlee. *Eds.*]

3. ["Autoruf" = auto-call; "Vulkan siebentausend" = Vulcano seven-thousand; *Eds.*]

4. [Whipped cream and cakes. *Eds.*]

5. [The Bruces were from Togo; see Rea Brändle, *Nayo Bruce. Geschichte einer Afrikanischen Familie in Europa* (Zürich: Verlag, 2007). *Eds.*]

6. [Children's home. *Eds.*]

7. ["this he did not any bad, any bad with it." *Eds.*]

8. [Julius Vosseler (1861–1933) was a German zoologist and director of the Hamburg zoo. *Eds.*]

9. ["Nero barks in the night." *Eds.*]

10. ["Come in the entrance." *Eds.*]

11. [Skating rink. *Eds.*]

12. [On January 11, 1923, French troops occupied the Ruhr after Germany defaulted on World War I reparations payments. The German government ordered a massive campaign of passive resistance, a general worker's strike, and the closing of factories and mines. The French troops were sent to reopen Ruhr industries. *Eds.*]

13. [Bernhard Nocht (1857–1945) was the director (1900–1930) of the institute, which was renamed in 1942 as the Bernard Nocht Institute for Tropical Medicine. The operation was conducted by Wilhelm Kotzenburg (1873–1940). *Eds.*]

CHAPTER 11

I MEET A NAZI ... AND MORE ON THE WORK OF THE CONSULATE GENERAL

F or three months after I left the clinic, a masseur was engaged to massage my hands every day for two or three hours. His name was Herr August Dunker, who became very fond of me and told me many exciting stories about pre-War Germany. Mr. Dunker was an old man with grandchildren and he looked very distinguished with his white hair and leathery suntanned skin. He belonged to the old German Conservative Party with all his mind, body, and soul. He was one of those who lost heavily on account of the war, and was bitter over the Versailles Treaty and the position of Germany in world affairs. Mr. Dunker impressed me greatly, but one afternoon he started acting as if he had seen a ghost. This ghost, as it turned out, was one of the senators of the city of Hamburg, who had come to pay my parents a visit.

Dunker told me the story behind the senators, saying that they were worth associating with, but did not like the rented Jewish house. He told of the events of the revolution of 1918, how Germany had not lost the war, and that the Putsch that had been staged in München would have succeeded. He maintained that what was being done to Germany was never going to be accepted by the Germans.

I heard Dunker's talks daily with increasing interest. He would bring me pictures of the activities of the various parties, and criticized anything that was not "National." He told me the backgrounds of President Ebert and the rest of the German officials. He criticized the fact that the people of another strange blood had the scepter in Germany and that another day would dawn. When Herr Dunker would leave, I would see and think politics. I would express his opinions, accepting everything he told me without criticism.

But then, the general philosophy of Nazism was very appealing, even to a child. I once asked a German friend who was principal of a Gymnasium, how he could so totally accept Nazism. He told me that he had to do so for his children, because telling them about democracy, love of humanity, and universal brotherhood did not seem real, but the fatherland and patriotism were something *greifbar* [tangible] to any child. I believed in essence that he was right. Only I don't believe that we should always teach our children things that they are able to *begreifen* [grasp] immediately. Training is preparation for life, and it is gradual. I believe that anything taught gradually, from simple to complex, can be made plausible to any child.

Herr Dunker was of the opinion that the French were Germany's greatest enemy and the worst people in the world. And, the people who allied with them were just as bad. The Germans who had signed the Treaty of Versailles were traitors to the fatherland. I remember asking Herr Dunker what he felt they should have done under the circumstances. He replied that they should not have signed and should have said: *"Wir wollen alle lieber sterben, als Sklaven sein."* ["We would rather die than be slaves."] I was, at some point, told not to listen to Dunker and to say nothing in response. But all of Herr Dunker's speeches were too exciting for me not to listen to, especially as the pictures he showed me helped explain events. I have long regretted not having saved all the literature he brought me. I am not certain what I would have become under Herr Dunker's influence if school had not started and directed my thoughts into other channels.

I have often alluded to the consulate, which carried out diplomatic service, but it was a little different as the representation was of a Black republic. While Europeans had previously represented the Liberian Republic in Germany, a Liberian held the position this time. This in itself gives the whole thing a different coloring. To give an accurate account of the work in Germany, the context of the times is necessary. This period was still dominated by the repercussions of Germany's loss in the war. German housewives were spending millions of Marks to prepare a single meal. New clothing for the average men in the street was a thing of the past, strikes for better working conditions were common, and there were demands for the establishment of a new ideology for the workers of the world. This weary old world was singing, "Yes, We Have No Banana."

Against the war-weary background, father had to keep a vigilant eye on the developments among the people and what he was surrounded by and confronted with. Thus he did not want second-rate places but the best locations that afforded full protection. No wonder the late Bishop Overs, bishop to Liberia, who knew father both in Liberia and visited the consulate in Germany, said the following of his work and appointment:

> After the World War, when President King planned to consolidate the trade relations with Germany, the largest consumer and most effective

distributing centre for Liberian raw material, he selected Massaquoi to initiate the project, and appointed him Consul-General, with headquarters at Hamburg. It was not an uncommon sight when visiting the little English church in that city, to see the Liberian Consul-General in his pew. He was always one of the first to leave his seat and humbly approach the Altar for his Communion. During his residence in Germany he spent much time writing, lecturing, and teaching, being a regular lecturer on African languages at the University of Hamburg.[1]

Not only were there important questions about the location and employees of the consulate, but also questions on how to represent Liberia and its diverse culture to the German public who hardly knew anything about Liberia. During the first years of our arrival in Germany, some people did not even know where Liberia was. When I would say "I am Liberian," I received a dumfounded look, with the reply, "you mean Siberian?" Thus, father lectured on African customs and languages to the few merchants and educated men who knew of them. As consul general, he received many queries on diverse topics about Liberia, which he answered, but there was also a lot of false information. In an angry response to a false publication, he responded that, a "certain almanac has published that Liberia is a protectorate of another state. Some journalists prefer writing only about the savages and cannibals of Liberia. Some call Liberians lazy and backward, while others do not even know where Liberia is situated."[2]

Thus after four years as consul general, father was compelled to produce a monograph in 1926 titled *The Republic of Liberia* to provide public answers to diverse questions asked and correct many misconceptions. It was hoped to lead to a deeper study and greater interest in Liberian history, natural wealth, philosophy, and ethnography to "dispel the century of gloom which has hitherto encircled Liberia and robbed her of the pure light of human sympathy and cooperation so much needed for her development."[3] He described this work as "a message from Liberia to the World's Trade and Commerce; but most particularly to Central Europe—a feeble endeavor to make clear what Liberia is, what the ideal is for which she stands, and what she offers to the world's market to perpetuate the progress of civilization and the advancement of the human race. If this message is clearly understood and accepted, the aim for which these pages were written is considered accomplished."[4]

In all of father's activities, everyone in the family helped. Father not only represented a government, he also had to look after a parade of Liberians usually coming to Germany for varied reasons and purposes. Ma Sedia and we children usually had the bulk of that work—taking them around to assist with accommodation, translation, and so forth.

For all of these people in the strange land, father and mother were their parents, while we children were their brothers and sisters. Father was also concerned with safeguarding the interests of those Liberians who lived temporarily or permanently in Germany. Lastly, we looked out for American Negroes and white Americans who had had connections with Liberia, and who often sought father's counsel while in transit.

As in Liberia, our family in Germany was large. During the five years or so we lived at the Johnsallee, I do not remember ever sitting at dinner on Sundays with less than 18 people at the table. Sunday was the only day when all of us were together for any one meal. Our ages and interests ranged widely, and we followed our pursuits at various times and places and so we could not be home at mealtimes on weekdays. What I mean by "family" is not what you mean by family. For instance, Fräulein von Bobers lived in the house and thus became a member of the family.

There were numerous Liberians, officials and nonofficials, who visited Germany and lived with us. My brother Ibrahim arrived in Hamburg shortly after Jaiah, and he was with us. In another year, Ma Sedia and Arthur had gone home for the winter, and returned with my sister Sie and my cousin, Mary Famata Roberts. There was Ma's brother, the late James C. Johnson. Later on, another cousin, Mary McCritty, and my friend and cousin, Victoria Johnson, joined us. There was my cousin Varney Tammuzy (my nephew, according to our standards) and a young man from the Kpelle ethnic group, Charles Bono Ketter, who had originally come to America but was not allowed to land. Not wanting the youngster to go into deep despair after being sent back to Liberia by way of Bremen, Germany, father had him come and stay with us to learn a trade. Even Grandma Johnson had come and spent a year with us, as did Angeline, her youngest daughter.

All of the individuals mentioned had not come during the same year. Some of them stayed in Germany for not more than a year or two. Some of them died. We also had three additions to the family in Germany, additions brought on by the stork. Besides all of the people named above, my brother Al-Haj made frequent visits to Germany and once remained as long as 18 months.

With such a large family, the problem of keeping domestic assistants was ever acute. We had to have three at the same time. Later on, when the family grew smaller, we needed only two. But for the first six years, we had to maintain the three: a cook, a general housemaid, and a nurse for the babies. This of course does not mean that I or my brothers and sisters or cousins did nothing. We had our various duties, especially my brothers, who had to help with heavy work such as moving furniture or with the heating. Having all these assistants made our home life even more complex.

The members of the family spoke various languages. There were some who did not speak many or any African languages. The assistants, too, were not always from Hamburg, and this brought a diversity of German dialects into our home. Since the Massaquois were already accustomed to a diversity of languages, this really did not create a real problem.

As in Monrovia, our lives in Germany were well disciplined. The boys, Jaiah and George, left early in the mornings to work for the apprentice examinations. Jaiah was preparing to be a *Hoch Und Tiefbau* [engineer] and architect. George was in apprenticeship as a carpenter. In the evenings, from 6 or 7 p.m., they had to be in school for their regular schooling. My brother Ali worked as an apprentice to an engineer before entering the *Oberrealschule*. After passing his *Abiturenten* [High School Certificate] examination at Easter 1926, he entered the *Technische Hochschule* [Technical University] of Berlin-Charlottenberg, where he pursued a course in engineering. Speaking of Ali, everyone, even the Germans, was astonished when he passed the Abiturenten examinations, since many Germans older than him did not pass the same examinations. My brother Ibrahim attended school to reach his objective in life, to be a dentist.

The two latter brothers mentioned attended day school only at first. Ali stopped working in the office because of his very strenuous schedule, while Ibrahim had to devote his afternoons to working in the office. Sie, after her arrival in 1925, attended the same school with me, so we had practically the same schedule during her first year in Germany. The next year I completed the work of the school and had to go to another. Mary went into apprenticeship in dressmaking, since she was beyond the German school age.

Our first Sundays in Germany were tedious. We did not attend church services since most of the members of the family did not speak German. But very soon father became acquainted with the rector of the Church of England, Rev. Charles Nibbs. We thus became active members in that church. Germans are not churchgoers; the majority attended church for special occasions such as baptisms, confirmations, and Easter. This, of course, does not hold true for Catholics. My point here is that my classmates at school would tell me on Mondays about the glorious times they had had at the parks and concerts on Sundays. This made churchgoing for me very monotonous. But, my parents were very firm in this respect, and we were never exempted from church.

Mary, Kobo, and I devised ways and means of dodging church. But father caught us when we lied about it, and we were punished. For the whole month, the three of us had to eat in the basement of the house in a room by ourselves. We were not allowed birthday parties or going out—in short, we were ostracized for having "unclean hearts and tongues," as father put it.

The Church of England that we attended in Hamburg was established for people in transit such as seamen when their ships were in harbor, as well as for the English-speaking people of the city. I really wanted to attend the German Lutheran churches in town, but since the majority of the family did not speak German, father thought that the family should attend the Church of England. Thus, it was in the church that I was confirmed by the bishop who came over from England, Rev. Nibbs having given the group all the necessary preparations in church dogma.

Our Sundays varied according to our plans and activities over the various years. Of course, the regular churchgoing was always a definite part of our program. Father took upon himself one Sunday after dinner, when the dishes had been cleared, to ask each of us to relate our experiences of the week. After this, he talked on a topic of the day and asked each of us to comment. Gradually, when a visitor would come to dinner, he would ask one of us to give a reading or a selection; sometimes he told us what to render. Later on, as we grew older, these programs diminished gradually, and with time died a natural death. I was not happy about it.

An interesting aspect of Sunday afternoons was to be invited, especially in the winter, to the home of some friends for the usual German 4 o'clock coffee. Sometimes these friends would have their coffee hours with us at our house. We also spent this time walking, ending up taking our coffee in a café while listening to music. Another special Sunday treat during the first three years in Germany, was a ride with my parents and baby Arthur in the old handsome Victorian cabs. Since I was the only girl in the house at the time, I had to go out with my parents whether I wanted to remain home and play with my friends or not. It was particularly interesting to hear my little brother express his life's first ambitions. He wanted to become a *"Kutscher"* driving the Victorian cab and wearing a tall silk hat. Today he is in engineering school at Howard University.[5]

Although my brothers teased me a lot, they depended on me for a great many things. I was the general darner for them. It all came about because father felt that if you wanted to make a contribution to the collection in church, it had to be the money you earned, and not what he gave us. Moreover, with my people, the girls and women usually have to wait on the male members of the family. Hence, since I needed money usually for the church collections and other welfare agencies to which I wanted to contribute, I had to work for the boys so they in turn could pay me. I had learned to knit and hence was usually seen sewing buttons on shirts for my brothers. They had a beautiful way of approaching me when they wanted something done. All of a sudden, I was "grandmother" and all the flattering names of the world.

My relationship with my little brother Arthur was quite different from that with the older boys. Arthur believed in his Tita, for that was the name he had given me. The family phrase *"Tita auch,"*[6] was ever prevalent. The little chap and I grew very close. I remember one night, when I had done something and father came to the bedside of the boys and pulled me away, Arthur, to whom I had been telling bedtime stories, was so angry that he jumped out of bed and went straight into the coat rack of the second floor and took father's walking stick and began beating my father, for what he termed, "beating his Tita." Arthur, and later on Tango Rex, Sie and I, had some grand times telling stories. Arthur's favorite stories were the "Max und Moritz" series.[7] I have cherished every moment; it took all of us, big and small, male and female, to form a family home life and sociable surroundings for which each member was as definite a part as the joints of a chain are to a necklace.

After having been invited to several parties given by my friends, I became eager to have a birthday party too. Until my life in Germany, a birthday was something unknown to me—and my birth date was simply not known. I worried so much about not having a birthday that my brothers one day wrote down all the names of the twelve months of the year and made me choose one. The month I chose was September, and of the thirty days, I chose eleven. During my first year in Germany I celebrated this date for my birthday—that is until Father received a written record from a niece who had noted our birthdays while he had been in the Gallinas. The birth date we had received was not all of one accord, by the way, there were reports of December 24th, another of December 25th, and still another of December 26th. Since father himself had said that he thought that I had been born on Christmas day, I placed that date on all of my papers from that day forward. And this time, my brothers gave me a real birthday party for the first time.

Our social life in Hamburg varied. We would often have a German or African dinner and invite friends to it (see figure 11.1). Since my parents were very resourceful, we often gave plays in an African setting, performing war dances and the like. But I wanted badly to be allowed to take social dancing lessons since most of my classmates had taken dance lessons and had been given an *"Abschlussball."*[8] So, for what seemed an eternity, the matter of being a "lady of society" had remained a dream until, suddenly, and without warning, my day came.

There had been talk of recalling the dean of the *Diplomatische Auslands Korps* [Foreign Diplomatic Corps]. The chairman of the diplomatic corps at the time, by the way, was the Italian minister. I was told that I would probably be invited, which caused father to let me take social dancing lessons. Of course, although my brothers teased me that I already knew all the dances, they had told the truth. There was hardly any social dance

Figure 11.1   Fatima in front row with father Momulu Massaquoi seated behind her to the center, ca. 1925

in Germany that I needed to learn. If the music is supplied, and I have a good partner, I could dance the bars to it. Well, the dancing lessons ended with a gala social dance at the house. Although officials were invited, this party did not impress me at all. When I went to thank my parents for the outfit and for having the occasion, I convinced them that I had been quite happy about it.

A few weeks later came the invitation for tea at the Hotel Atlantic, and the date was May 25. On the envelope was actually written *"Fräulein."* The invitation came at a somewhat inconvenient time, as far as Ma Sedia's health was concerned. Since she could not go with me to choose my dress, she gave father the general idea of what I wanted. Father then took me to the coiffeuse, and there I got an excellent work done of remodeling my hair and nails.

Every night during all this time, I read the invitation again and again and could not sleep. All my brothers arrived early from their various activities to see their sister dressed for the occasion. It was like the whole family had been invited. As father and I approached the car, I looked up and saw the heads of the members of my family sticking out the windows of the house. Not only their heads, but also that of Fräulein von Bobers, who had come to continue her speeches she had made in previous years when teaching me *was sich gehört* (what is appropriate). I was taught to properly greet various personalities, whether a lady or a man. A missionary, Miss Sarah Williamson, now Mrs. Coleman, who had been principal of the Suehn Mission in Liberia, and was at the time visiting with us, was also among the group looking on and she made me promise to come to her and tell her the story later. When I saw Miss Williamson in Washington in 1940, she and I had the biggest laugh over this first social function and how excited I had been.[9]

We were seated at the table with the Russian representative to Germany. He had watched me translating to father the speeches and toasts being made in French. He was quite amused with me, for he knew French beautifully, as I later found out. Father had been chosen to make the farewell toast on behalf of the diplomatic corps. I was to interpret his speech into French. My interpretation was impressive and I felt as proud as a peacock. After the tea, many officials assembled around us with congratulations. Of course, my friend, the Russian representative, remarked most enthusiastically. He never left my side for a moment during the rest of the time and the picture taken on that occasion shows him leaning over to talk to me.

The day did not end with the tea at the Atlantic Hotel. Upon our arrival home, the boys were all anxiously waiting on the stairway to ask father how I had conducted myself. This was one of the very joyous sides of my dear old man. He told the boys how I threw back my long neck and did not notice him since I had been out on the conquest of the Russian. Behind my back he mocked me for days to the boys, I know, because I caught them at it several times when I would enter a room where they were. But at the same time, their teasing did not get me into tears as it had done in previous years.

Our social obligations consisted not only in our being invited to attend receptions given by the diplomatic corps. We, in turn, made Liberia known by inviting the corps to see what Liberians were like socially. Thus, as Thomas Mann once said, "*Wir müssen die Feste feiern, wie sie fallen*" (we have to celebrate the occasions as they fall). The usual way for us to do this was on the occasion of the anniversary of the independence of our little Republic of Liberia, July 26. Sometimes the celebration took place at leading hotels in the city, at other times it consisted of an afternoon tea and a program at the house.

When these receptions were held at the house, I was allowed to participate. In fact all of us participated by wearing costumes to represent the various nations of the republic. In course of time, the boys scattered and grew away from the home site. This made me more and more the person for father to fall back on. When we were planning to commemorate the event one year, father asked me to welcome the guests. It was a great international gathering with people of the diplomatic corps, senators from both Germany and Liberia, and others.

The distinguished Liberians who were visiting Hamburg that year and were guests included: Hon. T. E. Beysolow, associate justice of the Supreme Court, Republic of Liberia; historian and author Hon. Rocy Dixon (whose position in the Liberian government I have forgotten); Hon. Anthony Barclay, member of the House of Representatives, Republic of Liberia; Hon. Richard Wiles, member of the House of Representative, Republic of Liberia; Hon. James S. Wiles, who by the way later became father's successor to Germany; Mrs. M. E. Barclay, wife of the secretary of state; and His Excellency Edwin J. Barclay, who later became president of the Republic of Liberia.

Having assured myself of a good African costume I proceeded to write my speech. This particular gathering took place at the Silver Hall of the Curio Haus on the Rothenbaumchaussee. Upon our arrival at the place of the reception, my heart leapt beat by beat. I saw the program, and on it the first item: "Introductory Remarks by Miss Fatima Massaquoi." I saw the mayor of the city arrive with his wife, the various senators, and as each group arrived I felt more and more that what I was going to say would be perfectly inadequate. Fräulein von Bobers, my dear standby, to whom I had shown the remarks, felt that what I had was excellent, but I was still not sure. Despite all the fear, when I arose from my table and walked to the podium to make the speech, I all of a sudden felt perfectly confident of myself. I kept saying to myself, "I am Fatima Massaquoi." I had promised myself never to be defeated, and I thought this was just a little gathering, that all of these people were human despite their ranks and positions, and they may not even be able to do as well as me in a similar position.

When I heard my own voice it seemed to come from another world. It was firm and unshaken. The speech ran like this:

Meine Sehr gerehrten Gäste,
Heute Abend haben wir uns hier versammelt, um den achtzigsten Nationaltag der
Republik Liberia zu feiern. Es gereicht uns zur freudigen Pflicht, sie im Namen
Liberias herzlich willkommen zu heissen, und Ihnen unseren Dank auszusprechen,
für Ihre Anteilnahme und Liebenswürdigkeit, die sie stets gezeigt haben, indem sie
an der Feier des Nationaltages anteilgenommen haben.[10]

My cousin and sister Victoria Johnson, now Mrs. Schaack, of Boston, Massachussetts, sang several verses of the "Lone Star Forever" with all of the Liberians singing the refrain to it. My other cousin Mary McCritty, now Mrs. Fiske, delivered an oration in English on the Liberian flag. German singers who had been invited sang solos to violin and piano, and we proceeded with a daylight dinner. This was followed by toasts and speeches, some on behalf of the city-state of Hamburg, others on behalf of the diplomatic corps, along with toasts to the health of the president of the German Empire. The Liberian officials present had their parts on the program—short speeches normally appropriate on such occasions.

After the meal and toasts, the orchestra began playing for the dance to begin. I was having so much fun talking to the guest at my table, and had already forgotten about my speech, when Mayor Peterson approached, taking both of my hands to congratulate me on my speech and my German. Many others did the same.

The press comments on the reception were interesting. Various papers spoke of the gathering and carried the pictures that had been taken and referred to the capable, handsome, and intelligent Liberian representative and his beautiful wife. They also spoke of their interesting and brilliant daughter and her share in the program. I was always very pleased with the comments about things I did in Germany that appeared in the papers.

In 1927, President King visited Europe and was received and feted in most of the European capitals and the Vatican. When the time approached for him to come to Germany, father visited the foreign office and the president of the Reich. The government gave father an official train to bring King and his entourage from the French border to Hamburg. Since the Liberian representative was based in Hamburg, it was to be the headquarters for the president's party. Father arranged to take the group to Berlin for an official reception later. A foreign office spokesman was provided to be with the president and the group throughout their stay in Germany. Quarters and suites were provided at the Hotel Atlantic for the presidential party, as were cars for their use. In short, everything necessary to color the visit of a head of state was provided and things proceeded according to plan.

There were many activities scheduled for the visit of the presidential party. Among these were receptions by the merchants trading in Liberia. There were fireworks staged on the Alster by the local government, which presented a picture of the Liberian Coat of Arms and the Liberian flag. Further, an entertainment house of the city, the Circus Bush, featured a play in which special reference was made to our dear homeland. Father gave a reception in Berlin and another in Hamburg on the eve of the departure of the party. We had all looked forward to the farewell reception. I remember that we girls wore shoes that pinched our feet.

Immediately upon our arrival, I was astonished to see a gentleman wearing several medals come to me and tell me that it was his honor to be my "Tischherr"[11] at the reception. His name was Karl Christian, Prinz zur Lippe,[12] who had come down from his home in Silesia, not far from

Figure 11.2   Hotel Atlantik, 1927

Breslau, for the occasion. He and father were good friends. We were all very surprised at this stranger offering me his arm. My cousin Mary, who was standing next to me and whose Tischherr had not yet appeared for her, exclaimed, *"sae,"* a Kru expression of surprise.

The reception was usual—a musical program, followed by speeches and toasts (see figure 11.2). President King once more reviewed the friendship that had existed between our two countries and gave a brief account of the aspirations or our little republic and her place in the great family of nations and as an African state. There were many distinguished guests present from inside and outside of Germany. The menu was splendid. Despite the splendor of the day, the deliciousness of the foods, and the glamor of the robes and precious jewels worn by the ladies, the best part of it was my new friend who was not too old to enjoy all of my childish humor, bad poetry, and composition. Father had told both Prince Lippe and President King at separate times that I had composed a song while I had been in the hospital just before the occasion. After all of the speeches, the reception ended with a dance. Consul Seyfried, Liberian consul to Bremen, invited us girls to a dance at the Hotel Reichshof. Our busy day ended well and beautifully, with us getting hardly any sleep that night.

At the reception, Prince Lippe told me of his *Rittergut*, (country estate), his mother, sisters, and fiancé, and invited me to come with him after the presidential party to meet his folks. He promised me a grand time and said I could recuperate at his castle, "Schloss See." I accepted the invitation two weeks later, after which time father came for me. I loved every member of his family. His sister took particular pride in having me tell stories to her girls and teach them necessary crafts. Not far from the Schlossee is the oldest Brudergemeinde, at Niesky, which we had to pass before arriving at See. His fiancée, Fräulein Maria von Trotha, was very kind and loving too. Her brother, Herr Bernhard von Trotha, was very polite and always played the violin for me.

The prince and I enjoyed discussing literature so much that he gave me one of Goethe's fables, *"Das Neue Paris"* (The New Paris), as a parting gift. He did this because he said that I must like fairy stories to be able to tell them so well. The prince gave me one of his own stories he had written of a cat, and had me write out about a dozen African stories for him. My contacts with this family lasted until I left Germany. Whenever I was near I would drop by, or one or the other of them would look me up whenever they were in Hamburg. I only regret that I know of their little son only by letters.

We kept touch with the homeland through letters and the fact that father's position carried with it eighteen months in the post and six months leave, which made going back to Liberia possible. The many Liberians who visited also provided information for us. It was interesting to watch the cultural differences between Africans and Europeans as seen in the attitudes of some visiting Liberians. There is the case of a native chief who was on a visit and we took him to the cinema. In the story, the wife of an unsympathetic husband almost succeeded in getting help to escape when the husband came in, told his wife that things would be different soon, and kissed her. I had the greatest difficulty in making our native African remain there to see the rest of it. He kept saying it was a lot of foolishness. To him kissing was nothing, while for Westerners this is the climax and sign that the couple loved each other.

Notes

1. Walter H. Overs, "Momolu Massaquoi: An African Prince," in *Sketches in Ebony and Ivory* (Hartford, CT: Church Missions Pub. Co., 1928), p. 10. [Overs was a Protestant Episcopal bishop in Liberia from 1919 to 1925. *Eds.*]

2. [Momolu Massaquoi, *The Republic of Liberia* (Hamburg: Advent-Verlag, 1926), p. 10. The book includes text in both English and German. An edition of the book was published in Danish two years later, translated by Harald Nissen, with the title *Republikken Liberia* (København: C. Th. Thomsens Bogtrykkeri, 1928). *Eds.*]

3. Massaquoi, *Republic of Liberia*, p.14.

4. Ibid., p.8.

5. [Arthur did not graduate from Howard University, although he did receive a BS in Mining and Metallurgical Engineering from Oregon State University. He later became the director of the Bureau of Mines and Geology for the Liberian government. *Eds.*]

6. ["Tita, too." *Eds.*]

7. [Written by Wilhelm Busch. *Eds.*]

8. [Akin to a "coming out ball." *Eds.*]

9. [Sarah Williamson Coleman (1899–1986) was an African American Baptist missionary. *Eds.*]

10. ["Dear Guests, We have gathered here tonight to celebrate the national day of Liberia. It is our joyful duty to welcome you in the name of Liberia, to render our thanks for your interest and your kindness, which you have always shown in participating in the celebration of the national day." *Eds.*]

11. [A gentleman who accompanies a lady to her table. *Eds.*]

12. [Christian (1889–1942) was a German politician. *Eds.*]

CHAPTER 12

HARD TIMES, "ISMS," AND SCHOOL

During the time we were in Germany, there was general unrest usually manifesting in strikes and demonstrations. Banners were carried by the Communists saying *"Wer nicht arbeitet, soll auch nicht essen"* ("He who does not work will not eat"). I wondered what it meant, and even though I asked my father and brothers for explanations, I remained in the dark about such movements connected with labor and wage disputes. One day there was a strike, and my brother George was beaten on his way to work. I overheard him tell the other boys about it, but I was unable to understand until much later.

Thus, at an early age, I had came in contact with these movements and strikes that were a mark of the times. Because of strikes schools were closed, trains and buses stopped running, and water supplies were cut off. In our Johnsallee residence, buckets and pots were filled with water. A policeman guarded our home. Abut and I walked around the block to see the beautiful trees and gardens when suddenly we found ourselves in the midst of a riot. People were shooting and fighting in the houses in the vicinity of the Binder and Schlüterstrasse, about five minutes walk from our home. I picked Abut into my arms and went into the dairy store where we had traded when we had lived in the Schlüterstrasse. Others also sought refuge there. To prevent Abut seeing the shooting, I covered his head with my coat, but he brushed it aside and saw people fighting with their fists and began screaming. I had a hard time keeping him quiet.

We remained in the store for what seemed like eternity. Then I looked and saw Ma Sedia in the street, walking as fiercely as only a heartbroken and desperate mother can do. I went to the door and screamed to her. She came to us. In no time father too arrived in a police car and we were able to go home safe and unharmed. Four days later, Abut began imitating the fighting he had seen.

The incident that day was not in Hamburg alone. That year I began keeping a diary, and my diary shows an item out of a newspaper from that day—April 5, 1925—showing that there were similar strikes in China and San Francisco. Later I realized that there had probably been this sort of social unrest all over the world.

Despite my contacts with these kind of movements, I was not affiliated with any of them until later on in the early 1930s. It happened one day, while I was preparing for the *Abiturienten* (High School Certificate Examination) to enter university, that a young classmate of mine brought some circulars and distributed them in class. This was for a lecture by his father, titled *"Gandhi Und Wir"* ("Gandhi and Us").

I knew nothing about Mahatma Gandhi and simply went to the lecture out of curiosity. The lecture was appealing and described the life of Gandhi from his struggles for the East Indian in South Africa, to the present struggle in India. The lecture ended with the similarities between the followers of Gandhi and the people who belonged to the lecture,[1] which was Gandhi's *"Selbstlosigkeit"* or "unselfishness."

I wrote a letter of appreciation to the old gentleman who must have been about 60 years of age, and received a reply a few days later with letters he wrote to Gandhi that he wanted me to translate. I was also invited to his other lectures—"Romain Rolland's Words and Life."[2] I translated several other pieces before I found out that the organization was more or less political. In reminiscing, I feel that though the brotherhood and equality of men was the main platform of the group, their other ideologies were not always clearly defined. At that moment it appeared to have been pacifist, yet at another, socialist.

The organization was definitely opposed to the idea of war. In this sense it was pacifist and believed in nonviolence. Nothing mattered to the group as far as the individual was concerned; what mattered only was what he did for his fellow man. It is perhaps not strange that this sort of belief should have appealed to me readily, since our people do things in terms of needs for the community, and not what an individual wants.

There were many avenues that this group opened up to me. I maintained personal contact with the old man until the outbreak of World War II and I have found that many of his teachings have come true as I travel along the road of life day by day. Recently, something he told me a long time ago struck me. He believed that nobody could acquire wealth without hurting and tramping on the rights and privileges of others in some way. I disputed with him regarding this philosophy, but now I can see his point.

My old friend was indeed brilliant and learned, and thought nothing of wealth and money. Despite his failed attempt to convince me to become a vegetarian, his wise words convinced me that we should learn from the experience of history. He approached the world like Plato, believing that the wisest men should run the affairs of state. Hitler, he maintained, was not wise or learned in the sense of Plato's Republic. He saw nothing more coming from the German war than despair and utter destruction.

This one man was a great teacher and a great inspiration to me. Once a week he gave me courses in historical research, Latin, and the fallacies of National Socialism. When I was about to leave Germany for the United States, I had one of my best recommendations from him. In his last letter to me he commented on the war in this way: "As long as men and women are grabbing and have no respect for the rights of the individual, and nations do likewise, we cannot hope for permanent peace and universal brotherhood of men. But, we, as individuals, should not give up the struggle, and perhaps fifty thousand years from now, mankind will realize this." This letter was dated April 20, 1940, and written in German. In Germany this essence is shared by millions like him, and they will survive the ordeals in their homeland and come out victorious and not sink into utter despair.

I guess you have wondered at what father thought of my interests in this connection. He gave me his advice in one sentence: "Be careful—I don't want you to become involved and implicated with German political life." I however listened to lectures given by the other movements in Germany: Hitler, Goebbels, Goering, Otto Strasser, et alia, although I could not, and would not, actively belong to these other movements in Germany. Although my circle of friends was afraid, I did not get into trouble before and after the *"Machtübernahme"* (seizure of power). I heard speeches by the politicians and listened to the *"Sieg Heils,"* which made me feel I was insane because I was not moved by what sent the whole gathering into frenzy.

National Socialism is known so thoroughly by now that there is no need to describe it. But here is an interesting fact about one of my friends who was a supporter of Hitler. I asked what she thought would come out of all of her ardent support of the system and how she could bridge adherence to the various women's organizations of the regime and her friendship to me. She had this to say: "We are not against Negroes or our friendships towards them as such. How could we when we are striving to have our colonies back? Our hatred is toward the Jew—and with right."

I also had active connections with and accurate knowledge of the Communists. My acquaintance came from the ship boys from Africa who were keenly interested in Communism as they often asked me to interpret for them. I was surprised to see the head of the Communist organization was an American Negro, who I learned to admire. This man told me about the group when he came to me to teach him German. My connections with all these movements were learning processes that allow us to grow, not in ideologies, but in strength and tolerance toward others that they afford us.

Perhaps it is quite natural that every human being at some point in life will be hit by Cupid's arrow. Ideas about the right man keep changing until they come full circle to the beginning point. Quite early in Monrovia I noticed my boyfriend, even if only in the mind. I did not dare tell that I was interested in boys—you know about my brothers and their teasing. My friend Dolly and her younger brother, Bobby, were born to a British mother and a German Jewish father. This family was living in a very impoverished condition in Hamburg. Bobby's family was so poor that the lad wore white suits in the winter. My brothers teased me so much about Bobby that whenever I saw the lad approaching I would run and hide.

My parents invited Dolly and her brother to have Christmas dinner with us. It was a traditional German dinner. When the fowl had been overturned and the dish passed around, Bobby took the largest lower backbone. Poor fellow, he was probably being modest in taking a bony piece and not the meaty part. But, unknowingly, he stepped on the toes of the master of the house. Father loved no part of the fowl more than this and no one in the home had ever dared touch it. His eyes followed the piece as the dish went around. The rest of us children understood this look, because this part was usually put away for the master of the house to eat later either at breakfast the next morning or for a midnight snack with his eyes half-shut. This was the end of Bobby as far as I was concerned.

Now, this particular Christmas was spoiled for him. We children laughed at him for days, and even Ma Sedia joined in. Father told us that we could invite the lad whenever we wished, but in the future we should count him out when we were inviting him. He told us in a dumfounded manner that he didn't understand why a little boy like that was not afraid to attack such a large piece of bone—what was he going to do with it anyway? Inviting these youngsters to eat was characteristic of my parents, sharing our Christmas with those who did not have this advantage. Father and Ma Sedia could dine with a street cleaner at noon or eat supper at home and feel good about doing both. I remember one Christmas in which a man came and begged for dinner; father actually had me set a plate for him at the table.

About the middle of the 1920s, the Garvey movement was gathering momentum. One Saturday, I was to attend the birthday party of a friend, Ingebeth Clauseson, and she asked that my brother Ali come to fetch me. But Ali had to collect some people from the United States from the steamer. These men were two representatives of the Garvey movement, a Mr. Strange and Mr. O'Meally.[3] They were on their way to Liberia. On Monday, after school, I was called to be introduced to the two gentlemen. I desperately fell in love with Mr. O'Meally. Mr. Strange, the older of the two gentlemen, dignified and quiet, did not exist for me. In those days, boys my age did not interest me since they had nothing worthwhile to say. Mr. O'Meally might have been in his thirties. All that week at school I did not listen to a solitary lecture or formula given by my teacher. I couldn't wait to come home so I could at least see him in the afternoons. Mr. O'Meally would ask me about school and have me tell him what was being taught, what I liked best, and so on.

One day I saw him go into father's office for a party consultation. I thought since he had manifested so much interest in me and since he wanted this conference with father without Mr. Strange, I thought he was going to ask permission to engage me, since with my people it usually happens that a man asks a girl's parents for her hand. I did not stop to think that Mr. O'Meally knew nothing about Vai customs. Well, I went upstairs to my room and actually prayed.

But then nothing happened. Since this was on Friday, I said to myself that father was probably waiting to make a formal announcement on the following Sunday, when the whole family would be assembled. Father had asked me to prepare a special program for Sunday. It helped that I was in charge of the program for that Sunday, so I put myself in the program for five readings as well as to play an instrumental solo.

When Sunday arrived, and I found out that I only had children's dresses, father said I should wear them. The Sunday dinner went very well. The guests, Mr. O'Meally and Mr. Strange, were asked to talk to us. Mr. O'Meally, like most Negroes in the United States, had the habit of tracing things back to Negro rights. He talked about the Queen of Sheba in ancient history, and he finally ended pointing to me, "Don't you know that Martha Moon Sheba, was no lighter than this child"?[4] Well, the reference to "child" absolutely killed my love. He never knew it, but when Tuesday came and they had to leave, I was the happiest soul in the world. All the time he had only looked upon me as a child. And, I had been thinking the whole time of an announcement of betrothal. As it so happens in childhood, I didn't even stop to think whether or not the gentleman was married. I knew nothing about him. Such it is with love, born as quickly as lightning, but usually dies in the same swift manner.

At various times in my life I would run to father and tell him that my dreams had come true. Finally, one day, it was really the truth. Although

I am too jealous to share thoughts of him with you, I would like to share with you one of his letters to father just to demonstrate the cultural differences between you and us. Some of my friends have told me that no one here would take such a step. In African custom, marriage is not an individual matter between two persons; it is an arrangement between two families. Therefore the families, especially the parents, have to spearhead it. But the influence of "western civilization" caused him to break the news to father in a letter dated August 18, 1926: "During my stay, my mother's namesake, both she and I fell in love with each other and seriously discussed the possibility of future marriage of which we mutually concluded might be happily consummated, if only your paternal sanction could be secured." He mentioned the difficulties we encountered in "how to approach 'the old man.'"

He informed his own parents who approved readily. He thus found the "courage . . . to inform [father] of my seriousness to wed Miss Fatima Massaquoi, your dear daughter, who had only temporarily accepted my proposal with the previous approbation, which I hereby earnestly and respectfully crave." He hoped that father would approve and give his permission. As can be recalled from earlier chapters about our culture, uncle-nephew relationship is special and symbolic, and marriage to an uncle's daughter is highly favored as "goat's head marriage," which was explained earlier. This is about the climax of my romantic life. We obtained father's blessing and, someday, we shall be together again. I have always believed in this despite the great distance of space between us.[5]

One of the primary reasons for father accepting the position of consul general to Germany was to educate his children, even though conditions in the Reich were difficult when I began attending school. Mothers complained of the scarcity of milk for their babies. Fathers had to turn in a basket of German Marks to meet the expenses of their homes. Schools often had to close for lack of heat. My brother George had to work as an apprentice during the day and attend a late afternoon session of an institution conducted by a Herr Dr. Wernser.

One day Herr Dr. Wernser came to discuss the boy's program with father, who asked him if he knew of any school for me. Herr Dr. Wernser recommended his little school and the Löwenbergsche Lyceum or the St. Ansgar Höhere Mädchenschule. Father thought I should not attend any night or afternoon schools. The Löwenbergsche Lyceum was a Jewish institution for girls located in a large villa in the block next to Johnsallee, where we lived at No. 22.

Father had preferred my attending a boarding school, but boarding schools, especially in North Germany, were either for children who were difficult to manage or for orphans and poor children. Well-bred families preferred to have their child at home, where she could receive *"eine gute Kinderstube"* (good manners).We visited the Lyceum and both father and I liked the old gentleman, Dr. Jacob Löwenburg. I already knew many of the girls there.

Meanwhile, my brothers and I were given intelligence tests. I don't remember who actually gave the tests or what they were like. I do remember that Dr. Löwenburg, instead of registering me, told father that I was to take two foreign languages and Hebrew. But father felt that as both English and French were foreign to me, Hebrew would be an added problem. So, Dr. Löwenburg's school fell through.

After Dr. Löwenburg's death in 1927, I came across one of his poems entitled *"Der Strassenbahn-Schaffner."* In it, Dr. Löwenburg described that fate of the streetcar conductor, who stands at his wheel, in rain, sun, cold, and late hours. This provided a glance into the lot of the working class, which I had never thought of. Now, I wanted to be a writer, writing stories for African children, not the saasaa player or missionary I wanted to be during my childhood.[6]

I asked my brother Ali one day why people had only painted the great buildings and left out people. The literature expressed the love for humanity and the achievements of the learned but never touched on the mundane like the matter of people saying after you in the streets *"Neger boy, Wasserscheu"* ("Black boy, scared of water"). I wanted to paint a picture of Europe, and my fight would be with the pen—we were certainly not "afraid of water."

One day, one of the senators who had promised father to do something for his "little daughter" suggested a school which was not a *"Volksschule"* (public school) but offered two classes higher than the "Volksschule" of those days. The girls who had been trained in this institution had usually been employed as clerks and sometimes secretaries. I found out later that only children of the bourgeoisie attended this school.

As it happened, a woman from the *Oberschulbehörde* called Fräulein Ahlmann came to see father in connection with the possibility of my attending their institution, which was named after St. Ansgar, the first bishop of Hamburg. I paid strict attention to all she had to say. The tuition fee would change from day to day—yes, hourly—because of the fluctuation of the German Mark, unless paid in coins, Thaler, Goldmarks, or in some kind of foreign currency. Before Fräulein Ahlmann left, she requested my place and date of birth but father could not give her my exact age. He promised to do some investigations and let her know. In the interior where I was born, no one kept a record of birth dates.

I was to start school the following week. Meanwhile, we went to the airfield, and father let me go up in a plane. I really enjoyed the flight. Everything seemed to be in miniature: the houses, the big commercial houses, and public buildings. People looked like ants. It was a great time and I was sorry when our 15 minutes in the air ended.

Before beginning school, Fräulein had asked that I come to school and become acquainted with the children. I was quite satisfied with my first visit. The girls came and looked at me as if I had stepped out of a story book, for they had never seen a Negro girl. But this was not my reason for satisfaction. The school building was large and quite elegant and I could tell my brothers about the school, I thought. Thus, for the rest of the week, no one in our home heard anything else from my lips but my anticipations for school.

On October 3, 1923, I began attending the school, which started at 9 o'clock in the winter term (figure 12.1). The summer term began around eight in the morning. Upon my arrival one of the girls accompanied me to the clothes rack and showed me where to hang my coat and hat. After remaining in the schoolroom for about 15 minutes, we formed a line, two-by-two. Since everyone was anxious to walk with me, I had to promise the various girls that I would walk with them the next day. But the girls loaded me with so many questions that we arrived in the chapel

Figure 12.1   Fatima at St. Ansgar Höhere Mädchenschule

in confusion and completely disorganized. Hence, we had to stand up during the whole devotional period. This was the very type of punishment I had dreaded at the mission, for something over which I had no control whatsoever.

When classes ended, Fräulein Ahlmann, who was my *Klassenlehrerin* (main class teacher) gave me a list of books for Algebra and Geometry, English, German, Spelling, Biology, History, and Bible. Fräulein von Bobers read the list in English and father did not see how I could take Algebra and Geometry, but Fräulein von Bobers reassured him that the courses would not be difficult, and that she taught me and knew that I could do the work. Besides, those courses were given early in order to give the children a great deal of time in school to become acquainted with the material and there were frequent reviews and repetitions.

I spent late nights memorizing whole chapters to cover the work and found it difficult to wake up in the morning to go to school. Father bought me an alarm clock and told me never to be late for school. This clock remains my constant companion and it is still in very good condition.

At the St. Ansgar Höhere Mädchenschule, history was a little difficult, but I understood the courses in Biology, English, Religion, and Math. In Literature, our class discussed the "King Arthur Saga," which I both loved and enjoyed immensely. I thought Geography most interesting and we studied the Norddeutsche Tiefebene (a geographical part of northern Germany). On the whole, I got along very well and was promoted to the *Zweite Klasse* (second grade) the following Easter, 1924, which is usually the beginning of the German school year.

If I had reasons to doubt myself before, they vanished in the Zweite Klasse. History and Geography had presented problems at the beginning, but they became my best courses. I remember when a new course was added to our schedule, called *Heimatkunde* (Local Studies) and dealing with the science of the home and Hamburg, I often achieved the best grades in the class.

In our Literature courses we had to recite and sometimes dramatize the poems we learned. There was to be a contest between students of various schools in Hamburg, and since I loved the literature classes and performed very well, Fräulein Ahlmann requested father to allow me to participate and represent the school. The poem she thought I could best dramatize was the "Frühlingsfeier" (Celebration of Spring) by Friedrich Klopstock, who as you know, is the author of the text of the Messiah. I could feel each emotion of the poet and deeply revered his sentiments to the Creation and Creator. The harp with which the poet sang the glory of God overwhelmed me with a love of nature and song, as only the songs of the Old Testament were able to do. I grew to idolize the author, reading about his life and his works (especially his stay in Switzerland), and followed him into exile to Denmark. I remember once, after school was out in Switzerland, and a girlfriend and classmate invited me to spend some time with her in Zürich, I found myself seeking the exact spot on which the great author could have stood to write his *"der Zürichersee"* ("Lake of Zurich"). So deeply had this poem affected me that it accompanied me through the years.

Aside from winning the contest with that poem that year, I had no more peace at home—for father made me recite it, even after I felt I was too grown to be reciting poems for people. In this way, I had to recite it for many of his colleagues who visited us. I had to recite it for Mr. Nissen, Liberian consul to Denmark and owner of the Danish line that went to West Africa. I had to recite it for His Excellency the secretary of state, who later became president (Edwin Barclay) of the Republic of Liberia. Hon. Marcus Garvey, who visited us in Hamburg, had to hear it at a dinner that father gave for him at the Hotel Reichshof, in August of 1928.[7] In Switzerland, I had to dramatize it in the home of the Sottiles, with whom I lived while attending school, and who represented Liberia at the League of Nations, when they entertained a guest who was a librarian at the Vatican.[8] In short, I had to recite the poem so much that I sometimes felt as if it was my very own production.

The poem nearly got me into the theater world. A Jewish friend of father's who lived in Berlin, "Uncle Hermann," as Abut and I called him, was interested in the transportation of elephant meat from Liberia to Germany. That was during the first years of his visits, when conditions in Germany were very bad. He asked father if I could go to a drama school, where he thought I could get a contract within a few years, or perhaps even six months. But father never wanted any of our names connected with the stage.

So back at school, we wrote two kinds of compositions monthly, a *Hausaufsatz* (Homework Paper) and *Klassenaufsatz* (Class Paper). The teacher would make us practice the ways of writing and the parts of an exposition: *Einleitung, Hauptteil, Ausführung, and Schluss* (Introduction, Body of text, Illustration, and Conclusion). These and a good *Überleitung* (transition) were the things she stressed. I discovered that the German educational system emphasized certain aspects of training more than anywhere else I have had the pleasure of attending school. People seeking employment could be ever so good in their courses, but if certain items in the question did not come to par, they were refused. These were: *Betragen, Ordnung, Aufmerksamkeit und Schulfleiss und Hausfleiss* (Conduct, Order, Attentiveness, and Diligence at school and home). These stood at the very top of your certificate. And if your grades were not very good in them, it was difficult for you to receive recommendation and employment.

How were the grades determined, you would ask? For Betragen or conduct, you could not cheat without receiving a little mark in your Verkehrsheft, which was a notebook in which the teacher wrote announcements of special events and when she wanted to see your parents. If you talked, there was also a little mark placed next to your name. These are counted at the end of the term and your grade is counted according to the number. If you had no mark against your name, you received "very good." Two marks or one brought you a grade of good, and more, an even worse grade. I was able to receive "sehr" good in Betragen, but in Ordnung, and in Aufmerksamkeit und Fleiss, good and very good. This was my situation throughout my entire stay at the school. The grades in "Ordnung" or "order" were based on personal attire and organization: being on time always, how neat your notebooks were, and whether or not you always had your materials and books with you at school on the days you should.

But there was something I did not like at all. This was that in spite of the fact that Fräulein Ahlmann and some of the other teachers at school had boasted of having shaped me and were proud of their experiment in this respect, I noticed that she did not wish me to excel in anything but English. Whenever I happened to go to the top of the class, she would say *"über"* ("over"), which made me feel keenly that she did not like it. I remember an expression she used, which today almost convinces me that I was right. She would say to the girls in a scolding tone: *"Fatima steckt Euch alle noch in die Tasche"* ("Fatima will be ahead of all of you"). It made me wonder whether she had thought that I was so mentally inferior that she expected me to be at the bottom of the class. This was one of the attitudes that I alone had to face and did not like. There were several other attitudes that also bothered me, but since on the whole my stay and studies at the school took on a very favorable and pleasant air, we had better let them go.

Along with the labor of preparing lessons and paying attention in classes, we had a grand time in school. We were no different from normal schoolchildren. We teased teachers, made fun of them, and did whatever else children of our ages usually do at school. One of the teachers we teased most was Herr Pastor Glage who taught Catechism to our class. He was fond of the song *"Schönster Herr Jesus"* ("Most Beautiful Sir Jesus"). One day when our class met, the *Drehorgelman* (barrel organ player) played outside, and the ears of the whole class were directed to this music. Herr Pastor Glage thought this was blasphemy on our parts. We loved Pastor Glage very much, and I cannot understand how we were able to anger him to the point of making him cry over our behavior.

We also teased Herr Pastor Jonas of the Johanneskirche, who taught us to read the Bible at school. Pastor Jonas is, by the way, a special friend of mine, as I very often attended the children's service at his church. I remember once when pictures of the school were to be taken, the principal, Fräulein Luhring, had the photographer come on the day he would be there to photograph my class, so he could have my photograph.

As we were able to tease some teachers, there were of course others we dared not tease, and some whom we loved dearly. We grew to adore the young Pastor Herr Rath, who had taken the place of Herr Pastor Glage for a while, in teaching us Catechism, as well as Fräulein Kochel, who taught History the year I entered, and also Fräulein De Fauquement, our singing teacher. I had my own preferences. Among these were Fräulein Kahler and Fräulein Hubner, who taught Church History. Even Fräulein Ahlmann was a hero for me to worship at one time of my school life. When I admired any teacher, I usually went early to school and went to the classroom of the present teacher of my choice and decorated her desk. I did this especially when the lilacs at the Johnsallee were in bloom.

Teasing and adoring teachers were not the only factors that made life at school pleasant and full of excitement. There was much fun, some provided by the school, and some we provided ourselves.

Notes

1. For the safety of the people in Germany, I think it wiser in this connection not to mention names or identities clearly. [The author almost certainly alludes here to Dr. Jakob Loewenberg (1856–1929) and associates. Loewenberg was a devout peace activist and poet known in international pacifist circles, with whom her family had a close relationship, and he is mentioned later in connection with a Hamburg school. *Eds.*]

2. [Rolland was a French novelist and fervent critic of Nazism, fascism, and nationalism. He was awarded the Nobel Prize for Literature in 1915 and later wrote a biography of Gandhi. *Eds.*]

3. [These men were associated with Marcus Garvey's Universal Negro Improvement Association (UNIA). James A. O'Meally was a New York City-based Jamaican UNIA "high commissioner" (referred to as "Sir James A. O'Meally" by Garvey), and William Strange was an engineer. They were in Hamburg to secure visas for Liberia, where they planned to travel to commence building a site for UNIA emigrants at Cape Palmas. Their entry to Liberia, however, was barred by President King and they returned to the United States. O'Meally broke with Garvey in 1925, with successful legal action against him over an unpaid salary, contributing to the bankruptcy of Garvey's scheme. Fatima Massaquoi's stepmother, Ma Sedia, was the daughter of Gabriel Moore Johnson, UNIA's titular "potentate" who was on the payroll of the UNIA and a stockholder in the Black Star Line. At the opening of the Second International

Convention of the UNIA in New York City, Johnson "wore a military-shaped helmet, with a large flowing white feather," and was referred to as the "President of Africa." Garvey and his Liberia immigration scheme were greatly opposed by the government of the United States, which spied on activities in Liberia and followed Johnson in the United States, and was aware of Johnson's connections with Momolu Massaquoi. In 1921, J. Edgar Hoover had written that Johnson was the "father-in-law of a very prominent ex-chief, who was ousted by the British as a trouble maker in Sierra Leone, but who now lives in Liberia." See The *Marcus Garvey Papers*, Vol. 3, September 1920-August 1921, p. 547. For an account of the failed UNIA scheme in Liberia, see M. B. Akpan, "Liberia and the Universal Negro Improvement Association: Background to the Abortion of Garvey's Scheme for African Colonization," *Journal of African History*, Vol. 14, No. 1 (1973), pp. 105–127. Eds.]

4. [Queen of Sheba played a very important role in Garveyism and the associated rise of Rastafarianism. Garvey had predicted that a black "Redeemer" would emerge as a king in Africa, and his prophesy was fulfilled in 1930 with the crowing of Ras Tafari, the precoronation name of Haile Selassie of Abyssinia (Ethiopia). Selassie was alleged to be a direct descendant of King Solomon and the Queen of Sheba. For Garveyites and emerging Rastafarians, both Garvey and Selassie were prophets, the latter being heralded as God incarnate. Eds.]

5. [The individual to whom Fatima Massaquoi had pledged her love was her cousin Kolli Tamba. Fatima Massaquoi would later be disappointed to find out that during their separation—while he was in Russia studying, and she was in the United States—he had married another woman upon a return to Liberia. In 1948 she married another man, Ernest Fahnbulleh, with whom she had one child, Vivian Massaquoi-Fahnbulleh (now Seton). Eds.]

6. [Fatima Massaquoi would later write a number of children's books with African themes and images. The first was Fatima Massaquoi Fahnbulleh and Artiste Doris Banks Henries, *Fatu's Experiences: A Liberian First Reader* (New York: Frederick Fell, 1953). By this time Massaquoi had married and taken on her husband's surname. While the book is meant to be a general reader, the names and images were based on Massaquoi's life (the name "Fatu" is a contraction of "Fatima"). Henries (1918–1981) was from 1951 to 1955 the director of the William V. S. Tubman Teachers' College at the University of Liberia, and had emigrated to Liberia from the United States. Massaquoi's second book, with the author named as Princess Fatima Massaquoi, was *The Leopard's Daughter: A Folk Tale from Liberia Translated from the Vai Language* (Boston: Bruce Humphries, 1961). She wrote five others including one on the history of Liberia University. Eds.]

7. [Garvey discusses his August 1928 trip to Germany in his association's official publication: "German Thoroughness Impresses Marcus Garvey," *Negro World* (New York), Vol. 24, No. 29 (August 25, 1928). As noted

earlier, Momolu Massaquoi's wife Ma Sedia was the daughter of G.M. Johnson, the key Liberian figure involved in the Liberian resettlement plan and the UNIA's "Potentate." Be that as it may, the plan for Liberia collapsed by July 1924 when the Liberian government, led by President C. D. B. King, banned the UNIA. *Eds.*]

8. [Dr. Juris Antoine Sottile (1883–1971) was an Italian who served as Liberia's permanent delegate to the League of Nations from 1929 to 1937 during the League's "International Commission of Inquiry to Investigate Slavery and Forced Labor in Liberia." *Eds.*]

CHAPTER 13

CHRISTMAS AND SCHOOL TRIPS IN GERMANY

Anyone who has spent a Christmas in Germany knows how much this nation has contributed to the joy and glorification of the Nativity. This is not only borne out by the fact that Germany has contributed more carols than any other single nation, but spending Christmas in Germany is an experience that no one should miss. Already four weeks before Christmas, the whole air is usually full of expectations, not only in school, but practically everywhere. I have never enjoyed, nor felt, the spirit of Christmas so much as in Germany.

In Hamburg, the beginning of the season is usually marked by the opening of the *Dom* (fair). There, we ride on carousels, eat frankfurters and candies, shoot for prizes, and have fun in a general way—that is, if you are not sensitive to the cold. The Dom grounds are in a large meadow, which is quite open, but for the temporary houses built there.

Father took us to the Dom about once a week. Sometimes, we also went with our class. Not only did we have the Dom and such outside activities to brighten our spirits for Christmas, but also many of our classes at school left off their various schedules to allow us Christmas activities. In singing courses, Christmas carols were practiced. In drawing, we made pictures of some aspect of the Nativity. In our literature courses we learned poems, which we were to surprise our parents by reciting them on Christmas Eve. One such poem we wrote in our *"Wunschheft,"* or our "Wish book." In this book, just above the poem was our drawing.

Four weeks before Christmas, I had to stop taking courses in the lower grades of the school so as to participate in the activities for Christmas. I then began singing in the "A" chorus of the school, the one with the best voices who sang on special occasions. My favorite carol, besides "Holy Night, Silent Night," was *"Fröhliche Weihnacht Überall"* (Merry Christmas Everywhere). I sang it so much at home that father fell in love with it and I had to teach him. I could hardly wait for the day to dawn to go to school and sing by lighted *"Adventkranz"* or wreath of advent, on which every week one more candle was added to express the ancient Teutonic pagan belief of light overcoming darkness.

I did something during that first Christmas at school that I am ashamed to tell. After we had sung several carols, Fräulein Ahlmann made a request for an African carol—a request she probably would not have made if she had thought about it a little. For, only those of us who have been touched by Christianity know anything about Christmas. So, there are no such carols among the Vai.[1] Ashamed to admit it, I stood there and made up one and actually sang it. But when the end of the piece came, there was a blank and I kept repeating the same line like a broken record.[2] Even Fräulein Ahlmann caught it, and asked, "what does *Basa mu la Kamba mean?*" I said, *"Leite uns Herr Gott"* (Lead us, Sir God), which is actually the interpretation of the song I had made up.

I had numerous friends at school, but Else Durkopp remained my most loyal friend throughout the years. She is now in China by the way. Else's mother is a niece of the famous expressionist painter Max Liebermann, and I don't think her mother will forgive me if I don't express this, because she was always talking of her uncle.[3] Else was the soul of invention and we played pranks. On our way home from school we would for instance look up all the persons with the name "Zieht" in the telephone directory and call them. After hearing the answer *"hier Ziehts"* ("here is Ziehts residence," but literally it meant "here is draught"), we would ask, "why don't you close your window?"

The curriculum and teachers of the St. Angar Höhere Mädchenschule have changed since I left. The school has become partly a state school, but in my days, it was supported by the Lutheran Church. It has also become a coeducational institution. Fräulein Kahler is now the principal, while my principal Fräulein Luhring has been pensioned, as has Fräulein Wilkins, my Chemistry teacher.

By Easter 1926, I completed *"die erste Klasse"* at the St. Ansgar Höhere Mädchenschule. There was a celebration for us to receive our *"Abgangszeugnis"*(diploma). I had looked forward with delight to this but was not able to witness it because I came down with my first and worst cold I had had since we had been in Germany. The teachers were sad and wondered whether or not my sister, Kobo, who had come to Germany in the meanwhile, and who had been in school with me for about half a year already, could go up and receive the credits for me. She and father went to school to witness the celebration. Kobo later told me that the teachers made good comments about me when she went up to receive my credits, while father went to the various teachers and thanked them, giving Fräulein Luhring a plant, and Fräulein Ahlmann some flowers. My grades on the *Abganszeugnis* pleased me very much, and I am forever grateful to this institution and all the teachers there for their eternal patience in aiding me.

German school terms were very different from American ones; Germany does not believe in long vacations. The German school year begins shortly after Easter and lasts until the week before *"Whitsuntide"* (Labor Day) when we come out for a week or ten days, the period determined according to the locality where the school is situated. Between Easter and *Whitsuntide*, we were usually off for *"Himmelfahrt"* or "Ascension Day" and for May Day (May 1). The next vacation was summer, five or six weeks between June and July. The school session following continued till the end of September. In this period there were no vacations except for August 11, the date of the Weimar Constitution. The next break for ten days to two weeks was for the Michaelis vacations. The next school term ran from October to December with only the third Wednesday in November free, which is the German *"Buss-und Bettag,"* which corresponds to Thanksgiving.[4] The Christmas break was for about twelve days to two weeks. From then until Easter there was no break until the rise of the Third Reich, when January 30 was included as a holiday. At the end of Easter came our grades, promotions, and finally vacations.

The average German is not a great churchgoer. As a matter of fact, in my circles, I noticed that aside from Easter, Christmas Sunday, a Baptism, Confirmation, sometimes a marriage, and at times a death, most Germans did not attend church. It is a remarkable thing, in view of this fact, to see Germans contribute so much church music and have a solemnity for Christmas that is unsurpassed. Woe unto the man in Germany who finds himself without a family on Christmas Eve. There are Christmas trees and the great voices of children and adults, sick and well, young and old, rich and poor, proclaiming the tidings of centuries ago.

Meanwhile various additions were made in our family. It is interesting to learn how we combined German culture with our own. This can be demonstrated in the naming of my little sister Leona Germania Keneja. She was given the name "Leona" because Grandmother Johnson, her grandmother, had just been with us, and it was thought that she should be honored in this way. "Germania," was after the German allegory, since the family was enjoying everything that it stood for. "Keneja," her Vai name, meant that she was born in a strange country, meaning literally "home of other people." But it seems that father had no luck with girls. When Ma went home for the first time after we went to Germany, she took baby Leona and Abut with her. Leona became seriously ill, and died onboard the SS *Wadai* of the Woermann Line. The captain, who admired father greatly, kept the remains of Leona in his personal quarters, instead of having her buried at sea, and we buried the infant at the children's' cemetery in Ohlsdorf at Hamburg.

On the same steamer that the remains of the body were brought, my sister Sie and my cousin Mary Roberts arrived in Germany. I was no longer the only girl at the house. Mary Roberts, by the way, is an older sister of Frank Roberts, whom you Americans know as Tonea Massaquoi. He has danced the stilt dance on various occasions for the American public, and Mrs. Hoffman made a sculpture of him for the hall of fame.[5] I remember Frank from the days when his sisters had been in school at Bromley with me. He lived in Monrovia with my parents, before eventually staying with President King.

Sie was still of school age, and I gave her lessons in German. She succeeded in this so well that she was able to enter the St. Angar Höhere Mädchenschule by the fall of 1925, and was only five classes below me. This made it possible for me to supervise Kobo's lessons. Mary wanted to become a dressmaker, and had an apprenticeship for the purpose. She took German and other types of lessons on the side, for she was above the German school age. My brother Ibrahim had arrived in Germany shortly before Ma, Leona, and Abut left to spend the winter in Liberia.

A month or two after I completed the St. Ansgar Höhere Mädchenschule, my little brother Friedericus Tango was born. This was on July 31, 1926 (hope the date is right). My parents gave the boy one German name at the insistence of Abut who greatly admired the German king Friedericus Rex and one Vai name, Tango, after a great warrior ancestor. The baby was thus named Friedericus Tango. Sister Victoria called him "Tango Rex," and everyone followed except Fräulein von Bobers, who is one of his godmothers, and calls him "Black Prince."

Upon the completion of the St. Ansgar Höhere Mädchenschule, father thought of placing me in a boarding school. But there were no boarding schools we knew of which could prepare me for the entrance to the university. So father began consulting people on the subject. The fact was that I could not enter the state school that prepared you for entrance to the university, because I had not taken French. Hence, a French tutor was procured in the person of Fräulein Leonore Schertel, a candidate at the university. I rushed, studying three lessons at a time, in an effort to be able to reenter school by that Fall. But, I just could not understand the examinations and was advised to return before Easter for the entrance examination.

There seems to be great class stratification in education in Germany. The public *"Folkschool"* or *"Volksschule"* is free of cost and gives you eight years of training in school and the age of admission is around six. After this, during the time of the Social Democratic Party when the Weimar Constitution was adopted in Germany, pupils from the Volksschulen could enter higher institutions of learning. Parallel to the Volksschulen, are the various private schools that charge fees.

The Volksschulen begin with the eighth grade and run through the first, whereas the St. Ansgar Höhere Mädchenschule began with the ninth and ran through the first. Thus, a person who finishes the seventh grade at the Volksschule and wishes to enter the St. Ansgar Höhere Mädchenschule has to be in the seventh grade because the seventh grade at the Volksschule is the eighth grade at the St. Ansgar Höhere Mädchenschule.

Fräulein Schertel who had studied at the Hansa Lyceum influenced my choice of her former school. While my application was in, the name of the school was changed to "Helene Lange Oberrealschule." Since I was then certain I would pass the entrance examination, I asked permission to be able to attend the naming ceremony. One of the greatest women educators Frau Schulrätin, who at one time had become Oberschulrätin[6] of the City of Hamburg, was principal of the school at my entrance. During the time I was there, her sister, Emmi Beckmann, also famous for women's rights and standards, became principal. I am today certain that all of these factors influenced my choice of my next school.

The renaming ceremonies of the school were impressive. On the rostrum of the big Aula of the school sat many prominent figures of the city. But I still recall vividly the closing words of the mayor when he dedicated the school: *"Möge die Helene Lange Oberrealschule, ihren Namen mit Würde tragen."*[7] With this ceremony I became, in my mind, a full member of the school and its standards.

I passed the examinations and was to begin school after Easter in the "U II C." This class is the *"Untersekunda."* The letter "C" was simply one of the divisions into which the class had been divided. "A, B, C, D" were all parallel classes of the Untersekunda and no one division was higher than another. The divisions are made so as not to have too many students in one class or in one room. Each of the divisions had about twenty-five to thirty students.

The schedule of work in the Oberrealschule, and particularly of this class, was very strenuous. I had to leave the house at seven in the morning to take the seven-ten tram car in order to be there at twenty minutes of eight. For, aside from half of an hour's ride, I still had a few minutes of walking to do. These cars ran every ten minutes and only two others left after that time to put me at school on time. I remained at school practically all day and did not reach home until after three in the afternoon, in contrast to being home between one-thirty and two while I had been at the St. Ansgar Höhere Mädchenschule. There was really nothing new which was offered than what I had had in the former schools. Only, the assignments and subjects became more difficult. This is one thing very characteristic of German education; once a subject is started, you have to go on with that subject until you know it thoroughly. The only new thing on my schedule was that I had French to prepare for. Otherwise, they were continuations of Chemistry, Biology, Religious Education, Physics, Mathematics, German (Literature, Compositions, and Philosophical Thought), Drawing, French, English (Literature, Grammar, and Composition), History, Geography, and History of Art.

Our French and English courses were divided into two divisions. In all four parallel classes, there were pupils who had started with English, and others with French. This being the case, we had to be divided up. Those who began with French had their classes together. Those with English took theirs together. I naturally fell into the group that had had English longer so as to avoid possible struggle with the French language. I now stood in great competition in every way.

One advantage which the state schools had over my former school was the fact that the classes for the Natural Sciences were very well equipped. At the Helene Lange Oberreaslchule we were well equipped and the teachers were all very good.

I was very fond of my History, German, and English courses—fond, because we had a lady teaching these courses who had been very strict and erudite. She and I had a little encounter one day, when she began the study of the American Civil War. She ended the study topic with this remark: *"Es war in der Tat, eine Kulturschande, andere Menschen als Sklaven zu halten."*[8] She looked around the room and caught my eyes. I interpreted this to mean that she meant well, but then at this very point came the antithesis: *"Natürlich, dass man den kulturel niedrigsten henden Neger nicht mit einem Europaer an einem Tische setzen kann, ist klar."*[9] I promptly heard the words coming out of my throat, seeming as if they came out of another mouth: *"Und umgekehrt, auch nicht."*[10] She became enraged and asked me to apologize for the disturbance. I did so, for speaking without putting up my hands, but not for what I had said. She demanded that I stand outside and wait until the class was over. Well, I took my belongings and went home. Only after a long conference between her, the Hamburg authorities, and father was I allowed to come back to school.

Inspite of this difference with her, I thought she was one of the best teachers in the school. She was brilliant and had received her early training in England and later her doctorate at Basel University. She knew how to make herself respected. Inspite of the strictness of her character, she just as well had the great faculty of making you her friend. These are qualities that we do not often find in any one teacher. It was therefore difficult for my friends to understand that I replied anything at all after she had spoken—no one ever dared contradict her. Well, some of them told me that they might have done the same in my position. At school, I became very group conscious. In History courses, all the wrongs that had been done to Germany were stressed and discussed thoroughly. This always made me conscious of what we as Africans and Liberians had as a right to demand and fight for.

The Helene Lange Oberrealschule, like other German schools, offered us many opportunities. Some of these were afforded in traveling, and traveling experiences and knowledge gained in childhood are far richer and longer lasting than all the books one is able to read. Every class at the school made trips in connection with their courses. In this way, we visited Munich to see the museum, art gallery, and other aspects of German cultural life. The same kind of trip was once made to Tirol, another to Köln (Cologne), and another to Helgoland.

In Geography, we studied the different earth formations, paying particular attention to the formations around the Weser River and mountains. In our religious classes, we studied destinations of ancient religious pilgrimages, some of which were located in the Teutoburgerwald.[11] There were so many things we studied in our courses that were worth visiting and seeing. So, with the consent of the teachers involved, we chose the area around the Weser River and mountains for our trip that year. Such a trip is called *"Studienreise."*

The trip was to cost each individual student about sixty-five Marks. Father had gone home on furlough while we were preparing for the trip, so Ma got me ready for it. But about a week before we were to embark, he announced his presence in Paris. I wrote to him about the trip with my class and he rushed back to Hamburg to see us depart.

On Monday, June 13, 1927, we assembled at the Altona Hauptbahnohf, or Central Station, with rucksacks on our backs, suitcases of prescribed sizes, bright cotton dresses and coats. Fräulein Grühn, our Klassenleiterin, and the gym teacher of the school, counted us. Father and my two cousins, Victoria and Mary, accompanied me to the station. At ten a.m., we set off, waving to my father and cousins, and soon forgot that I had left my folks behind, as I joined in singing the songs we had practiced for the trip. We sang *"Nun ade Du mein lieb Heimatland, lieb Heimatland, ade..."*[12]

Our first stop was Lübeck, where we visited the Rathhaus, or Council House. This city had many relics from the time of the Hansa, such as antique silver and other valuable objects which the Hansa pirates had accumulated. We then proceeded to Hannover, the home of Fräulein Gertrude von Bobers. I was sorry indeed that I had not asked for the address of her mother to thank her for a slice of birthday cake she had sent me. Our group visited school houses and churches, and we were amazed at the English influence of the city.

The ancient city built by Charles the Great, Hildesheim, was another city that we visited, where we saw a rose bush that was said to be one thousand years old. Both Hildesheim and Hannover had buildings known as *"Zuckerhüte"* (sugar cones), constructions that were wide at the bottom and became ever narrower at the top. The train next took us to our headquarters for the trip, Hessisch—Ohlendorf, an der Weser. We climbed a hill to the Jugendherberge or youth hostel, where we were assigned the second floor for sleeping purposes. The teachers were lodged on the first floor which had the living quarters of the Herbergsvater and Herbergsmutter (inn mother and inn father), as well as the kitchen and dining room for the students. In the basement of the inn were quarters for another class and washrooms for us to wash our hands and faces. There were no bathrooms.

The morning after our arrival, we rose at about four a.m. and went out of doors with the gym teacher to take our morning exercises. After this, we dressed and took a little walk around the mountains in the neighborhood. Breakfast was usually served at seven and we had to return for this. The inn food, we thought, was very poor, until we visited other places, where it was worse. We visited many scenes around the mountains and on the Weser. We saw the Porta Westfalica, a fortress built in the days of the Romans, near the Jakobs Mountain and Wedikind. All of these sights reminded me vividly of the sights around Cape Mount and Koobolia.

Our Herbergsmutter was Frau Schneider. She was very kind. One thing that puzzled me was the fact that although the German names were much easier, my name was the only one she knew. One day she even invited me to eat in her quarters and to tell her about Africa. I would always take one of the other girls by turn, as she had asked me to do. My special friends were Sonja, a Russian Jew, and Waltraute Wichmann, the daughter of a medical professor at Hamburg University. The three of us composed all the poems that the class needed for anything, including one for Frau Schneider to the melody of "unpaidiadai," and we also danced for her every night. Frau Schneider told us that there was never any class at the Jugendherberge which she had enjoyed as much as she had enjoyed our class.

We kept in contact with Frau Schneider for a long time. I remember one day when we went on another excursion, the teacher asked that I write her a postcard in the name of the class. I wrote these lines on the postal card:

> *In Reinbek, in schönster Waldespracht,*
> *Hat beim Reigen, beim Singen*
> *Und freudigen Springen,*
> *Die U II C Ihrer gedacht.*[13]

Our Studeinreise was a happy one in every respect. We left every station singing songs and would arrive singing as well. People on the trains would often join us. Before going on the trip, the girls asked me to teach them an African song. I began teaching them a Mende song, "To the Drum," but it took them much too long to learn the words and the song. So, one day, they read the text of a supposedly African song in the papers and taught it to me. The interesting thing about this supposed African song was that everyone believed that I had taught it to the girls.

Another song that likewise made no sense and which the group enjoyed singing was the following:

> *Do you speak English,*
> *O yes, I love you, I love you,*
> *Mister, Du sein garnicht nett,*
> *Sein brav Du, Du Schaf Du,*
> *Denn ich bin aus Berlin an der Spree,*
> *Nanunee, nanunee.*[14]

These nonsensical melodies won us many friends on the trip. People bought us cold drinks, sandwiches, and the like. Our traveling companions were never bored. We kept them entertained all the time.

Our longest stay away from our headquarters at Hessisch Oldendorf was the one we made to the Weser. We took the train to Hameln an der Weser, and then boarded a steamboat to Detmold in Lippe. There, we left our rucksacks and marched to the Teutoburgerwald to see the monument set to Herman der Cherusker, who won the battle of this forest. The great German hero who drove the Romans away stood looking down on the whole forest, sword upward, seemingly telling everyone that never shall a Roman dare to touch the same grounds again without feeling the sharpness of his sword. It was raining on the day we arrived at this monument, and, with the music of the rain on our steps, and the blowing of the leaves on our backs and heads, we marched in typical goosestep style to the forest, singing at its approach, *"Als die Römer frech geworden."*[15] Inside the figure of the monument there was a book for people to write their names, and, on June 24, 1927, I wrote my name in Vai and the names of some of my brothers and sisters in that book.

We rested in Detmold, visiting the castle that afternoon, where we had to leave our shoes outside and wear slippers so as not to soil the carpeting of the edifice. Early the next morning, we set out to visit the Exsternsteine, a sandcliffe formation that represents the sufferings of Christ. There were stone steps leading to a little chapel to which people in ancient days had made a pilgrimage to pray. I went up and offered a prayer, for what I thought in those days to be essential to my life.

Singing and marching through hills and valleys, the U II C continued her Studienreise and we visited Kloster or Convent Korvey an der Weser this way. Here in the garden of this convent lies Hoffmann von Fallersleben, composer of the text of *"Deutschland, Deutschland, über alles."*[6]

The whole trip was wonderful and we sent home letters and postcards of all we had seen. We stopped at Convent Corvey, built in 822 by the Benedictine Order. After that, our next excursion took us to that fashionable health resort in the province of Waldeck, where the Prince of Waldeck ruled. This house, the house of Waldeck, is the home of the late Queen Mother Emma, of Holland. The objective of the trip to Piedmont was not to visit the health resort but to see the carbon dioxide tunnel of that city. Here also is the castle of Waldeck, noted for the historical Bettstelle[17] of the Grafen von Gleichen. This is the story of the count who went into battle during the Crusades and married an oriental princess because she saved his life. Upon his return, his wife demonstrated her gratefulness to the princess by having a bed constructed for the three of them until one of the wives died. Though the castle and the sight in Piedmont were very beautiful, I left with a feeling of pity for the people who lived in the days of old. I was told how in ancient days castle prisoners were punished in cruel and gruesome ways, and this did not exactly make for a delightful feeling.

This glorious and most impressive trip ended on the first day of July, as our class was ordered back to Hamburg to witness a celebration of some kind at the school. As a Studienreise, we had to give an account of the trip. It is one thing to enjoy marching in fresh air and seeing scenes of people of antiquity, along with their artifacts and cultural monuments, but quite another thing to have to account to someone about them. So, we decided to prepare an album of the trip. We thought we would be quite complete if we divided ourselves into committees. We had a committee to be responsible for all of the sketches of types of doorknobs on various churches. We had another committee drawing types of constructions of castles and churches. There was another committee responsible for anything pertaining to data, religious, historical, as well as geographical. Another committee was responsible for all literary materials providing background.

Aside from the album prepared by the class, we had individual albums to prepare. We included details of styles of churches, as well as personal experiences of hunger, when the girls stood on the Detmolder Bridge and ate the dry bread like lions seeking and devouring a much awaited prey. The trip broadened our horizons and made us form valuable friendships. We learned to know and love many of our classmates, as we could never have done just sitting in the classroom. And, here, also, it made us work as a unit, from the beginning of the trip to the end. In this way, we also became much better acquainted with the teachers who accompanied us, for forever thereafter they became our friends, and not our tutors. The learning was especially valuable. Previously, in Geography for example, the various formations of the soil had been discussed. It had previously meant nothing to me but the drama of seeing our Geography teacher show the places where something happened, saying *"altes Gebirge, hochgeschoben"*[8] (by which she would carry her hands up high), *"gesunken"*[9] (carrying her whole body and hands downwards again). Now, all of these things meant something to me. This, I think, is the most important aspect of such a trip.

Shortly after our return from the trip, our summer vacations began. This was no real vacation for our class since this was the time to account for the trip. So, we spent the first two weeks doing this; it was a very busy summer indeed, and I hardly had a chance to take a little rest from school. Otherwise, the summer was spent as usual—on the beaches, swimming parties, restaurants, and other activities. But something happened that I never would have dreamed of. For the first time in my life—aside from my hands—I became seriously ill, and had to remain out of school for thirty-seven days. Thus, I was not able to witness the formal presentation of the large album prepared by the class.

After I returned to school, everything connected with school life seemed like Greek. I had to catch up, and some of the girls were very helpful and showed me what they had gone over. I was able to catch up in a few weeks except for Mathematics. Although I did well in all the other courses the end of the year, I took a poor grade in Mathematics. Next to Mathematics, Physics was my worst class. We had a new teacher, Dr. Lederer, whose southern German accent I needed to pay particular attention to. I remember one day he was lecturing on capacity and what it meant—"Energie und Kapazität." He did not say the "K" sound in "capacity," but pronounced it "Gapacität," which is frequently a southern German habit. I spent the whole afternoon looking up "Gapacität," and was astonished when I found out from my friends that this was just his way of pronouncing the "K."

I had an encounter with this particular teacher also. One day, I was struggling to be attentive to be able to cover the gap in Physics when someone near me spoke. Although I knew who had been talking, I couldn't tell it, and simply said that I did not talk. He said he had seen my lips move and my teeth glitter. Well, this was too much! I promptly replied, *"Das ist eine glatte Lüge..."*[20] I had forgotten the incident when my special teacher called me and said that I meant that a mistake had been made. I was then summoned to see the principal who was having a discussion with the professor. I heard her remark that so long as I had not gotten into difficulties, and because I was dealing with a foreign language and would likely confuse my expressions at times, the teachers should not take things I say so seriously. Then, seeing me, she said, "not so Fatima, you meant Dr. L. made a mistake, didn't you?" Well, that was that. I got off easily because the person who had talked was my personal friend and she went and confessed. We had much more work ahead before completing the Untersekunda. But it was nothing more than what was expected.

Notes

1. [The Vai, as a matter of fact, are overwhelmingly Muslims, about 90 percent. *Eds.*]
2. [In pre-digital times, music was played on a phonogram (gramophone) from a disc (record). Holes would develop from long use, and when the needle got there, it would not move to the next groove on the record and so kept repeating the last piece over and over until someone pushed it over the hole. *Eds.*]
3. [Liebermann (1847–1935) was Jewish and his sympathetic portraits of laborers led to a Nazi ban on his work in the 1930s. *Eds.*]
4. [Buss-und Bettag is a day of "Prayer and Repentance." *Eds.*]
5. [Malvina Cornell Hoffman (1885–1966) was a well-known sculptor and her bronze, entitled "Frank Roberts, Liberian Dancer," executed in 1937, is in the collection of the Los Angeles County Museum of Art, with its orginal mold at the Metropolitan Museum of Art. Frank O. Roberts was a featured dancer with the Hampton Institute's Creative Dance Group in the 1930s. *Eds.*]
6. [Senior assistant mistress. *Eds.*]
7. ["May Helene Lang Oberrealschule hold on to its name in dignity." *Eds.*]
8. ["It was indeed a shame in culture to keep other human beings as slaves." *Eds.*]
9. ["Naturally, that you cannot sit the culturally low Nigger at one table with a European is clear." *Eds.*]
10. ["And not vice versa." *Eds.*]
11. [Wooded area near the Weser river. *Eds.*]

12. ["Good-bye my beloved homeland, beloved homeland, good-bye..." *Eds.*]

13. ["In Reinbek, in lovely sylvan splendor, We of U II C, whilst singing and dancing and joyfully prancing, Our thoughts of you to you we render." *Eds.*]

14. ["Do you speak English, O yes, I love you, I love you, Mister, you are really not nice, Be brave you, you sheep you, Because I am from Berlin on the Spree, Nanunee, nanunee." *Eds.*]

15. ["When the Romans became obnoxious." *Eds.*]

16. [The national anthem: "Germany, Germany, above all." *Eds.*]

17. [Bedchamber. *Eds.*]

18. ["Old mountains, pushed up." *Eds.*]

19. ["Sunk." *Eds.*]

20. ["This is an outright lie..." *Eds.*]

CHAPTER 14

THE "INVINCIBLES," AND MY DEPARTURE FOR SWITZERLAND

I have mentioned that my best friend and seatmate was Sonja Schönfeld, whose parents had migrated to Germany after wandering all over Europe while she had been just a baby. She claimed her family were descendants of the tribe of the Levites and were orthodox Jews, though I don't believe that Sonja was.

Our friendship started because we noticed that we liked the same teachers and girls in the class. Besides, wherever there was prejudice, we noticed that it concerned only the two of us. Thus, it happened that nobody could touch Sonja without touching me, and vice versa. By the way, her name on the class list was really Sarah or Sarashka; however, no one called her by this name outside of the classroom. Sonja was definitely a leader. Waltraute Wichmann, who was a member of the group, and I followed her blindly, and thus, we formed a regular clique. Sonja had other friends outside the classroom, and she made us accept all of them. These were Hertha Nathan, the daughter of a German Jewish Grosskaufmann, whom we nicknamed as "Teddy"; Mira Goledetz, the daughter of a Russian immigrant family, whose real name is Mirusia, which we shortened to Mira; and there was Olaf, a girl from Stettin, who was in business school and older than the rest of the gang and, hence, never fully in the group.

It was much fun being with these girls. We had weekly meetings and dance parties, since somebody always had a birthday or was giving a tea party. Our group was dubbed the "Invincibles." We were so jolly and full of sunshine and mirth that even our respective parents and relatives came to know each other. For, naturally, they wanted to know the homes of our friends that we frequented. Thus, these friends were not only my friends, but those of my parents and their parents also. My two cousins, Mary and Victoria, joined in the gaiety. And we spent many good hours together this way. I remember when the Charleston was fast becoming the style, Sonja and the rest of us organized dancing classes and taught father a form of Charleston for the salon, a slow form. I don't believe anyone needed to teach an African the Charleston.

When we were on the Studienreise in Hessisch-Oldendorf, and when there was a Jahrmarkt, one or two of the girls went to the largest hotel in the village and told the manager that there was an African actress in the group. Since we were given opportunities to go to the village to purchase postcards and stamps, the girls thought I could dance at the place. I didn't really want to, but because of the spirit of the class I agreed. I was surprised to see the crowds of peasants gather who had never seen a "darkie," and came there for the sake of curiosity. I thus danced the Blackbottom and Charleston. I shall never forget the full rhythm of the song to the Blackbottom—*"Was macht der Meyer auf dem Himalaya..."*¹ But since our only drawback on this trip was the lack of food, we were able after this performance to purchase liver sausage, cheese, butter, rolls, and other items.

During the regime of the Social Democratic Party, there was a *Schülerausschuss* (student council) in all the schools, which decided punishment for various classes when they broke some school regulation. They also heard desires and wishes from the various classes, about such things as trips, work-free afternoons, and the like. The council decided and voted on the petitions of the various classes. The principal of the school was the faculty advisor for the body. Each class had a *Vertrauenschülerin* (student of trust or student leader), a vice *Vertrauenschülerin*, and a secretary who served as treasurer. All these persons representing the class were elected by the respective classes.

It was a great day in the Untersekunda on election day. Suggested names were written on the board and the ballots were secret. You wrote down the person you wanted to represent your class and the teacher counted the votes. I am sometimes amazed at myself. When Sonja suggested my name, I promptly went to the board and erased it. We wanted somebody who could argue, and at the time I felt that I could not do this.

I suggested Sonja and voted for her as vice Vertrauenschülerin. But, unfortunately, she did not win. There was too much anti-Semitic feeling in the class. One girl told me later that she would never have voted for her, and knew many others who would not have done so. I asked her why, and she told me that Sonja was a Jew and Jews have a habit of leading everything. I asked her if she would have voted for me and she said that this would have been a different matter, because Negroes are not usually as aggressive as Jews are in organizations. I have often thought of this conversation, which took place back in 1927. Inge Backhaus was voted unanimously as Vertrauenschülerin, and Ellen Spilling became her assistant. I really don't remember the names of the other officers, but I think the officers of the class were very good in their respective positions. Inge never brought any matter before our class teacher that she had not discussed thoroughly with the rest of the class. We were all in support of her in every respect. The class was democratic and the *klassengeist* (class spirit) very high. No wonder this was my favorite class during my entire life in schools.

My love for this class could also be attributed to Fräulein Grühn, our Klassenlehrerin, who was with us every inch of the way, even though we often provoked this statement from her: *"Kinder, das ist ganz schäbig von Euch."*² She told me in 1936, when I went to see her, that she had never enjoyed advising a class or traveling with one as she had enjoyed ours. She also teased me about mocking her favorite sentence in a play that the class had written. I drew her on the blackboard scolding us for something and holding her mouth in the position of "schäbig." One day she walked into the class and I did not see her standing behind me, until she said simply: "I look very good Fatima." Well, that was good sisterly Chlorus.

There was also Fräulein Dr. Arndt, a very brilliant woman, and one of the best teachers the school has ever known. She was very fond of our class, and although Fräulein Grühn was our Klassenlehrerin, Dr. Arndt taught us German and History. She also taught one group in English. Hence, we had a chance to really know her. She knew how to make you respect and love her, and at the same time make you do your duties. This is a quality not found in many persons in the teaching profession. Once when she was lecturing to the class, Ellen, who sat behind me, could not resist the temptation of sticking her pencil into my hair. She did this, by the way, because she was astounded at the ability of my hair to hold pencils, pens, or anything else she would choose to make my hair hold. At the time, my hair was very thick and woolly as I had not begun having it pressed and curled. So, Ellen had her treat, and the queer thing about it was that I would never feel the things she had put in it. That day, Dr. Arndt suddenly called me to do something in front of the class and found all the decorations. Ellen began to tremble for what she had done.

Speaking of seats and seatmates, at this school we sat wherever we wanted to sit and with whom we wished to be seated. In this way, Sonja was my seatmate in all the classes held in our room but Modern Foreign Languages. In the other courses like Physics, I had Traute as a seatmate and sometimes Else Volkmann. But the vital thing is that we chose our own seats. In the other schools, or rather in the St. Ansgarschule, we had been assigned our seats by the teacher, with the big girls at the back and the smaller girls at the front, although later, Fräulein Ahlmann assigned the seats according to her ability to check on those who would cheat sitting at the back. In this way, Erika Pflughaupt and I had the back seats. For me, I saw myself as much too competitive with the other girls to have them know that I would copy anything from them. There was always a time when Fräulein Ahlmann would make me sit in the front row for a period or so. She wanted the girls who sat like commas to see my posture.

Do you believe in premonition? Well, here is one experienced by our class. At the close of the school year, Dr. Arndt wanted to do us a special favor. She made us understand that our class could have no work-free afternoon as far as her courses were concerned, but we covered all the materials we needed to cover for the year. She thus sent some of us out one day, when we had two periods in succession with her, to buy cake and lemonade. It was a special program for her birthday, which was on March 12. After eating together we began singing folksongs. Then, suddenly, someone began *"An einem kühlen Grunde,"* which was one of her favorite folksongs, but which is sad and speaks of parting. Not an eye in that room remained dry; we were all crying. I thought at the time that everyone was sad because some of the girls were leaving that year and those of us staying would not be having any courses under her tutorship. But that turned out to be the last group and the last class period she was ever to teach at school. For, a week later, on March 19, she was dead. She had developed a cold and with it, something else.

During the Weimar period, the lady teachers received the title of "Mrs." For example, in speaking of Fräulein Grühn, I should have written Frau Studienrätin Grühn. They were thought to be married to their professions, and since Frau is the highest title for a woman, they had a right to claim it. That is if they had no academic title such as Fräulein Dr. Arndt, in which case the title was optional. This was the explanation given me.

As the Untersekunda is one of the stiffest classes in the whole German school system, I became afraid for the first time of not acquiring a certificate for the completion of this class. This fear was also due to the fact that I had spent such a long time out of school, and Mathematics had become quite complicated for me all of a sudden, but my teachers felt that I did not spend enough time on it. But I never doubted my not being promoted that year when in February, the examinations for those who were completing the work of the Untersekunda, and the Oberprima, were to begin. Since father was worried about my Mathematics, I did not tell him of the examinations which were scheduled to take place earlier than usual.

During this time, father had to make several trips. One was to Berlin to witness the fight between Max Schmeling and an Italian boxer—this period, you will remember, was the time when the Germans and Italians were working up some sort of friendship, and hence this great boxing match had been planned.[3] Practically the whole Diplomatic Corps of Hamburg attended the match, which was staged at the Winterpalast in Berlin. Shortly after that, father had to take a short trip to Leipzig to the Frühjahrsmesse, as he always attended both the spring and autumn fairs in Leipzig. It was due to these trips that he did not notice me doing my biggest reviews for the examinations.

One day then, while coming home, I met Traute, who told me that I and other members of the Untersekunda had passed with the exception of only two. I came home and fooled my father into thinking that I thought I did not pass. He surprised me greatly. He did not react to this news in the way I had thought he would. He pointed out that since I had always been promoted, and since I had been ill and had had to spend so much time out of school, he could say nothing against my inability to have my Einjährigen this time. But if I had passed he intended buying things for me, and that he was going to let me take a trip, since some of his colleagues in Leipzig and other places had invited me to spend some time with them, in honor of the event. Now he would have to write and cancel these invitations.

Well, I had totally forgotten to tell him the truth when I returned from my violin lessons one evening to find a great surprise awaiting me. Father addressed me in Vai which he spoke when he was in a very good mood, saying *"Mba koloee, musu baa, mbe, mu i ma a fo nje? Mbe mu i ma towonaa fo nje? Naa so wi fo ke, ke i wele dawoaa mbe malo"* ("My great lady, my mother, great woman, why didn't you tell me the truth? I knew that you wouldn't let me be ashamed of you"). I went into the living room where many of our friends were gathered, including the Wellmanns (Romanians who manufactured wine in Hamburg), some of father's colleagues, and others. They had come to congratulate me upon reading in the papers that I had been among the candidates to finish the course. Wine, cake, and coffee were served, and father promised a party when Ma Sedia, who was visiting Liberia for the winter, returned.

Although we expected Ma daily, she did not return until April 5, and since the people had been greeting us by phoning, sending flowers, and coming to greet father in general, he decided not to wait too long to give the party. So, my "Einjährigen" party was held on March 28. We took some pictures, with all the members of my class whom I had invited, as well as the members of the "invincibles" sitting on the floor in the front row. Father kept all his other promises made to me too.

The reception of the Einjährigen certificate at school was impressive. This examination or qualification is, I guess, the completion of the Lyceum, and might correspond to high school. But when looking at the curriculum of the American high school, I don't see how the two could be compared. The Einjährigen originated with the training of young men for military service after their schooling, and spent one year to obtain a standard qualification. This section of the German educational system is reached, however, after ten years of schooling.

Having the Obersekundareife meant ever so much in being considered educated in Germany. When it was difficult for Germans to obtain jobs during the years of the Depression, the familiar question, *"Haben Sie das Einjährige oder das Abitur?"*[4] became more pronounced. Only people with these two qualifications were able to obtain available jobs. Thus, with the Einjahrigen, I had passed another milestone toward the great fountain of knowledge. But there were still many more to pass.

After Easter, work in the next class, die Obersekunda, began. This time, we were in the O II a. Herr Dr. Hartleb, whom we called "Bubi" as he had the face of a baby boy, became Klassenlehrer for this class. Those of the members of my original class who remained my classmates were Ellen Spilling, Marieche Wobbe, and Ilse Huhnecke. The few of us were to be placed with one of our greatest rival class members of the "b" group, who had previously teased us and blamed us for all the noise on the floor. This new change was not pleasant. As with the new classmates, we had new teachers, with the exception of Bubi, who still taught Physics.

The subjects were more or less the same as in the previous class. The only new course was Latin, which was optional. But I had to take Latin, since at the time I was planning to study medicine for which it was required, as well as for other sciences. I had to leave our domicile at six o'clock in the mornings for about four days of the six days of school, in order to take Latin, which was offered an hour on the four days before the time for chapel. The course became stricter and harder as more and more work was demanded of us. Our new teacher in Mathematics, Fräulein Dr. Sturm, did just what her name signifies—she stormed us continuously with calculus and other mathematical formulas. In short, school was no fun, just hard work.

A very important event, to me at least, was the celebration of the birthday of Frau Dr. Helene-Lange in April of 1928. It was her seventy-fifth or so. By this time, I had acquired a new friend, our Latin teacher whose name was Frau Studienrätin Helene Hauenschild. Dr. Lange came to Hamburg, and the homage that the women of Hamburg paid her was stupendous. There were torchlight processions from the train station to the residences in the Neubertstrasse, where she had her domicile with the two Beckmann sisters, Emmi and Anna. I have never seen such a long procession of girls and torchlights. We sang and marched straight to the door of her residence. The sort of hero worship and honor Dr. Lange received reminded me much of the time in my childhood, when father would visit the interior and the people would dance all night.

Although I do not intend boring you with other trips made in Germany, or anywhere else in Europe, I would like to describe the weekend spent in Cologne, because I notice in my diary that the trip awakened numerous depths of emotions in me, as new scenes and people always do. We went sightseeing, and beheld the city from beginning to end. It is often said, "from Rhein to Rhein," since the town seems to form a ring, beginning and ending with the Rhein. We visited the university and were narrated its history from the foundation in 1388 or thereabouts, through its years of total inactivity, to when Napoleon closed its gates. It was not reopened until after World War I. It was not these facts, however, that formed a lasting impression on me. The inner town with its narrow streets, and the outer one, with its residential quarters as well as the churches and chapels of the city, were all superb. It was the *dom* (the cathedral) that made me bow in deep humility.

In receiving all the information about the Dom and the centuries it had taken to build it, I began wondering about man—how he in this edifice had lifted his heart from common everyday occurrences of the earth toward the skies. The height of the Dom symbolized exaltation to me. The deep bows and curves of the windows and Gothic-style construction seemed to tell me that man soars in his heart but must physically bend before the Great Unknown, whose eyes he does not feel he is worthy to meet, and hence bows in humiliation for all of his sins.

As a result of the Einjährigen, many colleagues of my father invited me to their respective homes. Since the vacation around Easter was very brief, I could not honor these invitations. But the summer vacations enabled me to do some traveling. I went to Leipzig where the consul of Liberia, Julius Haeuber, resided. There were many courtesies shown me and I made many valuable friendships, which lasted throughout the rest of my sojourn in Europe. In Leipzig I visited the grave of Johann Sebastian Bach at the St. Thomas Kirche, and the *"Völkerschlacht Denkmal."*[5] What I wanted to see, above all, was the university at Leipzig. From literature I had learned of the great German personalities who had sat within its walls. I thought of Goethe's pronouncement, *"Mein Leipzig ist ein kleines Paris, es bildet seine Leute."*[6] From Leipzig, I proceeded to Dresden, then to Berlin, and finally to Zoppot. The celebration of July 26, Liberia's Independence Day, demanded my presence in Hamburg again.

Nothing much happened in the Obersekunda, but for one incident, which was the result of a growing tide of prejudice in the schools. While the teachers at the Helene Lange Oberrealschule had been very liberal, there were others who belonged to parties that were not liberal. Upon Dr. Arndt's death, another teacher, who belonged to the Conservative Party, took her place, and so too was the History teacher, who was not in favor of the Jewish students and me. In teaching Civics, she often referred to the fact that we were not paying enough for our schooling, even though we might be paying the highest tuition fees charged. Once, when she had a review staged, she asked a question to which she said my answer was wrong but later on, when the same answer was given, she said it was correct, saying that she had to cut the rest of the students down, including me. Simultaneously the whole class replied that I had given that answer before. The teacher simply said "so." Although the other girl was not allowed to go up after the teacher discovered her error, I was not asked to cut down the two students who had missed the question before me.

Although circumstances at the school were otherwise pleasant, and I was progressing in every way, our physician recommended that I should not spend the next winter in Hamburg because of the severity of the climate. Thus, father obtained a year's leave of absence from the school for me, and arranged for me to go to boarding school in Switzerland.

My school started around the end of August, but I could not leave since I could not obtain credits for the school term until late in September when the Helene Lange Oberrealschule closed its term. September 30, then, became my last day at school, and I bade the teachers farewell. I stood with Fräulein Arnold, looking into the yard, watching the other girls play. Fräulein Hauenschild stood before me like a statue when I went to say goodbye and thank her for all she had meant to me. Dr. Hartleb, with all his views on tolerance, was there to give me a handshake. So I hurried and walked down the steps, looking into each classroom with its green walls—green, which the Germans say is the sign of hope, which awakened in me the hope that I would return soon again. I thought, when I returned, I would be speaking French, and all the teachers would be proud of me. As I proceeded down the street in the direction of the tram-car, I heard Fräulein Dr. Sturm, who taught Mathematics, surprise me with a box of handkerchiefs.

I was busy the last two days at Hamburg buying things on my school list. I also had to go to the doctor for a physical examination, since the certificate had to be sent to Switzerland before our departure. On Wednesday,

October 3, 1928, father and I boarded the train for Switzerland. Friends were at the train station with many gifts—handbags, flowers, candies, chocolates, and many other items. The compartment on the train was so full of gifts that had it not been nine o'clock at night, I would have bought another suitcase for them.

The trip to Switzerland was delightful in every respect. At about midnight, father left my compartment for his sleeper. Between the time he left and his return in the early morning hours, a pair of twin sisters entered the compartment. They were teachers in Freiburg, im Breisgau, and had been vacationing in Stuttgart. Father joined the conversation when he arrived, and I was quite happy when he came, because these sisters had been kind enough to invite me to see Freiburg at a later date. These teachers knew nothing about Liberia; in fact, they claimed not to have seen a colored person before. As such father promised them his booklet on Liberia published in 1926.

When the sisters left the train, father began a long speech about his days as a student in America, during which I discovered how sad he had been for not meeting his mother alive after his return from America. It sounds queer indeed that I should have been chosen for him to pour his heart out to. This is the very same thing that happened to me later; I lost him while I was in America. A great admiration for my father piled up in my thoughts. This was the same man who at one time had given a party, and a German friend who had attended the function, came the next morning to thank him for the party, but thought to make light of him, saying, "Your party and sense of statesmanship was splendid and you looked wonderful in your uniform—no European statesman, could have done better or represented better (see figure 14.1). But, in looking at you last night, the thought kept occurring to me how far could you be from cannibalism, in spite of all the dignity and poise?"

What brought on my admiration was how father received the statement. You see, in those days, I would have become enraged at the insult. But he had another answer. With a broad and beautiful smile, and in perfect calm, my father replied, "I don't suppose I am very far from that stage." As our friend grinned with satisfaction into his mustache, father calmly added: "But who can tell how far anyone here is from cannibalism"? After the gentleman assured him that he was certain that he had never had any kind of contact with this practice, father asked him whether he would be able to tell how much of the human flesh Heiman, who had just been executed in Hanover for making sausages out of human flesh, had consumed. The man said that of course he could not be certain. Well, those of us standing around were all quite pleased with the embarrassment that our friend felt. The joke was on him.

Figure 14.1   Rachel and Momolu Massaquoi, ca. 1925

On the morning of October 4, we arrived in Basel. My dreams came true. I had seen in these visions that I was in Switzerland, walking among the narrow passages of the mountains. You would think that people here would feel squeezed at any moment because of the tightness of the mountains over them. The Swiss have managed to keep out of wars, in spite of two great recent wars waged by their neighbors. They have known how to cement the brotherhood of man and are willing to become a great center of democracy. They had for this purpose opened their doors and invited the nations of the earth to come to terms with their brothers by settling their grievances through pledges of honor, commonly called "Covenants," rather than by fighting.

Father attended to the passports, while I wandered around thinking about the people with whom I was to become associated. I am going to learn French, and in this way once more become another person, in speech and attitude. Will I also learn Esperanto, so as to be like these people in acquiring the brotherhood of one language—this universal language?[7] What of the Center of the Red Cross, the emblem for the relief of human suffering? Will I have a chance to attend any of its conventions?

We traveled through tunnels and up and down hills. Father asked me why I had been so quiet while he had been attending to the passports and identifying my trunk, which was to enter Switzerland free of inspection as diplomatic luggage. After hearing some of the things I had been thinking, he warned that I should never make up my mind as to what the place or people would be like, for fear of being disappointed. He reminded me that we had often criticized people who happened to be on their way to Africa and knew all about the situations and what they would write and speak about. "Try," he said, "to have your heart, eyes, and mind open—open to observe."

Upon arriving in Neuchâtel, we made reservations at the Hotel Terminus and went sightseeing. The same taxicab that took us through the town, soon found its way along a countryside road and we arrived in Montmirail. Victoria had arrived here from Hamburg at the opening of school in August to be in boarding school.[8] We asked for her to be allowed to go and spend a day or two with us in Geneva. We passed the night at the Hotel Terminus and very early the next morning we continued to Geneva, along with Victoria.

Geneva was a beautiful sight to behold. Father began pointing out the various buildings of prominence. He had been in Geneva a dozen times or so, and knew the place very well. At the station, called la Gare Cornavin, stood Baron Lehmann, who at that time was Liberian minister accredited to the League of Nations.[9] His giant size, posture, and sternness reminded me of Frederick the Great. He was not feeling well that day, but nevertheless still looked like a statue. The baron had been in Geneva to attend the last September sessions of the League of Nations. His residence was in Paris, but he had remained in Geneva because father had informed him of his coming. With the baron was also his attaché, Mr. Nico Ooms, who upon the former's death that same year became the Liberian representative to France.[10] The fact that these gentlemen were there to meet our train flattered my vanity to no small degree.

Dr. Antoine Sottile, who at the time was consul of Nicaragua and Liberia in Geneva, also promised to be at the station. But the baron and Sottile did not like each other, I later learned, so since the baron had come to take us to his quarters at the hotel, Sottile left the station before our arrival. We climbed into the baron's car and headed for the hotel. Passing through the Rue de Rive, with its fashionable jewelry stores, we soon crossed the Pont de Mont Blanc to the other side of the Lac Leman and then to the Hotel Beau Sejour, which was situated almost on the outskirts of the city. On the way, father and the baron discussed the events of the day. They talked about the last sessions of the League of Nations, but my thoughts were elsewhere. At the time I considered myself a historian, a lady of letters, one who was keenly interested in the lives and activities of great men of the past. What, in this connection, did I expect to see in Geneva?

I was quite eager to meet the Sottiles, who had asked to be my guardians during my sojourn in Switzerland. I had for a long time corresponded with Madame Jeanne Sottile, who was of French descent and had been trained in Austria, and hence spoke and wrote German well. Dr. Sottile was an international lawyer, and founder and editor of the renowned journal *La Revue du Droit International*, the second of only two such journals at the time. He had received his training in Italy, his home, as well as in Lausanne and Brussels.

After lunch, I called Madame Sottile, whom I had telephoned long distance from Neuchâtel, announcing our arrival in Switzerland. I had an African cloth to give her and could hardly wait to do so. Besides, I wanted to find out whether she was anything like her letters, which for the previous eighteen months had been a great source of joy to me. We were then invited to have tea that afternoon with them, at their residence at 105 Route de Chene, close to the French border. Madame was very pleased with her cloth and served tea on it at once.

I liked Madame and Monsieur Sottile instantly, as well as their house. The home had three stories and was built with double windows and had quaint furnishings with antiques, all of which intrigued me very much. The arrangements of the kitchen especially interested me, which I later noticed was the style of kitchens in the Italian homes I visited. After a delightful visit, we returned to the hotel.

The next morning, Dr. Sottile accompanied us to the boarding school, "Hirondelles," it was called, in Champelles, which was on the city outskirts. Since I had an academic career in mind, the principal and father decided that I attend, instead, the Ecole Superieure. Hirondelles was primarily a finishing school, and French would have been the only new item on my schedule, which would not have meant much progress for an academic career. We left the Hirondelles that afternoon, with pouring rain providing music to our steps, and drove back to the hotel. That evening we went to the opera, to hear La Teresina. The setting of the opera was the time of Napoleon, and La Teresina was the name of the heroine. My French was good enough to understand that much of the opera.

It is queer how a person's taste for certain types of cultural things can develop. To hear me speaking now of enjoying an opera of the type that we heard in Geneva that night seems so contradictory to me. I remember the first opera that father took me to, and how I felt all throughout, thinking that the people were not singing but continuously yelling and screaming. At the time, the only opera I could enjoy was "Carmen," for the music in it had more rhythm and it had more action.

After our night out at the theater, we went to a variety show and, thereafter, to a restaurant for a midnight snack. This was a significant event in that father had now accepted, and I felt, quite grown up to be taken out to an after theater amusement. Well, this meant to me that my days for "early to bed" were over.

Mr. Oomes, father, and I went to see the director of public instruction for the Canton de Genève the following Monday, as the principal had advised. The minister of public instruction, Monsieur Marché, made arrangements with the director of the École Supérieure pour les Jeunes Filles Étrangères,[11] Monsieur Henri Duchosal, to see us the same day. My credits were presented to him in his rue Voltaire office where sat a gray-haired man with white moustache, who remarked "She is a very good student, according to this." I could notice that my father felt proud, but just then Monsieur Duchosal cut in, "but, oh, mathematics..." which jolted me. Monsieur Duchosal told father all about courses and costs, but we could not meet my teacher, Mademoiselle Long, as she was not there.

Monsieur Duchosal recommended a pension[12] for me, where the mother of the minister of public instruction was also staying. He knew the lady of the house well and thought I should be very happy and safe there. The proprietress, Madame Jeanne Dancet, was very friendly. Her residence was at the Rue de Lyon and her pension famille was called "Clos Voltaire," in honor of Voltaire who was believed to have lived there. My room was on the second floor. During my sojourn there everything was delightful, as I soon became the pet of the house, with Madame Dancet dubbing me "bébé." Even after I left her home, she helped me and followed my progress with ardent interest.

Meanwhile, as there was nothing much to do again to assist father, Baron Lehmann and Mr. Oomes left. My cousin Victoria too had left for her school earlier in the week. Father remained a couple of days more in Geneva with me so that we could purchase books and make arrangements for me to follow activities that were not a part of the school curriculum. Finally, it was time for father to depart. At the station stood the Dancets, some people from the school, and Madame and Dr. Sottile. I went and whispered in father's ears that I didn't want to go to school in Switzerland. He promised to come back in six weeks, at which time we would discuss in detail. Everyone became concerned. The Sottiles promised to take me out everyday if I liked, and the others made promises too. But nothing anyone could say at that moment was able to console me. Suddenly, the engine of the train began to puff and I brought forth a loud scream, which startled even me. Father turned away to keep from looking at me. The Sottiles and the Dancets spoke anxiously. But father asked them not to worry about me, saying that his daughter had a bucket of water under her eyelids, which on occasion could turn into a very free and resourceful fountain. With this, everyone managed a forced laugh. Then, at about 2 p.m., the most wicked train in the whole world rolled unmercifully on, bearing my all.

With my broken heart, a heart which I thought at the time could never be cured again of its hurt and pain, I got home and crept into my bed and fell into the arms of Morpheus for consolation. I didn't go home with the Sottiles as they had asked me to do. I must have slept very long, for I knew nothing more until I heard the sound of the gong for six-thirty supper. I went down to supper, laughing and joking with the other members of the household. I almost forgot about my father, but then it was only sleep, a greater medicine there is not, that cured my broken heart.

Notes

1. ["What does the Meyer on the Himalaya..." *Eds.*]
2. ["Children, that's very bad of you." *Eds.*]
3. [Max Schmeling (1905–2005) fought in Berlin on January 6, 1928, against Michele Bonaglia, the Italian light heavyweight champion, who he knocked out in the first round. Schmeling became the first European to become the world heavyweight champion (1930–1932) and he knocked out African American boxer Joe Louis in a 1936 fight in New York, and this success was appropriated into Hitler's Nazi propaganda. Louis easily defeated him in a rematch in 1938. For comments on Schmeling by Fatima

Massaquoi's nephew, see Hans Massaquoi, *Destined to Witness: Growing Up Black in Nazi Germany* (London: HarperCollins, 2001), pp. 91–95. *Eds.*]

4. ["Do you have the one-year degree of the Abitur?" *Eds.*]
5. ["Monument of the battle of the people." *Eds.*]
6. ["My Leipzig is a small Paris, it is educating its people." *Eds.*]
7. [The artificial language Esperanto was invented by Dr. Ludovic Lazarus (1859–1917), a Russian-Jewish philologist, who first published his schema of the language in 1887. *Eds.*]
8. [Victoria Johnson, a family relation who had previously lived with them in Hamburg. *Eds.*]
9. [Baron Rodolphe Auguste Lehmann (1870–1929) was permanent delegate of the Republic of Liberia to the League of Nations (1920–1928) and Liberia's ambassador to France. *Eds.*]
10. [Ooms had spoken before the League on Liberia's behalf at the beginning of the investigation into charges against President King's administration of engaging in slavery in Fernando Po. In 1929 he stepped down from the position, being replaced by Antoine Sottile. *Eds.*]
11. [School of Higher Education for Young Girls. *Eds.*]
12. [Sometimes also *pension famille* or *pension de famille,* French for boarding home or residential hotel. *Eds.*]

CHAPTER 15

L'ÉCOLE SUPÉRIEURE ET SECONDAIRE (SWITZERLAND), AND ROUGH TIMES ON MY RETURN TO GERMANY

The branch of the institution I attended in Geneva was a large edifice located on the Rue Voltaire. My session was almost entirely for students with a foreign language background. My classroom was on the second floor and my class teacher, the "maîtresse de classe," was Mademoiselle Margret Long. This department of the school offered French in all forms. The regular courses for my section began at 9 a.m. and lasted until 12 noon. We studied diction, grammar, etcetera. We used *Le Petit La Rousse Grammaire Supérieure*, and in later years I found this grammar very helpful. Two hours on Fridays were devoted to scientific expressions. The teacher lectured in French. Mademoiselle Long showed an excellent sense of justice and took great pains in teaching girls who had come from all over the world, including Italy, Armenia, Brazil, Denmark, Germany, United States, Switzerland, and many other places.

There was a ranking system at school based on our monthly average. A girl from the United States had held the first place in the class for a month or so. I had reason to rejoice over a victory I am about to relate. I was told this girl had raised some objections about having a Negro in the class. Although I was late entering the school during the first term, I surpassed her after a month or two. One day, as luck would have it, she had to bring me her poetry album to sign. She requested I write in the album in Vai, so I wrote: *"a ko mu mo wele ja tiye I bo kai la he,"* which is "one does not cut eyes at his comrades." By this my people mean that you do not judge a person until you have given him a chance to prove his worth—in this case, according to his or her race or color. I don't suppose this girl ever knew what I wrote. She and I became good friends later, and she even invited me to her place and visited me at my domicile. The point is that I was fighting against her not wanting a Negro, and this really pushed me to get the highest ranking for that month. Such is my spirit.

The regular courses in school were not enough for me since I had planned studying French in that one year. Father was not sure whether he would return home for good, or take the job of Baron Lehman (who died in December that year) at the League of Nations. I thought I might have to enter the University in Geneva, and Mademoiselle Long thought I could take additional courses, which she arranged for me with her sister who prepared students privately for matriculation. But father saw all of these extra courses in the bills I sent him and advised that I drop them.

Every day, except Thursdays, which was a work-free day for the schools and called "petit dimanche" or "little Sundays,"[1] I went to school from 8 a.m. to 12 noon. On Tuesday afternoons I had violin lessons, and on Mondays, Wednesdays, and Fridays I returned to school in the afternoons for my extra courses, which now had to be dropped. I therefore joined the physical education classes on Wednesday afternoons. Thursday afternoons usually found me in the theater, la Comedie Française, where I held a weekly subscription that father had given me. During the whole period I held the subscription, only plays of Molière were presented.

I took violin lessons at first with a Mademoiselle Andrée Doret, a young Swiss who was reputed to be of the Swiss aristocracy. She had just returned from school in England, and she was amiable and more of a friend than a teacher of mine. She and I lived in opposite directions of the town and met at the apartment of a friend of hers. Later, when I moved to the home of the Sottiles, even this place proved too far for me for lessons and so she recommended a Madame Minkoff, who was virtuosité du violin du conservatoíre de Genève. Madame Minkoff was a Russian immigrant and very strict. She totally broke me out of playing pieces by ear. She claimed that I would never be able to read notes so long as I continued playing everything that way.

While in Germany, I thought I knew French, and I had interpreted for father on several occasions. But it was one thing hearing a language spoken and a different matter to have to use it daily. I remember in this connection, some of the difficulties I had earlier with German, and how my friends laughed at me. Madame Sottile once asked what she should serve as an appetizer, when she was expecting Ma Sedia and the children. I promptly replied *"des angelures"* (meaning frostbite) instead of *"des anchois"* (anchovies). During my sojourn in Switzerland, I usually spoke cautiously, pausing to search for words. The little trick, I thought, was to pause between words and say *"n'est ce pas."* Soon, my friends began calling me Mademoiselle *"n'est-ce pas."* But the matter of utter limitation of words for daily use did not last long, and as a matter of fact, I filled the missing links very quickly, not only in speaking, but in all of my courses.

In general, I made good strides in the courses I took in Geneva. I received a certificate at the end of the year with *"moyen bien"* (good average), with a comment from the teacher that *"Mademoiselle Massaquoi a fait de reel progress pendent ce second semester."*[2] Mademoiselle Long told me that my progress in the second semester had been astounding, and she was particularly surprised because I had entered the course so late in the year. School closed that year in June, and since I had already left for a journey through Switzerland, my certificate had to be mailed to me.

When father left me earlier in the school year, he promised to spend either Christmas or New Year with me. But then Baron Lehman died suddenly in Paris around Christmas, and the Liberian government asked father to officiate at the funeral. It would be easier to come to Switzerland and spend Christmas with me. I expected him all Christmas Eve, but he did not arrive and I gave up. I had had Christmas Eve dinner with the Sottiles and returned to the pension home to go to bed. When I was fast asleep, Madame Dancet came and tried to wake me up; father was sitting downstairs and it was already around 4 a.m.

I dressed hurriedly, and went with him to the hotel where Dr. Sottile had made reservations for him. I spent the rest of the night on the couch of his living room, but there was little sleep, for I kept father up talking until I fell asleep on the couch with clothes and all. The reason father had not arrived at Geneva the time we expected was because he had dozed off on the train and later disembarked in a strange town. He had not been aware of his whereabouts until he mounted a taxicab and stated his destination.

Father, the Sottiles, and I spent Christmas quietly, since the people in Geneva do not make as much over Christmas as the Germans do, but celebrate New Year's as the French, instead. The day after Christmas, father and I went to Caux, Glin, and other places of interest where there were winter sports. We wound up in Montreux, where we awaited Victoria. We were also expecting Mary, who was to arrive from Hamburg and would soon enter boarding school at Villa Petit Port in Lausanne. The Sottiles asked father to let me board at their home. So, I moved in with them shortly after his departure for Hamburg in January. Life with the Sottiles was beautiful and Madame and I became very close friends. Even after I left, they often invited me to spend some time with them, which I did in spring 1932 and again in spring 1935. I returned to them whenever I liked until 1936, when I planned my voyage to the United States.

The severity of the winter in Hamburg caused the doctor to recommend a warmer climate for Ma Sedia and the babies also. They spent two weeks in Paris, then moved to Nice, to San Remo, and ended up in Geneva to spend three weeks with me. She advised me to write and ask father to take me to Italy, where he was planning a trip. I wrote father that I wanted to go as his interpreter. Well, since Italian was not at all on my bills, he wondered of course how I had learned it. I bought Otto Sauer's *Italienische Konverstions-Grammatik* and plunged myself in the study of the language. A friend, who noticed my efforts to speak, aided me. Thus, father was never able to know that the day I wrote him that letter I did not know one word of Italian.

Immediately after school closed, father sent me my fare to return to Hamburg and gave me permission to visit a few friends in Switzerland and other places. But since I went to other countries before visiting my Swiss friends, I was very much behind schedule. When I returned to Switzerland, first to visit with the Kuenzlis, I found a host of telegrams from father asking me to return home immediately. Both of my cousins, Mary MaCritty and Victoria Johnson (Mrs. Fiske and Mrs. Schaak, the latter now residing in Boston, and former in Liberia), had already returned home in May or June. I had made trips to Lucerne, Beinwilam, and See, where I saw Marta Harri, now Mrs. Hintermann of Arrau.

Since I had spent the money father had sent me twice to return home, I had to sit in Olten and wait for him to send some more. In this way, Mrs. Kuenzli, to whom I did not explain my situation, suggested she take me to Bern to see the entertainments being staged there in honor of King Fuad of Egypt. This was early in July 1929. My next visit to Bern was not until May 1936, when I visited the grave of the late Johann Büttikofer, who had been a friend of my grandmother's, and whose widow was living there and had invited me. This was the same family we met in Rotterdam on our way to Germany from Liberia.

Mrs. Kuenzli and I returned home the next evening, and there were telephone calls and telegrams from father, as well as some money. I had to be in Hamburg by July 7, since 8th was Ma Sedia's birthday and they were planning a surprise party for her. Early next morning, Frau Kuenzli-Bauer and Herr Kuenzli-Bauer—the Swiss usually carry the maiden names of their wives last—accompanied me to Basel, and from there I journeyed to Hamburg.

I arrived in Hamburg late on the night of July 7, and father and some friends were at the station awaiting my arrival. My parents had moved to another residence on the Schlüterstrasse, but not to the same one in which we had lived before. On Sunday, July 8, we had a combination birthday celebration for Ma and an open house. After a few days of rest in Hamburg, I found myself becoming restless. Every day I would go to the office and fetch father during the lunch hour, doing this chiefly so that he might get some rest. Father had had a serious operation in May and was weak; hence he could not come to Switzerland to fetch us. I decided to myself that he should not be working.

The purpose I had in mind for fetching him was to make it possible for him to come home for lunch so he would get a nap in the afternoons at least. While fetching him one day, I noticed I had to wait for him a long time in the outer waiting room of his office. When I went to his private office I did not see him. I looked into the employee office and there stood my father, stamping consular manifests. The general typist and clerk of the office, Miss Bismarck, had gone to lunch, while Mr. James, another employee, had gone on an errand. Fräulein von Bobers was on her six weeks of furlough for the summer. Herr Consul Berends, his attaché, had phoned me saying that I was not a child any longer and had to work somehow to show my gratitude for all the good things I had been receiving. For, by this time, I was the oldest child near father, since all of my brothers had gone back to Africa.

In stamping the manifests and invoices, I noticed that father stopped after each and sat down. He was tired, so I offered to help him if he would show me where to stamp the papers and what to do. He sat near me and showed me, step by step. From that day onward, whenever I was in Hamburg, and until 1935, I worked in the consulate general in various capacities.

All of this brought about the beginning of the job, and I began accompanying him to the office in the mornings. Finally, I spent all of my mornings there, then, gradually, all day. After five months of helping out in the office, father wrote to Liberia and informed the authorities of my employment at the office. By that time I was not putting in a full day anymore since I had already started school again, but would work in the office after school hours. My first five months at the office, even though I was there all day, were without remuneration. Nobody thought of money. I was all too eager to learn the work, and in those days I had everything and never gave a thought to money. Even when I began drawing a salary, it was rather small. I had often obtained that much from father without working for it.

Since father was expected to have his furlough and since I had become interested in the work of the consulate general, it was thought that I should attend a school that would give me ample time to be able to do both work. Although I had previously only obtained a leave of absence from my studies at the Helene-Lange Oberrealschule, I did not reenter the school because it would have meant devoting all of my time to schoolwork. Professor Carl Meinhof, whose advice father sought on the matter, suggested the Studienanstalt Jessel, where his secretary had just obtained her maturity for the entrance to the university.[3] The Studienanstalt had people who worked and for the most part had been out of school a long time and desired advanced studies. This type of school is what the Germans call *"Presse,"* and the courses were in the mornings and evenings. Since father did not wish me to attend any form of evening school, I attended the day classes.

In an institution such as Jessel, activities like sewing, singing, drawing, and gymnastics were not offered, so there was more time to devote to regular academic subjects. In this way, the school is able to cover materials for a whole year in only a half a year. The students are for the most part grown men and women and know what they are after, so they don't need coaxing and regulations to go about their duties. Father and I went to see Professor Herr Jessel, and it was agreed that I begin around the middle of September.

The courses offered at the Studienanstalt were a continuation from the Helene-Lange-Oberrealschule, from where I had left for Switzerland. The difference was that we were expected to cover the materials in half the time required for the state school. I learned in this period what the term "presse" meant for this type of school—the "pressing" of formulas into your head. One great difference I have noticed between the German educational system and others is that although a course may be listed by a certain name, there are many subject matters taught under its name. In German Literature, for example, we were not only taught the history of literature of Germany, but also that of all the foreign contemporaries as well, such as the French stylists and Shakespeare. The same was true for Philosophy, where we studied Hegel, Schoppenhauer, Kant, Fichte, and others who wrote in German, as well as John Locke. With all these streams of philosophical thoughts and writings, you can imagine how much we had to study.

Essay writing was practiced vigorously in these courses, to prepare us for the examinations. Herr Theile, who taught German and Latin, usually gave us topics for discussion. One topic I wrote on was *"Europa, Land und Leute, Wie Ich sie sehe."*[4] On this subject, I told all the good and the bad that I had observed in Europe. He must have discussed the things I had written with some of the other teachers, because one of them, Herr Spohring, with whom I had often walked and talked during the recess periods, said to me that he believed when I one day leave Europe, I would feel differently. Herr Spohring said that people tend to forget the bad things they observe, and remember only the good. I believe today that Herr Spohring was right.

One day during a Biology class, I sat next to a young man with whom I worked on experiments, using the same microscope. My hand was under the lens of the microscope. He looked down at it and told me that the skin under the microscope was as brown as smoked and dried meat. I promptly asked him to place his hand under it and, seeing his skin, I told him that his skin looked like that of a hog. He told the teacher and other students that I had said his skin was hoggish. And it did look like a hog, with all the big pores and hair of a hog. Of course, while I did not mind telling him this, I certainly felt embarrassed for the teacher to hear what I had said.

There were twenty-three students in our class. Of these, about five or six of us were women and girls, and the rest men. We had many masquerade parties, a Christmas party, and we went together on February 8, 1930, to witness the launching of a ship—the *Europa* or *Bremen*. I don't know which of the two was launched on that day, but my class decided to witness it, and in spite of the bitter cold outdoors, we sat in a boat and watched the giant steamer take her first dip into the water.

In those days, there was not much prejudice in Germany. In fact, whenever father and the boys took me and my cousins out, Germans came to mingle with us, perhaps out of sheer curiosity more than anything else. European prejudice and segregation differs from that of America. Of course I don't believe that Europeans—that is to say, a certain class of people—believe in intermarriage between races. But they would go with you to parties or sit with you in the theaters and public places (see figure 15.1). No one looks down on that. That is all.

With regard to attending dances, I have only one unpleasant incident that I recall, which bordered on prejudice. Father and my brother Jawa once took me to an official dance. As soon as father took the floor and was dancing with me, the band changed the music quickly and played *"der Neger hat sein Kind gebissen, Oh...Und hat es an die Wand geschmissen, Oh!"*[5] Contrary to his usual tolerance, father protested, and the officials apologized for the insult.

Not only did my brother Abut come to see me sometimes at school, but also my little baby sister, Fascia, asked her nurse to bring her by and play on the Moorweidenstrasse, which was not far from school. Once while on such a visit, a photographer made color pictures of her. Some of the young ladies and young men of my class were in the habit of bringing chocolate and flowers they would place in her hair.

One day, then, one of the young men brought her a watch, made of chocolate. She first placed the clock at her ears to see if it would tick. Then she examined it in various ways. We did not notice that the photographer had taken pictures, showing her examining the clock. Thus, when her pictures appeared in one of the illustrated papers, we were all quite surprised. It is not the pictures that caused me to remember this incident, but the caption under the pictures, printed at a time of the rising spirit and tide in Germany. They demonstrated an aspect of German prejudice, because they showed little Fascia and stated that her father was from Togo. I took the paper and the caption to Fräulein von Bobers and asked that we reply to it. In those days, unpleasant articles in the papers increasingly appeared mocking blacks. The matter of not

Figure 15.1　Fatima and friend, Germany or Switzerland, ca. 1932

mentioning Liberia with the cute baby, normal as any other child, is a case in point.

This was not the first time that we saw articles that gave rise to a battle of the pen. Father had waged one for a long time with an explorer who had been to Liberia before World War I, and on his second visit after the war obtained a rare stone the Vai consider precious. He brought the stone to Germany, and the Vai protested to the Liberia Government, which in turn asked father to look into the matter. The stone was in the shape of a crocodile.

The explorer maintained that he had bought the stone from a private individual. Father pointed out that no one could buy from an individual something which belonged to the public. In the end, the court decided that the stone must be returned to the Liberian government. This fight with the pen was not a simple one, for every evening there was an article on the stone in the paper, either by father or by the explorer in question. In the end, the law settled the matter. A replica of the stone was made, as the court requested, and was kept for the museum.[6]

Thus, when I showed Fräulein von Bobers the photographs of Fascia, and suggested answering it, since the writer of the article was hurting the national pride of all of us, she suggested that it would be a long drawn out process, just as with the stone. Besides, she said, there was a tide which no one would be able to combat easily.

I spent a rather short time at the University of Hamburg, only three semesters. The national mood was changing and perhaps the less said about it the better. But, I feel grateful that I ever got to the point where I was privileged to sit in the university at all. So, I shall leave it at that.

As a child, Hamburg University was only a term to me and nothing more. But father developed a deep and close friendship with two professors at the university—Professors Meinhof and Klingenheben.[7] Dr. Klingenheben studied the Vai language. He came regularly on his bicycle after office hours to the Consulate General to take his lessons. My brothers, Ali, Jawa, George, and Ibrahim would be called into the office for Dr. Klingenheben to study their various pronunciations in Vai, which were somewhat different from father's. The various pronunciations seemed to depend on the influence of the other languages that they happened to speak besides Vai. I was never called in. Before long, Vai was added to the curriculum of the university and father held a regular lecturing position at the Seminar für Afrikanische Sprachen.[8]

I remember that the inscription on the building of the university inspired me greatly, *"der Forschung, der Lehre, der Bildung"*—the university was dedicated to "Research, Teaching and Education." I then made up my mind that I shall in some way sit in the round red-capped building some day. I was going to search for knowledge. At first it was medicine, inspired by the mystery of the surgical operation performed on my hands and by the herbs of Mama Jassa to cure the sick. I was now among Prof. Muhlens,[9] who had discovered a cure for malaria, and Professor Bernard Nocht, who established a hospital for the cure of tropical diseases. That is what I thought I wanted at the university.

But after three semesters, things changed. My dreams were shattered and I felt it keenly. What followed was a period of self-analysis. Did I really want to study medicine? Had father not often said that I would make a better teacher? Finally, I heard of a course of the old seminary-type offered near Hamburg, where scientific methods were offered. I was told by the director that I would not be permitted to live out there but if I were willing to follow the courses, I could be a student. Since I wanted the knowledge and wasn't interested in the paper, I became a student there for a while. Thus, my despondency disappeared in the pursuit of my daily tasks. Soon I was able to tell myself that a weak woman does not want medicine anyway.

My entire family, including my parents, left Hamburg and I was living at the Heim für Junge Mädchen in the Rothenbaum-Chausse 32.[10] I was in bed with a cold one day when Fräulein Meyer, Herr Professor Meinhof's secretary, came to my room and brought me a message that Herr Dr. Meinhof wanted me to be an assistant at the university, and particularly in the Seminar für Afrikanische Sprachen, of which he was director. My appointment had gone through with the proper authorities and she said when I was rid of the cold she would like me to go and speak with Herr Professor Meinhof. When leaving Hamburg, father told the professors at the Seminar für Afrikanische Sprachen that I knew as much about the Vai culture and language as he did. Well, this is somewhat exaggerated.

The Heim in which I lived was under the auspices of the Lutheran Church and Fräulein von Bobers, who was my female guardian, took me there and made the necessary arrangements for my stay. I remember when she accompanied me to see the Pensionsmutter, Fräulein Hoche, who was from Elberfeld, and whose father had been a mathematician. She told Fräulein Hoche that she would find me very independent. I lived at the Heim while I attended the university, worked at the consulate, and also worked at the new job, which I am now about to describe. Life at the Heim was beautiful. I became an active member of the family life there immediately after my entrance, where I became particularly fond of the cook, Fräulein Pflahler. The girls, Ilse Sierck and Margaret Marquardt, had told me that Fraulein Pfahler would be having her birthday in a few days so I wrote a song for her serenade, the first verse being:

In der Rothenbaumchausee,
Fräulein Pfahler ist die gute Fee.
Schlägt die Glocke punkt halbzwei,
Strömt das Essen schnell herbei.[11]

I started work as Sprachgehilfin,[12] but at first I was ashamed because the people whom I was teaching were doctors and great learned men, some of them with hanging beards. Professor Meinhof was personally very kind to me and often told me that I should not fear to correct them. I heard indirectly his comments to the effect that a few years back, he had seen me playing in the sand boxes in the park, and now, I was doing a valuable service.

I learned a great deal about my language while working at the seminary. For example, I had never stopped to consider any grammatical rules in Vai. Now, when I had to explain anything, I would suddenly become conscious that there were rules that guided speech as with any other language. The greatest difficulty was usually to make the Germans differentiate between the pronouns for something acquired and for natural nouns. Let me illustrate. We have a separate pronoun in Vai for things and substantives like father, mother, sister, brother, hand, mouth, eye, and etcetera. The Vai consider these nouns natural, because you did nothing to have them, and hence, there are possessive pronouns for them. Nouns like wife, daughter, husband, lamp and the like have another group of possessive pronouns. The Germans always maintained that a wife is something natural and hence should belong to the natural group. But the Vai feel that you don't have to have a wife, or a husband, or a child, unless you cared to—hence, they are acquired.

When times became very disturbing in Germany, Professor Meinhof wrote me a letter saying that my services at the university could no longer be continued, adding *"für diesen Dienst den Sie der Forschung und der Wissenschaft geleistet haben, haben Sie den dauernden Dank des Seminars erworben."*[13] In this same letter of thanks, he announced the publication of the stories, which some of the members of the class had recorded and which were published in *"Zeitschrift für eingeborenen Sprachen."*[14]

When I was about to leave for America, Professor Meinhof wrote a letter of recommendation for me to President Lane of Lane College, where I spent the first year or so in America. He described the work I had done on Vai and how valuable "the Massaquoi family with their widespread knowledge" had been. He added that "all of this could not have been accomplished if Miss Massaquoi had not mastered the German language thoroughly." I was glad that he had been pleased with my five semesters of service to them.

Notes

1. [This continues to be the custom in many French-speaking countries. *Eds.*]

2. ["Miss Massaquoi made real progress in her second semester." *Eds.*]
3. [Carl Meinhof (1857–1944) was a famous scholar of African languages. From 1909 until his death, he was a professor at the Kolonial-Institute in Hamburg. *Eds.*]
4. ["Europe, Country and People, how I perceive them." *Eds.*]
5. ["the Nigger bit his child, Oh...And threw it against the wall, Oh!" *Eds.*]
6. [The lawsuit is fully described in an article which appeared in the *New York Times* in 1924: T. R. Ybarra, "Accused of Theft of Sacred Stone," *New York Times* (July 13, 1924), p. 15. The byline of the article was "German Movie Operator Stirs All Liberia by Removing Venerated Emblem," which was not taken from Vai country, but rather from Gola territory, near Balomah. In the lawsuit, the German explorer and filmmaker Hans Schomburgk (1880–1967) was accused of stealing the artifact (he claimed he bought it for £1) and smuggling it aboard a German steamer out of Freetown, after it had been stolen from its sacred place and smuggled over land from Liberia by one of his servants. It is not known by the editors if this stone occupies its sacred place among the Gola today, or if the German copy of it is extant. *Eds.*]
7. [August Klingenheben (1886–1967) was an important scholar of African languages in Hamburg and Leipzig, and was introduced to the Vai language and script by Momolu Massaquoi. Klingenheben published a number of influential articles on the script and language. He visited Liberia several times over the years, first in the 1920s, with his last visit coming in 1962, when he participated in a conference on the standardization of the Vai script at the University of Liberia run by Fatima Massaquoi-Fahnbulleh. *Eds.*]
8. [Seminary/Department for African Languages. *Eds.*]
9. [Dr. Peter Mühlens (1874–1943) is known for his advancements in study of malaria although his legacy also concerns dubious experiments in which he deliberately infected patients with malaria without their consent. *Eds.*]
10. [A home for young girls. *Eds.*]
11. ["In the Rothenbaumchausee, Miss Pfahler is the good fairy. Rings the bell one-thirty sharp, Food flocks quickly to the scene." *Eds.*]
12. [Language aide. *Eds.*]
13. ["For this service which you rendered research and science, you acquired the everlasting thankfulness of the Seminary." *Eds.*]
14. [*Journal for Native Languages*. *Eds.*]

CHAPTER 16

DEPARTURE FOR AMERICA

Now that a career in medicine seemed out of question for me, I turned my attention to the possibility of a teaching career. But, while a person can practice medicine almost perfectly without great knowledge of the language of the country in which he intends to live, this is not the case with any other branch of knowledge. Hence, since my ultimate objective in all the training I had received was to work in Liberia, father and I had to turn our attention seriously to the matter of my knowing English as much as my own mother tongue. The first possibility was to study in England, but father ruled it out because of the growing menace of war in Europe. I didn't feel that the war might include Great Britain, but father did. He felt that war in Europe—and in the whole world—was inevitable. After giving up England as a possibility, our only alternative remained America.

About this time, an old classmate of father's, Dr. J. F. Lane, who was president of Lane College in Tennessee[1] obtained his Hamburg address and contacted him through his wife, Mrs. J. F. Lane. Since father was not at the office, I replied and forwarded the letter to him. In this correspondence I learned that another classmate, Dr. Mattie Howard Coleman, was dean of women at the same college.

I was particularly happy to learn of Dr. Coleman, ("Aunt Mattie" as I later came to call her) for father had spoken so very kindly of her. From the cradle, I had learned about father's experiences at Central Tennessee College.[2] Although Aunt Mattie was not father's girlfriend, I learned that she bore all his romantic quarrels, as he always turned to her when his love affairs went wrong. As she expressed it to me, "I was not yellow enough for him, but he always made me think that I was the best girl after he had a quarrel with another girl, and he would not miss taking me out then. He was often very convincing, until his affairs were patched up again." At once I began defending my father saying he would not permit this as he was a model himself. She replied that she was glad I thought so, because Momo was as mischievous as he could be, though underneath he was a fine boy and everyone loved him at school.

I immediately wrote to her expressing my burning desire to meet her and the rest of father's classmates. I told her that I would think of it as a great pilgrimage to behold the faces of father's friends and the scenes upon which he had trodden. But all of this would indicate my getting ahead of my story. For, it was more than a year before I could have this pleasure.

The time was nearing to bid Europe farewell. I went to Switzerland, and, after spending about a year there, it was clear dark clouds were looming, with the League of Nations apparently failing. The Geneva Disarmament conference of 1932 was not a success, and by 1936, the certainty of war made the League appear hopeless, causing us non-Europeans to feel sure that Europe was no longer the place for us to follow our pursuits in safety.

After a glorious time with the Kuenzli Bauers in Olten, where I rested a while, I returned to Germany to await the steamer. The parting from my German friends became very difficult indeed. There was Fräulein Peemoller, with whom I had resided for a time after the "Heim fur Junge Mädchen" was dissolved. As with her love for vegetarianism, so too was Fräulein Peemoller's admiration for Theoder Storm. This love I did not share, for I had by the time I knew her completely outgrown my curiosity about writings based on the saga and customs of the North Sea coast. I remember once when one of the most famous works of Storm, the "Schimmelreiter" was made into a movie, she would run to each section of the town in order to see it. I myself accompanied her on three such occasions and was able to count six other visits she made to the cinema to see this particular show. But that was just Fräulein Peemoller, simple in taste, deep in things spiritual, old-fashioned in dress. I shall never forget some of the gowns she was in the habit of designing herself, and how happy she was whenever I admired them. Although I was sincere in my admiration for them, I knew I would never wear them myself. I admire her great spirit and friendship shown to me during my later years in Germany.

Although I could count numerous friends of the family as well as many of my own in Germany, there are a few I find myself thinking of during the calamities over these few years. From these thoughts, I realize how much these people have really meant to me. One family which I particularly became attached to was the Osterburg family. Frau Osterburg typified for me the perfect German Hausfrau. She would keep house, sew, knit, love, and care for her children, and was keenly interested in human beings. She became for me a kind of big sister. Many afternoons I would arrive from the university or the seminary, and as soon as I put the key into the door, I would hear her familiar cry, *"Fräulein Massaquoi der Kaffee ist fertig."*[3] I would then quickly dispose of my books, take a craft of some kind—knitting, sewing, crocheting, and the like—and proceed to her home, where the most beautiful and neat little table would be set for coffee for two. We would work and drink coffee and eat cake, sharing our experiences of the day. Her children, Gerhardt and Claus (the latter we called Tucki), became my constant friends whenever I was home. This did not give me much time to miss my own little brothers and sister.

I remember once when they were about to go to Kiel for the summer, and Claus cried bitterly, wanting to be left with me. Since I was on vacation, I promptly agreed and I have never enjoyed a child more. My neighbors, of course, felt that I was being made a nursemaid. But I knew better. Claus was very obedient. One time I told him to go outdoors and play with some of the other children, when to my surprise I saw the children trying to operate on a frog. I quickly called Claus to come and not participate in such a wicked game. As he attempted to come up, I heard the other children telling him how soft he was to obey a "Negress." When I looked and Claus had not come up, I went down only to find him fighting with some of the children, telling them that I was "Fräulein Massaquoi" and *"keine Negerin."*[4] Well, I don't know what was in his mind up to this point as to my identity.

Herr Heinrich Osterburg was a businessman, but his love of music remained. He and many of his business colleagues formed quintets, quartets, and trios, to which he would invite me, since he found that I loved music too. He played the violin and "Bratsche" beautifully. At one time, when he thought I was neglecting my music, he offered to help me, in exchange for teaching him languages. Frau Osterburg always invited me in the evenings when her husband was home, for she maintained that her husband was very fond of me. This was something to take note of, since he was not generally fond of girls of my age, who he usually thought were dumb and only thought of dresses. He liked talking to me, though, and since his wife respected his knowledge of human nature, she had to doff her hat to me.

Mrs. Osterburg's mother and sister often invited me to Kiel, and I also met members of Mr. Osterburg's family from Hamburg and Braunschweig. The Osterburgs even had dinners and entertained special guests of mine from Africa, in spite of all my protests. I was also fortunate to be a friend to Frau Else Osterburg when her little daughter, Ellse Maria, was born. I was the very first person Herr Osterburg phoned to notify, and I went running to the hospital as if it had been my own niece who had come into the world.

Loyalty was a quality that my father admired and at the same time criticized in me. He often felt that I was too loyal to those with whom

I associated and feared that someone might someday hurt me in this way, by not reciprocating my loyalty. Be this as it may, I have so far only had two occasions to regret having been loyal. Besides, if something is in your nature, there is nothing you can do about it. My motto, you will remember, was "I live for those who love me, whose hearts are kind and true."

Alas, the day for my departure came. With numerous friends at the station to bid me farewell, I boarded the train to take me to Cuxhaven, where my ship, the S & S *Hansa* of the Hamburg Amerika Linie was docked. The Seminary for African languages was fully represented at the station, as were girls and teachers from each of the institutions I attended in Germany. I had thought that the parting and gift giving would end at the station, but to my surprise, at the pier in Cuxhaven, many other friends were waiting also to say goodbye and see me board the ship. Well, I have practically done nothing else all my life, but meet and love people, only to part from them.

I was the only colored passenger on the *Hansa*, but I was also the only person who was cosmopolitan. This was particularly true in the sense that I had the ability to converse with everyone that I had the chance to meet on the ship, putting my finger in almost all activities; a group of Germans or German Americans would want me to play bridge with them, then another nationality wanted me at the pinochle table, while still another group desired my company for deck activities like dancing.

I was so absorbed in the activities of the ship that I found little time to write anyone except father, whom I wired from Southampton that I was on that ship and wrote a letter from Ireland. My friends back in Germany were so distressed about my safety that they phoned and went to the Liberian Consulate General to ask Hon. James S. Wiles what had become of me. He, in turn, wrote Consul General Walker of New York, asking to know of my whereabouts since my friends had been anxious about me.

As the *Hansa* approached the shores of New York, and with every force with which she pushed her way through the Hudson, my vision of America overwhelmed me. I dreamed as I stood on deck and observed the Empire State Building, which seemed to ask the skies for a living space. I thought of my days at the mission, when Victoria and I had dreamed of visiting the United States. I had learned many numerous and strange things about this vast country, and I had finally lived to see the "promised land."

I gazed upon the Statue of Liberty, as she stood there erect, telling the world that though she was of the weaker sex, she was there to dare anyone to disturb the peace of those living within the walls of the house over which she had been made the mistress. The crown she wears on her head, stood for the justice of the wise who wears one, who loses herself in service and noble deeds. But as she stood there, she was not only telling me that she would defend such virtues for the sake of her own people, but for the whole world. She evokes the desire of being a light and guide to those entering her hall, leading to the walls of her home, with torch in hand. She lifts the torch to the skies, asking the heavenly elements, light, moon, sun and stars, to assist her in doing this duty. With the vastness of the gardens behind her walls and the fertility of her expansive soil, she hopes to feed all. She also wishes to protect her children from the cold, and therefore wears a robe, which, when unwrapped, will put out warmth and comfort for all. The Statue of Liberty overwhelms with awe all those who dare to gaze upon her.

Although the sight of the statue and that of the city in general were impressive, I was quite disappointed in New York harbor proper, for it was nothing to compare to Genoa, for example, in cleanliness. The ship's officers came on board to inspect passports and other papers. I stood on deck a long time, looking at the activities around the harbor, since American citizens were the first to be attended to. Soon, Rev. and Mrs. E. T. Woods, who were at the time pastors at the Williams Institutional C. M. E. Church, and who President and Mrs. J. F. Lane had asked to meet me, and to whom I had directed my last telegrams and correspondence with regard to my arrival, came on board to meet me.

After the regular routine of passport inspection, we disembarked and I went with Rev. and Mrs. Woods to their parsonage in Harlem. This was not accomplished without many strange sights as we passed through the streets leading to Harlem. The bridges and the number of cars as well as all the hustling and bustling of New York did not fail to leave a lasting impression on my mind. But more than anything else, I was astounded to see so many people of color. Although I knew the statistics of the colored population of the United States, I had not expected to see so many. Outside of Africa, I had only seen a few people of color in Germany. As a matter of fact, they we were so few in Europe that whenever any of us chanced to meet a colored person on the street, we automatically greeted them. Thus, I remarked ever so often to Rev. and Mrs. Woods, "Oh, there goes a Negro." To this he told me that he was taking me to a section of the town where I would see many of them. It was quite strange to see so many colored people together in a cold country. I felt related to everyone I saw.

Parties, dinners, teas, and calling friends of father were among the many activities that filled my days in New York. I was glad to greet Mrs.

Julie Stuyvesant Chanler, promoter of the New History Society, an organization that had been closely affiliated with a similar one in Germany
back in the days of my belief in pacifism. Both she and Mr. Mirza
Sohrab, founder of the New History Society, did not fail to have a tea
session on my behalf. I had met Mr. Chanler while he was in Hamburg
in 1932. I had been asked by the Hamburg organization to accompany
their founder, Mr. Sohrab, to his Hamburg hotel, to interpret for him
and Mrs. Chanler.⁵ I think Mr. Sohrab will not mind my inserting a particular incident from Hamburg here, since he did not even know that I
knew of it. His hotel, the Shuman hotel, was very fashionable, and he
expressed surprise after I had left that I had been allowed to enter at all.
I wonder what he would say if he knew that father had a surprise party
celebrated there for Ma Sedia's birthday on a Sunday afternoon long ago,
with Grandma Johnson, little Abut, and all of us there. These friends in
America were very kind to me indeed, and I was able to tell them many
of the things that their German friends had not been able to tell them.

Mrs. Manet Fowler, director and founder of the Mwalimu School of
Music, organized a party for me.⁶ At that time she was organist for the
Williams Institutional Church, where we had met. Her share in making
me comfortable in America was great. The pastor, Rev. Woods, arranged
for me to speak at his church and others. It struck me as strange when
Mrs. Woods had me take some of my clothing and jewelry, which she
thought were odd, and stage an exhibition at another gathering for
young people. I had felt that my clothing was something highly personal,
but saw that the curiosity-seeking American mind wanted novelty and
information so as to grow. I complied with her wishes, but not to contribute to this growth, but rather out of my ardent desire to oblige her.
As far as the speeches I made, whether at the Williams Institutional
Church or at other places, I have often wondered what was in them to
make people profess their delight. I also wondered why the audiences
were so attentive, for I spoke hardly any English, my knowledge of the
language not being adequate to address an audience. But interestingly,
apart from the extreme interest people showed in the events unfold-
ing inside Germany, they also considered me an authority on African
culture.

My activities were not limited to speaking and being entertained
while in New York. Father's friends, including my godfather, Dr. Waller,
called to take me sightseeing. All of this could not have been possible
unless I felt perfectly at home. Being Eve's descendant, the day after my
arrival in New York, I went to the hair dresser and had my hair pressed
and waved for the first time. I had longed to see how I would look, after
seeing American Negroes who had visited our home. Now, I wanted
to see myself treated by a beautician. Well, great was my satisfaction

when the Hughes sisters gave me a Marseille wave. I was ready to see America.

There were a great many discussions as to how I should be routed to Jackson, Tennessee. My old friend and acquaintance, the late Mr. William N. Jones,[7] with whom I had spent many pleasant hours in Germany, had written Rev. Woods to notify him about the steamer bringing me. He wanted me to make the trip via Baltimore. Mrs. Lane, on the other hand, wanted me routed by way of Chicago to meet one of the missionaries of her connection, or by way of Cleveland, to meet Bishop Phillips. I was very anxious to settle down at last, and asked Rev. Woods to plan a trip that would not mean many days en route. He decided that I should go by way of Chicago, meet the missionary and take the night train out of Chicago for Jackson.

I left New York after a late dinner engagement and arrived in Chicago around ten the following morning. Upon my arrival, I discovered that the letter Rev. Woods had given me for the missionary in Chicago, Mrs. Lena Jones Rice, was without an address. There I was in the station, completely lost. I did not even know all of the names of the lady, except the Rice part. I certainly couldn't arrive at Jackson and tell Mrs. Lane that I did not meet the lady she had wanted me to meet. After checking my violin and typewriter, I searched her name in the directory. Well, anyone who knows the Chicago telephone directory can imagine what I was up against. There were more "Rices" in Chicago than the whole population of the Vai nation! I searched and phoned one Rice after another, but none of them was from Jackson, which I believed to be her home.

No one I phoned knew Mrs. Lane, or anything of Lane College either. After choosing the names in the directory that the woman in the restroom, Mrs. Ida Boyles, had told me might be colored, I decided to go and look for Mrs. Rice. Great was my search, with some people slamming doors in my face. I did not see Mrs. Rice. All this time, my yellow cab was running, and the taximeter, which I had not been aware of, was registering, going higher and higher. Finally, after running back and forth, I asked the driver to take me back to the station. "What station?" he asked. I had not even bothered to notice at what station the Pennsylvania Railroad stopped. Hence, I was at a loss as to what station the driver should accompany me to. Not wanting the driver to notice my stupidity, I told him to drive me to the same spot, whence we had started the trip. By this time, the taximeter of the car, and my diary recorded it too, had made me waste eleven dollars and sixty-five cents.

I returned to the lounging room and took paper and pen and wrote my father the bitterest letter I have ever been capable of writing. I was surprised, though, when my brother Abut told me last Christmas (1944) that he never told the family that particular experience, saying that father would think that I could never live that down. Well, that was my first acquaintance with Chicago. Union Station was the worst station in the world and the most dreadful place ever created. Finally, though, I boarded the train and continued my trip southward.

Notes

1. Drs. Lane and Coleman have since traveled to the great beyond, and I count myself most fortunate for having known them [Dr. James Franklin Lane (1874–1944) was the son of the founder of Lane College, becoming its president in 1907 and serving for 37 years. *Eds.*]
2. [Central Tennessee College (1870–1900) had a Methodist association and was founded for freedmen in Nashville under the direction of Union Army chaplain, John Braden. The name of the school changed to Walden University in 1900 and by 1925 it closed. Later the land where Central Tennessee College once stood was purchased by Trevecca Nazarene College. *Eds.*]
3. ["Miss Massaquoi, the coffee is ready." *Eds.*]
4. ["no Negress." *Eds.*]
5. [Chanler (1882–1961) and Sohrab (1893–1958) were spiritual leaders in the Bahai faith. In 1939 they were expelled from the organization for ideological reasons. *Eds.*]
6. [Manet Harrison Fowler (1895–1976) studied at the Tuskegee Institute and Chicago College of Music, directed the Mt. Gilead choir and for a time served as the president of the Texas Association of Negro Musicians. She was the founder and director of the Mwalimu Center for African Culture in New York City. *Eds.*]
7. [William Nesbit Jones was editor of the Baltimore *Afro-American* and a devout Pan-Africanist who nearly a decade after the Liberian government had banned the UNIA Liberia scheme, attempted, in the early 1930s, to rescue the program. *Eds.*]

CHAPTER 17

WELCOME FOR A "SAVAGE" AT LANE COLLEGE, AND DEATH OF FATHER

After a delightful night, that is, as delightful as nights on a train can be, I looked out of the window and beheld the plains of southern Illinois, which were followed by the hills of Tennessee, with a short stretch of Kentucky in between—all of which, but for the names, meant nothing to me whatsoever. Around ten my train arrived in Jackson. Mrs. Lane, who knew me from photographs, was at the station with several of the girls from the school, along with another young woman from Jackson, Mrs. Effie N. J. Payne, who took a liking to me immediately and has been loyal in her devotion to me ever since. Mrs. Lane then came up, greeted me, and introduced me to the rest of the girls. Among them was her niece, Catherine Johnson, who also became one of my best friends during my sojourn in Jackson. We then drove to the campus, which I had been dreaming about for the past year. Now I was really in America.

I know Mrs. Lane will be surprised at the incident which I am about to narrate, for I don't believe I have ever told her about it and don't know whether she noticed it on that day. However, some of the girls at Lane, upon hearing that I was from Africa, decided to stage a reception for me that would make me feel at home among them. My arrival had been anticipated week after week and month after month, and in spite of this, these girls had not given up on preparing a warm welcome for me.

As our car stopped in front of Cleaves Hall, the girls dormitory where I was to live, I stepped out of the car and looked up to gain a first impression of the dormitory. But what did I see? There were the heads of girls, standing straight up like wires, with their faces painted in all sorts of colors, from the loudest red to jet black. After washing their heads so as to make the hair stand up, these girls had decorated their hair with feathers, which represented every color of the rainbow.

Later in the year when I had made acquaintances of the girls, I asked them why they looked so bizarre on the day of my arrival. I was told that they had thus decorated themselves like savages, so as to make me feel at home. They added that they had also collected tin can drums which they were going to beat to accompany my steps to the hall. But, after seeing me in my black Hudson seal fur coat, Marseille waves, and French pumps, they felt embarrassed and left the window quietly without the demonstration. Of course I know full well that this demonstration could never have been staged without the offenders receiving their just punishments, for however small a college Lane may have been reputed to be, the code of behavior for the faculty and students was rigid: *"esse, non videri."*[1]

Mrs. Lane then had the dean of women, Mrs. Annie Mae Pempleton, give me my keys and accompany me to my room. With a host of girls there, along with Mrs. Lane, I proceeded to unpack in a very jovial manner, with Mrs. Lane sitting on a chair beside the bed asking me questions about my trip. The girls asked questions about every piece of clothing or anything else I had in my luggage. I noticed that as Mrs. Lane kept asking questions, so did the girls keep laughing, but when I mentioned dancing and bridge playing on the ship, they got more audible, for these were strictly forbidden at Lane.

But how could I know? Besides, what was the use of hiding things that you would do anyway? If I think it is a good thing to dance then I should not attempt to hide it. In those days, I danced for the fun of dancing, and I never found that it made me any worse than I am. Of course, had I known that the institution was against it, I never would have mentioned it, although if I had been asked about it, I would never have denied it either. There is nothing worse in this world than deception. So, this was my first mistake in this New World and my new environment.

After the unpacking of my things, Mrs. Lane asked me to go to her residence, where President Lane was awaiting me. He was very cordial, and he showed that he was very happy to see me, and asked for news of father as if the latter had been his own brother. Shortly after supper, I sat in the office of Dean Pempleton, when the dean of the school, Dean Paul, came to welcome me. I mention all of this because they contributed in no small degree to making me feel at home. I had no idea that I had made an impression on Dean Paul with my handshake. He later sought my permission to comment on the firmness of my handshake to some of his classes.

That first day at Lane was spent in meeting new faces. I met the Home Economics teacher, Miss Modeste Duncan, the English teacher, Mrs. Pembrook, the librarian, Miss Muriel Osborne, and the voice director Mrs. Stevens. I met Professors Beck, Carrothers, and Jeans, as well as the coach Mr. Clemons, Mother Robbins who was the dining room matron, and Mr. Tuggle, the professor of Sociology. Others I met were the late Fr. Rodgers, who was treasurer of the college, and Mrs. Susan Porter, professor of Education. All the members of the faculty, as well as their husbands and wives, received me well, and I felt obligated to reciprocate. And, at the close of the first day at Lane, my resolutions at bedtime were to do my best to agree with the principles and people around Lane. I felt keenly that night that a great day had dawned and passed pleasantly in my life, and for this I was very grateful.

My second day at the college was a Sunday, and it was on this day that I noticed all the varieties of lipsticks used. The girls had promised to fetch me some for church, but I had promised to go with the dean of women, Mrs. Pempleton, who, from that day onward, became my constant companion at Lane. When the girls were ready for church, some of them came to the room to bid me farewell. Their lips were painted in such a way that I had cause to ask whether they were going to the zoological garden. Well, I was told that the preparations had been made for church, and nobody asked me why I thought it should be a trip to the zoo. So, no explanation was necessary, and it probably saved a great deal of embarrassment.

At St. Paul C. M. E. Church, where the student body of Lane attended services, the pastor was Dean Paul. The preaching was grand and different from what I had known elsewhere. That Sunday afternoon, Mrs. Lane asked me to accompany her to Milan, Tennessee, where she had been scheduled to speak at a program arranged by one of the graduates of the school there.

On Monday morning I arrived in the chapel, and President Lane called me to the rostrum and formally presented me to the student body and members of the faculty. Among these were some whom I had not yet met, such as Registrar Stevens and Professor White, who taught foreign languages. I was asked to speak in the chapel again. In making such speeches, I sometimes had to pinch myself to see whether I was really speaking in English for the benefit of the public. But, I have recently adopted a philosophy that when the opportunity comes, anybody can do anything. The chapel periods at Lane were and are usually quite inspirational. And, my first day formed no exception in receiving this impression.

I did not begin courses at Lane immediately upon my arrival. I had planned coming during the summer of 1936, but I had had so much curiosity about the outcome of the rising conflicts in Europe, and had remained in Switzerland so long, that I had simply kept wiring and writing the Lanes and changing my schedule. There had been other issues that had held me up, such as a conflict I had with someone regarding the advisability of my coming and therefore had to reach some agreement with regard to our destinies.[2] There was also the matter of Lane not being approved by the American Consular Services as a school for foreign students, which required that I wait for permission from Washington regarding my application to go to Lane. Due to all of these factors, I was slow in making the final decisions and taking the final step. Hence, I did not arrive in the United States in time to be in school for the first term of school year 1936–37. Since I arrived about four weeks before the close of that term, I had a lot of time to simply get adjusted to it.

Dean Paul told me that while I could not register for courses, I could visit classes if I wished until the beginning of the following term. This was quite fortunate for me because, in spite of all the lectures I had been giving during my ten days stay in the United States, I had to adjust to the various regional speech variations (accents) of individuals with whom I spoke, for the next three or four weeks. In fact, there were not ten people with whom I could speak or listen to for an hour without the greatest strain. This strain expressed itself in the strange headaches I would have at the close of the day at four o'clock, when I would take an aspirin and go to bed for an hour or more.

The courses I attended during this period and later when I registered were interesting in terms of methods and topics. At Lane I enrolled chiefly in courses to which I had hitherto not had much experience. These included Sociology, American Literature, Government, Psychology, English, and Education. I also enrolled in a course in practice teaching in education. I had told Mrs. Porter that I wanted to teach Geography in my practice teaching at the Merry High school and the experience was great fun, although I felt sorry for the children. It must have been laborious for them to listen to someone who they probably could not understand very well. One of the girls is now a sophomore at Lane, and in November, 1944, she told me that I was wrong on that score.

There were numerous differences in teaching methods in the American school system as compared to the systems that I was accustomed to. For example, in Europe, text books were only used as aids to learning, but in America I found that they were central to teaching. I also found great difficulty with "objective tests." I still maintain that a thing may be false in one sense and can be true in another, and unless a true or false statement leaves out all other possibilities, it is unfair. Most teachers do not have questions or statements that can truly be answered with "true" or "false." Also, the matter of answering a question with one word is unjust to students. While that one word may be accurate or has been used by a special class, there are often numerous words that can describe a topic or serve as a keyword. I have felt keenly all along that teachers who give objective tests do not wish to be bothered with reading and grading too many written papers. They take the road of least resistance. But, it is not for me to criticize a great system, so let those believe in it do as they so choose.

All in all, I did very well at Lane, even though I did not receive a very good grade in American Literature, since I had no background in it. But I am satisfied with what I was able to achieve. On May 26, 1938, I received a Bachelor of Arts degree from the institution. This was significant because during all my studies I had not received a degree, Europe not being as degree conscious as America.

At Lane I was asked to take charge of the extension school classes in French. It was great fun working with all the experienced women of the area, although they must have suffered, since I attempted to teach French at first on the same basis as I had been taught. One lady told me that she wanted French expressions, believing that these explain everything. I found out later why it was difficult to teach French because the students did not know English, their own language. How can you explain a French declension to someone who does not know what a declension is in English, or speak of the various conjugations to a person who has no accurate conception of a conjugation in English? A person who does not know what a mood is would be unable to use a subjunctive in French. In brief, we had to define these terms in English in order to study them in French.

In my last year at Lane, I had a French class that was much better in most respects than the classes for adults. This was the sophomore class in French, which that year had more than eighty pupils, and was divided between Professor White and me. In this class there were a few students who exhibited great linguistic interest, so we worked expeditiously.

Life around Lane during the period that I spent there was on the whole conducive and I was able to make a quick adjustment to American habits. Mrs. Lane was never tired of mothering me, and although sometimes this was taken to extremes, I still feel that her intentions were good. She took me to several places and had me meet many of the leaders of her connection. In this same way, Bishop and Mrs. Phillips had me at their home and invited me to attend various convocations held in his district. For the contacts and spiritual uplifting and fellowship based on them, I have always found a cool fountain of refuge in times of stress to quench my restless soul. With them, I attended the laying of the cornerstone of one of the churches near Cincinnati, where my name was included on the list of the names laid in the cornerstone of the church dedicated on that particular day.

The faculty and student body were very kind to me and untiring in their courtesies. I was happy indeed when I received this in a letter from father: "Mrs. Lane informs me that each and every member of the faculty loves and respects you highly." I was glad that father knew that much on my activities at Lane. The student body and the girls, Mary Lois Peyton, Lillian Wright, Theresa Jones (Tee), Emma La Rue, and many others, constantly teased me. The members of my class who received the bachelor's degree with me are all ever so vivid in my mind. My friends in the city, Mrs. Bush, Merry, and Payne and numerous others were also kind. All in all, I had a splendid sojourn. But, after the degree, I wanted to press on.

After the school closed in May 1938, father and I were making plans for further pursuits. He planned to come to the World's Fair in 1939. Meanwhile I left Jackson for Memphis, where I went to spend a few days with Mrs. Mattie E. Smith, whom I had met in Jackson, and also with the Rev. and Mrs. J. L. Campbell of that city. It was while I was enjoying myself and attending parties and speaking in churches that a registered airmail letter arrived for me in July. I cancelled my appointment with the hairdresser in order to wait for my letter, which had come the evening before from Jackson.

When the letter was brought early the following morning, I wondered why there was no letter from my father, who had never before missed writing me. I couldn't believe what I read; I handed the letter over to Mrs. Campbell. She said simply and sincerely, "Yes, my dear, something has happened to your father." I don't know what followed, or even remember how I returned to Jackson.

What a terrible blow for me. It meant, in the words of Stefan Zweig, that "a bridge had blown into two." But before long, I determined to at least be able to put my feet near his shoes, as I am not worthy to step into them. What did he want of me? How should I proceed? Am I ready? These were the questions that kept crossing my mind. I was certain that he had been pleased with what I had done with my life so far.

A comment from one of my brothers, Ciaka, gave me the assurance I needed more than anything else: "Father's death makes me think of you keenly. The last time we spoke of you, we were speaking in Vai, and this was his comment about you: *'Musu mu batoma Famata la.'*" When the Vai man says that somebody is a "woman," well, that woman can feel very proud. Father's comment translated means: "Mother's namesake Famata is truly a woman." There were many letters of condolence, some prettier and more beautifully put, along with letters from people in high stations of life. But this comment from Ciaka was the sole one to put me back on my feet, because I knew that my dead father had challenged me with this comment. Father's comment told me that there was no soft way out now. Although I neglected reading the letter for all these years, here are portions of it, for I think the writer beautifully expressed the situation of announcing the death and challenging me to push on.

Monrovia, Liberia,
June 25, 1938

Now, Dear Fatima, I want you to know...that "motion" is the immutable rule of the universe; there comes a time in the life of every individual when radical changes must be made, without reference to his or her wishes, and the only reasonable manner of receiving the situation is to adapt one's self to it. Nothing remains permanent—you know this very well; otherwise, we might have met Adam and his Eve and they might still be with us; otherwise, one family alone would constitute a whole nation; otherwise, you would have met Old Lady Sandimanni, or King Lahai, or King Jaya. Momolu Massaquoi, your Father, was in the United States (as you now are) when his mother was besieged and her estate devastated. But he came and adapted himself to the situation, and afterwards became a great man in the truest sense of the word "great."...

Are you prepared to adapt yourself to a similar circumstance?...I believe you are made of a stronger fiber than that. And knowing this, I am not afraid to tell you...that on the 15th day of June, at the hour of 5:20 p.m., your darling Papa, my beloved Uncle, Momolu Massaquoi, slept his last.

On the 13th of June, I went to see Uncle, and seeing his condition unsatisfactory, took him to a doctor [who] declared that Uncle [needed an operation]...that same day....The operation was successful and we took him on a stretcher to the Baptist hospital; here, to our great consternation, while all of us—Jawa, Al-Haj, Nat, Arthur, Sedia and I were at the hospital—he quietly slept, to wake no more; May he rest in perfect peace....

Do not weep....At present everybody seems to be confused, civilized[3] as well as aborigine. The great leader is gone...and the question now is who shall succeed Momolu Massaquoi as native leader in the country?...Of course, you did not expect it...but so it has come—let us try to adapt ourselves to the situation and be men and women.

The above letter will explain why I felt challenged, as so many people expected something of me. Father had written to me himself, saying that he would like to see me do graduate work. But how could I do this in the face of the changing circumstances. I went on a short trip in order to have time to make up my mind as to what to do. I could have returned home at the time—for some portions of the letter I quoted above mentioned this as an alternative, although I did not deem this necessary to relate the circumstances suggested with regards to my return home. But the point is that father was dead and buried. So, I thought, I should do graduate work after my travels. And thus, I welcomed the chance, when an opportunity was offered me.

Notes

1. [Latin for "to be, rather than be seen." *Eds.*]
2. [The author alludes here either to Kolli Tamba (her cousin, studying in Russia) or her German boyfriend, Richard Heydorn (then in Liberia or Germany). Heydorn was the son of Wilhelm Heydorn, founder in 1930 of the *Menschheitspartei* ("Humanity Party"), which was outlawed by the Nazis. Richard Heydorn spent several years conducting linguistic research in Liberia before subsequently completing a doctorate in African languages at the University of Hamburg in 1940/41, only to die in military service on the eastern front in 1943. For information on Richard Heydorn, we are grateful to Wilhelm Heydorn's biographer Rainer Hering (personal communication, 30.7.2002). Although Fatima does not mention it, she and Richard Heydorn lived together from 1932 to 1933 and she is credited as the inspiration for his linguistic research in Liberia and Sierra Leone. For details of their relationship, see Rainer Hering, "Richard Heydorn," in Franklin Kopitzsch, *Hamburgische Biografie*, Vol. 5 (Göttingen: Wallstein, 2010), p. 187, and Wilhelm Heydorn, Iris Groschek, and Rainer Hering. *Nur Mensch sein!: Lebenserinnerungen 1873 bis 1958* (Hamburg: Dölling und Galitz, 1999), p. 420. *Eds.*]
3. [A condescending custom that has persisted in referring to "westernized" people and the Americo-Liberians in contradistinction from the "natives" who were looked down upon. *Eds.*]

CHAPTER 18

THE FISK UNIVERSITY SAGA

I am at a loss when I try to write the story of my encounter with Fisk University that turned out to be a contradiction for all the possibilities it offered me, as well as the difficulties that have ensued as a result. This is not an attempt to defame anyone, because I know full well that I am not in a position to do so. As all too often happens in life, people are sometimes quick to believe those in authority rather than some insignificant person. But, there are such things as facts, from which one cannot get away, even if they be ever so important.

In June 1937, while father was still alive, I was looking for possibilities of doing graduate work since Lane College did not have any. When a Lane College bus was taking a class trip to Nashville, I went in order to see the town, but more importantly, to speak with Dr. Charles S. Johnson, Head of the School of Social Sciences at Fisk University, about further pursuits in social research. Dr. Johnson was very cordial and suggested the possibility of studying at Fisk, where one of the professors was interested in the study of African languages.

Upon my return to Jackson, I took up the matter with father. Although he wanted me to study at Chicago University, he wrote that I should spend the year at Lane College as the Lanes had wished. But when father died in June 1938, the situation for me changed dramatically, and I knew that it would be impossible for me to consider any further pursuits in this country. I don't know exactly what I wrote Dr. Johnson, but I reported the death and related the predicament caused by it. On July 22, 1938, he replied that he was "quite distressed" to learn of father's death for whom he had "the highest respect."

About my plans, he said: "I have been discussing the matter with Dr. Watkins, who is also interested in having you come because of your knowledge of the Vai language, as well as your knowledge of German and French." He thought that it was possible find a way to cover the $150 tuition cost a year, and an additional $20 a month that, he said, would be enough to cover board and lodging.

However, when I checked the catalog of the university, I discovered that board and lodging would be approximately $32. Thus, I hesitated

Figure 18.1   Fisk University, 1943

greatly, as I did not have the finances to contribute much to the living expenses. Since I had applied to two other schools for a fellowship, I was torn between accepting any offers and just finding a way to return home. But Fisk was giving me a chance to work for what I was to receive, and I thought it better to work than to accept scholarships. I also believed that the work might enable me to gain further experience and other skills in dealing with African languages, in addition to what I had experienced at Hamburg University.

On September 20, 1938, Dr. Mark Hanna Watkins wrote to me confirming discussions with Dr. Johnson and that "although your letters are none too encouraging," they still looked forward to my coming to Fisk. He added that "the assistance offered you will be sufficient to meet your needs here, I can assure you." But more importantly, he went on,

> I am depending on you to serve as "informant" in a course in African Linguistics and shall have to know definitely and immediately whether or not you are coming before students can be assigned this course. You will not only be receiving pay for the work, but receive academic credit as well.

If you still have doubts, come at any rate for an interview immediately, and if it is necessary we will pay your return expenses. If you can come within the next day or two, we should be able to avoid the late registration fee of five dollars.

With this letter sounding somewhat encouraging, I decided to accept the offer and have something to do by way of school and work to heal my wounds. I wired Dr. Watkins immediately, and on September 22, I arrived in Nashville, where I found both he and Mrs. Watkins, who received me cordially. That same afternoon, I registered in the university. The Fisk University catalogue, on the basis of which I entered the school, required thirty hours leading to the Master of Arts degree. The departmental requirements were the same number of hours, but although unwritten, there was the further requirement of having to spend two years, instead of one, for the Master of Arts degree at the school.

I was required to take statistics, which, with my very poor mathematical skills, became my worst disappointment. But the other courses were good. My favorite courses were the Race and Culture seminars, which were directed by Dr. Robert E. Park, an eminent sociologist.[1] I also enjoyed the social-psychological courses of Dr. Dai and some others (figure 18.1)[2] I studied for the other courses, but more or less there is nothing significant that I can remember about them.

But I soon got engaged in writing an autobiography that became fraught with problems and difficulties. At this point in the narrative therefore, it is important to explain how and why this autobiography came about, as well as the conflict that followed. For a very clear understanding, the saga will be presented in chronological order. I shall try to paint as unbiased a picture of the persons involved as best as I can.

As can be seen from the two letters quoted above, I was employed to teach Vai, or to be an informant for one of the classes. For this, I was to receive my expenses to do graduate work. After six weeks in school, our checks for the work we had done came. I did not have the one hundred and fifty dollars for tuition along with the twenty towards my living expenses, as I had been promised. Taking the school year at ten months, this would have amounted to a total of about three hundred and fifty dollars for the year, one hundred and fifty being tuition and two hundred for living expenses. Instead, I was paid thirty dollars per month that first year. Out of this, I had to pay every week, about three dollars for my room and another three dollars for my board of two meals per day. When you deduct the sum of about ninety dollars for tuition, which I had to pay during the first semester at Fisk, you will see that I did not have quite thirty dollars from which to defray my expenses of board and lodging, as I had expected before coming to the university.[3]

Apart from this, I was to work for Dr. Watkins as an "informant" in the course, but he had arranged some twelve hours of schedule, according to which I not only served in the course, but taught him Vai as well. However, I thought not to say anything about this, since they had created an opportunity for me to continue school, and Dr. and Mrs. Watkins were personally kind and good to me. I did not pay my board and lodging very long when Dr. Johnson called me in and told me of some plan whereby I could move to the Bethlehem Center and work there toward some of my expenses.

I moved to the Bethlehem Center in the middle of November. Miss Margaret Marshall, then the head resident of the institution, told me that I could have a room, but since appointments for work toward room and board had already been made, I should pay for my board. This took me by great surprise as it was not what I had expected. I had only thirty dollars left after paying my expenses of tuition and boarding (twelve dollars a month) and lodging (also twelve dollars a month), before moving. This put me in desperate need of money. I am relating all of this, because now that I sued for the autobiography, I am told, and others are told, that I was too poor and have very little money of my own. Meanwhile, the work with Dr. Watkins continued on the same basis, attending the courses, providing Vai vocabulary and teaching him.

In the second semester that year, I was appointed as a full fellowship worker with both room and board. The point here is that I expected the classroom work to take care of room and board, as well as tuition, but now I was doing three things for it. During my second year, the university finally gave me a scholarship of $150 for that year, which was applied toward my tuition, as well as ten or fifteen dollars per month. And, I was also reappointed to return to work at the Bethlehem Center. All of this work was in excess of what I had been promised. But, since my studies were not really disrupted, I did not complain.

Meanwhile, Dr. Bingham Dai, a Chinese scholar, joined the faculty in the fall of the school year, 1939–40. He offered a social psychology course on "Personality and Culture" for which he required us to write several papers. At one time, he took one of my papers before the class and asked whose paper it was. He commented that out of the whole class, my paper was the only one different, providing him evidence to confirm the place of culture in the development of personality. Dr. Dai subsequently assigned an autobiography as a term project. With all of the other work I had to do, I could of course not write the autobiography in detail as I have done here, but rather made a detailed outline.

Dr. Dai promised the class that the term paper should be written freely, as it would be treated very discreetly and returned, if requested. I was already having difficulties accumulating materials for my thesis, "Nationalist Movements in West Africa," as the library did not have enough materials on this topic. Also, that past summer I had sent out questionnaires to some areas of West Africa, but due to the outbreak of hostilities in Europe, materials from the various colonial countries were heavily censored. Thus, everything I needed for my social unrest thesis was cut out. I talked to Dr. Dai about this, and he told me that the autobiography which I had written in the first semester was very good. As a matter of fact, he told me that I was the only person in the class who had written one. I remember that the students probably did not take an interest because they considered the assignment was born out of inquisitiveness.

Dr. Dai then suggested to me that I turn the autobiographical material into a thesis, a suggestion he drew the attention of the faculty members to. But he thought that my style of writing needed improvement. Since I had only had contact with Dr. Dai that year, I didn't come outright and refuse. As a matter of fact, I said nothing.

In the spring of 1940, Dr. Lorenzo Turner, head of the Department of English at Fisk University, was planning a trip to Chester County Pennsylvania, to do some work on *Africanisms*.[4] I requested to come with him to interview some West African students, about fifteen or nineteen, who were at Lincoln University. They had invited me to pay them a visit. There was not enough time to do long interviews so I handed some of them questionnaires. The students Mr. Okongwu and Mr. Ikejiani from Nigeria, Mr. Desou, Mr. Ako Adjei, Mr. Jones-Quartey from the Gold Coast, and others.[5] Prince Manbongo was also there visiting them as we tried to form an organization of African students in this country.

Upon my return, I used the information I had received and developed an outline, which I took to Dr. Watkins, my thesis adviser. He asked, "Are you still trying to write a thesis?" I said, "yes" because I didn't see how the autobiography could be one. He then told me that the autobiography had been recommended for publication, and that I wouldn't need a thesis, if I could write a book. I pointed out that I didn't wish to sell the autobiography so he asked me who was buying it from me. I said if I give it in exchange for the degree, that would be selling it. To this he pointed out that I owed it to the school to let them publish it, since Fisk had become my school. He was willing to edit the book free of charge. I was not to discuss with anyone, any arrangement made to me about it, and that the book should only be published under the auspices of the school.

Since I had promised him that I would not discuss his promises with regards to the manuscript with anyone, I simply went to Dr. Dai and told him that I wanted the manuscript turned over to Dr. Watkins, which he readily did. By spring, Dr. Watkins did not appear to have put much effort into the editing—well, I don't think he was entirely to blame for that, for he had other obligations such as his regular teaching load. In addition, as professor of Sociology and Anthropology and head of the department at Fisk University, he also had administrative duties like pre-registration, registration, other theses to advise. He told me that he was unable to do the corrections and asked me to remain there to work on it that summer. I told him I had no money to stay, and that I wanted to accomplish something else in the United States. He told me that he would tell the authorities my stand about the autobiography, and that since I was not going to complete my original thesis, he and Dr. Johnson would write the publication of the book. But of course I never saw what they wrote, if anything.

On June 3, 1940, the degree of Master of Arts was conferred on me, at the Sixty-Sixth Annual Commencement of Fisk University. The program shows "Nationalist Movements in West Africa" as my thesis. I had refused to place the autobiography on my application, as he had wanted me to do, saying that as long as there are other agreements with me I don't see why I should put anything of the sort in my writing. The Nationalist Movements was my thesis, and if that was completed, the school could have it, but not the autobiography.

However, before school closed, Dr. Watkins promised that they would take care of my living expenses so I agreed to remain and work on the manuscript during the summer. But I could not live at the center that summer because Miss Marshall was closing it and going to take some courses at Western Reserve. I went to Dr. Mattie E. Coleman, who then had her home on Wharf Ave, in south Nashville, and whom I had promised to spend some time with. She had charge of the Vocational School for Coloreds, and told me that I could live with her.

Her home was very spacious and a week after I moved in, Dr. and Mrs. Bone and their three daughters returned from Chicago, as Dr. Bone was to take his position on the faculty of Meharry Medical College. With these, I had a grand time. I had moved to Dr. Coleman so I could reduce my living expenses since Dr. Coleman herself did not stay there, but only came on Sundays. However, when she did come, she and I had a good time with her stories of the old days with father at Central Tennessee College.

That summer I lived with Dr. Coleman, I was paid about 12 dollars per month to work on the manuscript, while still teaching Vai to Dr. Watkins. During the two years that I was an "informant," he did not keep the regular schedule he had given me. Besides, it took him almost all of that time to become well acquainted with the sounds in Vai. There was no question of accurate knowledge of the musical pitch of the language. Neither had we ever, up to that point, recorded stories. These points are important. And, today, I can see clearly why he wanted me to stay on.

As work on the manuscript began in the summer of 1940, Dr. Watkins corrected two pages, and commented that the spaces between the lines were not large enough for him to insert all the expansive materials which I would dictate. Then he told me that he would rewrite it. I then asked him how much he would be contributing in rewriting it and he replied, "I am only editing it and will write the introduction to the book." Dr. Watkins taught summer school in the morning hours, so I went to work in the afternoons on the manuscript.

By the end of that summer, as Dr. Watkins and Mrs. Watkins planned to go to Mexico, and I planned spending the rest of the vacation in Boston, only the first chapter of the manuscript had been edited. This was the story of the Vai migration to the coast that I had written, which we went through and translated into English. He then asked me to return to work on it the following year. On his return from Mexico, I wrote to him from Boston that I was coming to work on my thesis. The arrangement for returning was they would take care of my living expenses, which I found out to be $20 per month.

I was no longer at Bethlehem Center, but lived at Dunn house, which was the building for the university's graduate women. At first, I was charged two dollars and seventy-five cents per week for the room and sixty cents per week for laundry. The balance of six dollars was hardly sufficient for food, and I often went as long as three days without eating at all. I am sure you get the idea of what taking care of my living expenses was in reality. I went to Dr. Watkins and told him my predicament. But, still nothing more than twenty dollars was paid during that whole school year. The difficult aspect to the payment situation was the fact that I had no redress, since the promise of paying the living expenses was made verbally.

In February, I became so ill at Dunn house that I thought I would develop tuberculosis. At that time, I had been asked by the AKA Sorority Graduate chapter to be their Founder's Day Speaker. Mrs. Bingham Dai was to speak on Chinese women, and I on African women. When Mrs. Watkins, who was then Basileus of the Sorority, came to my room and saw that I would be in no condition to speak, she began nursing me in every way to have me well enough to be able to appear. It was then that Dr. Watkins asked Dr. S. H. Freeman, a local physician and member of the faculty of Meharry, to pay me a visit. Dr. Freeman examined me and wrote prescriptions, telling me that I could not get rid of the cold if I did not eat. How could I tell Dr. Freeman that I had nothing to eat?

However, I was well enough to be wrapped up and went to the home of a Mrs. Harris where the AKA's had their Founder's Day Celebration. During the whole meeting I had to remain upstairs on the couch, until my turn to speak came. My stomach had shrunk together in such a way that it was not possible for me to partake of any of the good refreshments they served.

When I was well enough again to go to work, I told Dr. Watkins that I simply could not stay. He told me that from that point on he would take care of the board, and that I should reconsider. He paid Mrs. Charles Wilson, who had charge of the little cafeteria, where I had had my meals once in a while, ten dollars for my food, which left me only to pay two for the month of February or March. Later, he paid five dollars of it, and aside from taking care of the prescription and the doctor's fees, that was the extent of the aid he gave that year.

Meanwhile, the actual work on the manuscript was negligible. Either Dr. Watkins had no time, or when I did go to work, most of the time would be put into teaching him Vai. I observed the situation closely, and made up my mind that the best thing to do was to leave and get myself back in school, if I could obtain a fellowship of some kind. Having made this decision, I contacted the people at Boston University, who had promised me an assistantship. With the arrangements completed, I told Dr. Watkins to give me my manuscript, edited copy and all, saying that I was going on to Boston for school. He asked me not to accept any offers definitely, and that he would speak to Dr. Johnson, and he was certain that they would lighten his teaching load and give me more money.

When I went to Dr. Charles S. Johnson for a conference, he also told me to let my scholarship at Boston University ride for a while, and asked whether I thought $350–500 would be enough to take care of me until the work on the manuscript was completed the following school year, 1941–42. I said I thought it would. After working the whole of the month of June with Dr. Watkins, all I heard was Vai dictionary, Vai dictionary. Although I did not completely trust them, my gratitude and my chance to work on the master's degree and receive it, however difficult the circumstances, made me decide to give them another chance. So, I agreed to return, if the promised amount could be secured for the following year, forgetting all the mental apathy and drudgery I had suffered in the previous year.

To publicize the book project, I was sent to the university publicity agent, Miss Bowles, to take my photograph and discuss the book with her. I recorded songs to be transcribed into sections of the autobiography, and worked with Dr. Watkins for one month on his Vai dictionary and the manuscript. I also recorded stories from my original manuscript so that he might be able to edit them. I then left Nashville for Birmingham, where Mother Fannie Turner, president of one of the districts of the Women's Society Christian Service of the Methodist Church and her husband, W. L. Turner, had previously invited me to spend the summer with them.

My impression as I left in the summer of 1941 was that the Fisk authorities would let me know whether or not they secured the funds for my expenses. If not, then I would take up the offer at Boston University. Although I was skeptical of returning, I have the bad habit of seeing anything I start to the end. But I now realize that too much confidence in people is never good. I guess this is what my father meant when he used to warn me against my extreme sense of loyalty, predicting that someday somebody might not appreciate it and I would be deeply hurt.

In the summer then, under the belief that the biography was mine, I shared any materials that I received through family letters, and went over changes, corrections, and interpretations. All of this was done on my own accord, and never under the advice of anyone. To be quite fair to Fisk, I must say that up to my entrance or re-entrance the following school year (1941–42), as a matter of fact up to the second semester of that year, I had entertained the utmost optimism that they had my welfare in mind.

As I was anxiously awaiting better conditions under which I could return to Fisk for the following year, I began a vigorous correspondence, so as to cancel my other plans in time to avoid embarrassment to any party involved. Here are some excerpts out of some of the correspondence with regard to the work on the manuscript. On July 26, 1941, Dr. Charles S. Johnson commented on my writing as "beautiful and well expressed" and wanted my "comments on the small towns of the South and I quite agree with your estimate of their aesthetic qualities, or rather the lack of them."

Although this has no bearing on the matter of the autobiography, I thought to quote it, because, in order to make light of my work, I am supposed not to be able to write, and my manuscript is full of incomplete and "unintelligible thoughts." Well, let us proceed. This is just a little food for thought. He continued that "there is a small amount ($50.00) on deposit here for you when you return for the fall, as result of Miss Bowles correspondence with certain individuals on behalf of your continued work to the completion of the manuscript with Dr. Watkins."

Then, on August 9, 1941, he notified me that "[money has] been deposited with the comptroller. This makes a total of $100.00 as a result of Miss Bowles' letters, and should serve to ease somewhat the strain of your living during the next semester." This was followed on August 29,

1941, with another letter stating, among other things, he would send me a copy of a letter "received from Dr. Thomas Jesse Jones, in response to an earlier note from me about your work. It should at least provide you some psychological security as you set yourself for the completion of your manuscript here, with Dr. Watkins."

The letter had been written to Dr. Johnson on August 21, 1941, but the copy sent to me was unsigned and therefore could be denied. But I took the risk anyway. Parts of the letter stated:

> I have now read the outline [written by Miss Massaquoi] and discussed it with several friends interested in Liberia and African life....
>
> We are all favorably impressed by the topics. They seem to us comprehensive, vivid and realistic, with a happy combination of the personal and the social, and also the informal and the scientific. Your high recommendation of the general content and style, of course, adds to our interest in the proposed plans for publication....
>
> Dr. Stokes shares my desire to assist Miss Massaquoi....We are wondering whether a grant of $100 would be of any help? If so,...should [it] be toward the publication or toward her educational expenses. [*sic*] Unfortunately, even this small grant would not be available until our next fiscal year beginning December 1st.

In spite of the announcement of the additional one hundred dollars, making a total of two hundred for the following year, I was not inclined to return to Fisk and spend a penny of my own money. My resources could not allow me to work on the autobiography or on Vai with Dr. Watkins. But, Dr. Watkins returned from Mexico in the meanwhile, and after the announcement of the $200, wrote me on September 10, 1941 that "...now we have assurance of much better funds than were available last year and am glad to learn that you are willing to work during the coming semester. We should be in position to work consistently at least beginning with September 29th and should be able to complete the biography as well as some texts."

Since Dr. Watkins was in a position to know of the amount of money available for my work at Fisk, and since he expected me to work during the first semester, I was naturally led to believe that the amount announced was only for the first semester and not the whole year. It was in this belief that I returned in the fall to proceed with work on the manuscript. But to my surprise, the amount of the time—or the lack of it—placed on the manuscript was the same. Moreover, in October and November respectively, I received fifty dollars per month toward my board and lodging. Believing that I had more money than I actually did, I began taking three meals per day instead of two as I had done previously. I began decorating my room with better curtains, a floor rug, and the like. Little did I realize that this newfound joy was not to last.

When we did work, it was still for the future dictionary. I had earlier told Dr. Watkins that I would not be willing to provide texts, since I was not being paid for that, but only for the language. He now thought that I could provide them, since my living expenses were to be taken care of by their having "much better funds," hence his reference to the completion of some texts in his letter. In brief, I thus began giving animal stories and some proverbs, not contained in the autobiography, and certainly not the story of the "How the Vai people Descended to the Coast," which was given to be translated into the first chapter of this narrative, as I did for the very first chapter of the book.

With regards to the money situation during the year of 1941–42, I received the stated $50 per month for the first two months and when the $100 from Phelps-Stokes came, it was handed out in various ways throughout that whole school year. For both the first and second semesters, I received only the two hundred dollars, which had been intended for the first only. Thus, distributed over the year, this amount was exactly the same $20 per month as before.

The epiphany moment caused me great dissatisfaction and I tried getting into Boston University for the second semester, but failed. I then wrote the Liberian Consul General in the spring of 1942, making a serious attempt to go home. You see, I had no intention of being "fried in my own fat" anymore by paying any part of my living expenses in order to continue the work. The Liberian Consul wrote me at the time that the steamships were not taking any women.

I then went to Dr. Watkins and asked for more money, since I had to remain there for the second semester. His reply was that I had money, referring to one hundred dollars which I had received that previous fall, with which I had opened a postal savings account in Nashville. I told him that I was not going to spend that money and was going to keep it for some other purpose. His argument was that I shouldn't make a distinction as to the "source" of the money.

In the summer of 1942, I remained for six weeks on the further promise that the work would be completed during that summer. They paid me another $20. But again, the work on the manuscript was irregular. And, there was no hope of its completion. Thus, when leaving for the summer, I told Dr. Watkins that we either had to complete the rest of the manuscript by correspondence, or not complete it at all, unless they disclosed the definite sum they had for me to return for the whole year. I was not going to accept his promises anymore.

I went to Illinois for the rest of the summer, and received a card from Dr. Watkins that gave no assurances. I made up my mind to accept my scholarship and began correspondence toward this end. When I wrote to Dr. Watkins, asking to please let me know what I was to expect, he replied on September 26, 1942, that "Dr. Johnson assures me that at present forty dollars will be provided for you this month and perhaps next month if necessary, until we can complete certain arrangements which now are in process of being made."

With the uncertainty and lack of definite commitment, I accepted the Boston University fellowship. This, I did, the very day his letter arrived. They had been kind to me, but the perennial problems and difficulties that came with their kindness was becoming a hindrance in my way for acquiring as much wisdom out of my American sojourn as I possibly could. I was grateful for their having made the scholarship at all possible during the first two years. But, no matter how much a person feels obligated, it should not be one-sided and should end at some point.

When they did not hear from me, Dr. Watkins wrote to my friend, Miss Barbee, with whom I had been staying in Illinois on October 4, 1942, that they were holding a room for me and needed to know my plans. "We have in prospect a rather extensive program of research on African languages and if she remains associated with us, she should find a good position in this respect." My friend gave him my Boston address and told him just how I felt. Meanwhile, I also wrote him and others concerned. There was a series of communications but I will confine myself to excerpts that relate to my manuscript.

Dr. Watkins wrote me on October 15, 1942, that he knew my difficulties but was not sure I made a "wise choice" and went on to explain the situation in "detail":

> This year, strange as it may seem, your opportunities with us are better than ever. The special funds for my work have not been secured yet, but Dr. Johnson feels assured that they will be forthcoming and, moreover, he will pay you from the regular budget at the rate of forty or fifty dollars per month while the other plans are maturing. Here, you would be listed as my assistant in research work in African linguistics. The program of research which we have planned is rather extensive and will include the use of several informants over a period of at least three years, we hope.

Upon the receipt of this letter I wondered how much more he expected me to know of the situation there. Had I not spent two whole years and three summers? Much of the correspondence concerned finances, but not the issue of the book, which caused me so much distress and heartbreak. In the same letter, Dr. Watkins informed me that he had finished "the notes... on your life story and cannot go further. My teaching load was lightened this year in order that there would be more time for this work. Yet you had to run away. Everyone here seems anxious about you."

The reference to "notes" and "dates" frequently used in connection with the autobiography is amusing, when all Dr. Watkins did in editing the manuscript was to read it, ask me questions, tell me to elaborate this or the other item with full explanations to enable Americans to understand. Also, in rewriting from my manuscript, he made earnest efforts to retain all of my own expressions, wherever he could, telling me constantly how good my expressions and descriptions were. I wondered then at all of this, but I was to understand later.

From the above letter, it was clear to me that he did not want to understand my problems realistically. Hence, I wrote telling them one or two things that had dissatisfied me. Among them was the problem of money. Of course, when a person has no reason to explain anything in detail, you always fear for hurting the feelings of those with whom you have been associated. Hence, I wrote as tactfully as I possibly could. But I did say something. Let us consider Dr. Johnson's reaction to my letters from Boston, embodied in his letter of October 26, 1942. He conceded that "it is true that our stipends have been unavoidably small," but that I was not under any threat of being "wholly resourceless." And there were plans for the "establishment of a language institute," which would get "adequate funds for before the end of this year." As such, they were "counting on you as assistant to Dr. Watkins in this work."

I wondered what Dr. Johnson considered as "resourceless," after I had gone through the drudgery of the previous two years and three summers. I wondered what else they expected me to do. From the tone of their letters, I thought that the time had come for me to talk to them. In every letter I wrote, I stated more and more how I felt. In response, Dr. Watkins acknowledged my difficulties "and admire you for your courage" on November 23, 1942. But he still emphasized the completion of the "biography as it should be of considerable financial benefit to you. Whatever profits there may be, will be yours entirely."

To this, I remember writing that I never thought he wanted anything out of the autobiography. But there were further developments. Thus, in seeing my hesitation about returning to them, Dr. Watkins informed me on February 3, 1943, that the research in African languages and cultures had "a definite promise" of substantial funding to the extent that "we can guarantee you immediately fifty dollars per month, with strong possibility of increasing it to seventy-five, and pay the expenses of your return. Our first task would be to complete the biography, after which we could resume the language study."

Dr. Watkins also promised that arrangements were being made for an Africa program "to prepare students for participation in the post-war representation as it will pertain to various problems in Africa. This will involve the study of present-day contacts, and interaction between Africans and 'Westerners,' self-determination for Africans, to take more active parts in the shaping of their nationalistic trends, preparation of Africans to take more active part in the shaping of their destinies, etc." Although this was in the formative stages, he saw a place for me there as well. With all these opportunities, "I hope that you will be inclined to give this your serious consideration and prepare to return at the earliest convenience."

This letter gave me mixed feelings, debating on whether I should return or not. But since I had previously given my permission for the autobiography to be published, I thought the decent thing to do was to accept and see that work come to a successful conclusion. On the other hand, there was the issue of repeated broken promises, poor work environment with consequent academic inactivity, and the mental anguish I suffered. And above all, I had a suspicion that Dr. Watkins would maintain the same old dreary way of doing things. But I also thought about the money. In earlier years I had only thought of money in terms of my needs, but the last years must have taught me the value of the most potent power in America—the greenback. So, I thought I should wait. But the same letter of February 3, 1943, had this other encouraging portion:

> If you do not see any possibility of returning soon, could you send additional data for the biography? I shall be glad to pay the carriage charges for such material. However, I think indeed that if the remaining part of the biography is to equal that of the first portion, we shall have to sit down together and formulate it as we have been doing. Surely it should not be allowed to stop at this stage. Please let me hear from you in some positive manner, as I have to give Dr. Johnson some definite information. He says that we must have some African person for our project soon, you or someone else. Since already I have made some progress in studying your language and the culture of the Vai, I should prefer you over others.

The fact that they planned to do something for Africa and the possibility of giving me more money to make up for what I had spent heavily out of my own pocket during the years that they had not paid me while I worked, made the proposal look positive. But I still entertained fears that seem to have been addressed when Dr. Watkins on May 12, 1943, asked I should come early to work with him much of the summer "so that by September we may have completed the first writing of the biography... If you cannot come for ten months, please arrange to come this summer so that the manuscript may be completed.... we can work on a schedule similar to that of last summer."

I have quoted out of enough letters for you to have an idea of what to expect with regard to my autobiography. There is a further telegram from Dr. Johnson, stating that they had received the grant, and, another letter, where he gave me permission to attend the luncheons held in New York for the two Liberian presidents, who visited the United States upon the invitation of President Roosevelt. Dr. Johnson also sent my fare to return to Fisk.

With the assurances that this issue about the autobiography would be finally settled once I got back to Nashville, I had great hopes as I left Boston arriving in Nashville on June 17, 1943. But my hopes were dashed, turning instead into conflicts and ultimate disappointment. From all the communication, one would have expected a rigid schedule for completing the work. But this did not happen; as a matter of fact, I sat in Nashville for four long months, until October 19. Since no work had been done on the autobiography, I went to Dr. Watkins on that day and told him that if he was not going to keep a schedule on the manuscript, he should return it to me since I was in the position now to edit my own writing. Well, I shall not discuss all the insults, humiliations, assaults, etcetera that followed this request during the rest of the school year, 1943–44.[6]

On that day, Dr. Watkins told me that the autobiography was not mine, having been paid for it. Upon asking whether he thought ten and twenty dollars in the past had been payment for the manuscript, he said that I had agreed to it. To this I told him that he should complete the chapter he was working on, but that thereafter, he would not receive another line from me, without an affidavit. By the end of January 1944, the chapter was still not completed due to the same lack of planning. When he asked me to bring in more chapters, I then reminded him of my demands.

Meanwhile, on February 5, 1944, Fisk President Thomas E. Jones called a conference to hear a report of the African Institute after its first semester of existence. The meeting comprised Dr. Watkins, the other two young Africans, Mr. Ako Adjei of the Gold Coast, West Africa, Mr. Motsi of Bechuanaland, southern Africa, along with Dr. Edwin W. Smith, special consultant of the African Institute, Dean Taylor, and myself.

When my turn came to report on the African Institute, I related some of my difficulties and told President Jones that I was going to leave. He urged me to stay. I am sorry that at this meeting I did not tell all of my grievances. But it is difficult, I suppose, to associate with someone for years and then at the first opportunity spill out everything he had done wrong. At least I felt too embarrassed to do so. However, I said enough to indicate that I was not satisfied with the existing conditions. Once again, I thought to have a talk with Dr. Watkins and perhaps iron out things with him without taking the matter up with President Jones. But I just met with further insults. I then went to President Jones to give him my decision about not working with them any further.

All this time, I kept teaching the Vai class with Dr. Watkins, doing so until I had further guarantees regarding my manuscript. I didn't know at the time how much of their promises they would honor. Doctors Johnson, Jones, and Watkins would all tell me that the manuscript was mine, and therefore I should finish it, yet no one was willing to put anything in writing. I took them on their word before, only for Dr. Watkins to tell me the manuscript was not mine. For my part, I had always refused to sign the book over to the school, by giving them the title or putting it in writing in any way. The period that followed was full of conferences, all to no avail. The more I conferred with them, the more I learned about the whole miserable truth.

Dr. Watkins even gave me a phony guarantee, that:

> It is my understanding that we have agreed that your autobiography will be completed by your bringing the other materials and discussing them with me so that I then may write. After it is completed three copies of the summary or abbreviated form will be given to the library in fulfillment of the University's thesis requirements for the M.A. Degree. The unabbreviated form will be published as a book for which I wish no monetary reward. The Department of Social Sciences will type all copies without cost to you.

This document was not signed but was in Dr. Watkins's handwriting. From this I could interpret many things. Until this time, there had been no mention of a thesis. Dr. Watkins in his November 23 letter did not use the pronoun "I"—"Whatever profits there may be will be yours entirely." I could not get Dr. Watkins to stipulate what type of reward he wanted, but my worst fears came true when a girl showed me an announcement of the autobiography in the *American Sociological Review*, No. 67, August 1943, p. 453, titled "Morning Beam, the Autobiography of a Vai Noblewoman," by Mark Hanna Watkins. The arrangement was that he would be the editor and thus write the introduction, but it appeared that he was claiming the book. Dr. Watkins could not satisfactorily explain this to me.

The original text of the first chapter of this manuscript about the migration of the Vai people to the coast, I had originally written in Vai. Dr. Watkins used this text for classroom material, which I objected to. He responded that it would do no harm for that little group to use it, since it would not be published. But I had been told that before, namely, in 1941, on the occasion of the seventy-fifth Jubilee of Fisk University. I went to work one day, and Dr. Watkins had my manuscript opened, including some materials, which I had asked my brother Ciaka to send me in order to correct some things I had thought I did not remember correctly. He had these in front of him and began asking me questions. I then asked him what he was doing and he told me that Dr. Johnson had wanted him to write an article on the "West African Bush School," and since, he knew nothing about it, he thought of using those materials.

When I objected, he told me that my reading public would be so much wider in comparison to the few who will hear him read the paper in the seminar on that occasion of the seventy-fifth jubilee. Later, while making a trip to town, I asked him to bring me a hot plate, which cost one dollar and ninety-eight cents. When I went with the two dollars to repay him for the hot plate, he asked me to let him have the original copy of the paper my brother had sent, saying that he wanted this for sentimental reasons, since my brother wrote in the same style that I used. When I returned from Boston I saw the article published in his name. I asked him about it only to be told that I had sold it to him or that it had been acquired with my cooperation. This article appeared, by the way, in the *American Journal of Sociology*, May 1943, entitled "The West African Bush School."[7] How could I have any more confidence in promises made to me by someone in whom I had had the utmost confidence? If I had given the musical pitch on the words of the Vai text, which I had written for the autobiography, so as to have an accurate account, "only to be used by this little bunch of students," I would have later been told that I had given those materials also as an "informant."

Since promises and actions were so divergent, and since the affidavit or written guarantee was not forthcoming, I thought to sever all my relations with Fisk. Besides, I had sacrificed too much of my energy and time into the manuscript to leave it with Fisk. I couldn't do all of that work, compile a dictionary, etcetera, and be told how poor I was, or that I would be deported to Liberia if I didn't complete it. So, I began taking steps to obtain my materials. As all the conferences had merely resulted to naught, and I had obtained only my originals, and not the edited copy, I proceeded to contact higher authorities—Board of Trustees, and others.

When these attempts failed, I sought the advice of a lawyer. Speaking of lawyers, I learned a great lesson—there are gentlemen lawyers, and others who may know the law, but certainly have no professional ethics. I went to a lawyer who was reputed to be very good. Instead of telling me that he could not take the case since he was obligated to some of the parties involved in some other matter, he assured me that I could obtain my materials. He read the letters and the evidence I provided, but to my surprise, he refused afterwards, telling me that I had no case. I decided that he was not the only lawyer. So I turned to another lawyer, Attorney Coyness L. Ennix. He saved me years of pain and hard labor. After reading what I presented, nothing could persuade him not to fight, and I am eternally grateful to him. I am a stranger here, and, although he knew nothing about me, he believed me and stood by me to the last.

Forced to respond, the university published denials that were untrue. I did not live at Bethlehem Center since the spring of 1940, yet in the denials, I was supposed to have done so. Furthermore, the salary of seventy-five dollars was paid only one month out of the five years I was connected with Fisk. Then finally, from the agreement Dr. Watkins drew up or from his letter of November 23, 1942, you can judge for yourselves whether or not they were ever interested in publishing the manuscript. Besides, why would Fisk beg me to come back every year and work on something for which they had no use?

Well, this has been a hard blow, not so much because of the years I wasted, but because of my disappointment in human beings. Were it not for the denials and other smears, I would not even bother to ever mention anything connected with Fisk. But surely they did not have me here out of love or for my beauty. There was a hidden agenda that could only be fulfilled if I could be used as the main tool. At this point, let us permit Fisk to go her way.

Notes

1. [Robert Ezra Park (1864–1944) taught at Fisk University from 1936 to 1943. *Eds.*]
2. [Chinese scholar, Bingham Dai (1899–1996), taught at Fisk from 1939 to 1942. *Eds.*]
3. [Working from the figures of ten months per academic year, $150 for tuition, lodging and board at $6 per week (for 40 weeks), the bare minimum for surviving one school year was roughly $390, which does not include any other expenses like laundry, books, etc. *Eds.*]
4. [Lorenzo Dow Turner (1890–1972), author of the influential *Africanisms in the Gullah Dialect* (Chicago: University of Chicago Press, 1949). Fatima Massaquoi served as Turner's Vai language assistant in this monumental work (p. 292), helping to identify a number of Vai retentions, perhaps most notably Vai-Gullah songs sung by Julia Armstrong of St. Simon

Island, Georgia, and Eugenia Hutchinson of Edisto Island, South Carolina (p. 257). These women had been unaware that certain words were Vai, which had survived for perhaps centuries in the traditions of their families. Turner departed Fisk in 1946 for Roosevelt University in Chicago, where he worked until 1967. He visited Fatima Massaquoi in Monrovia in 1951. *Eds.*]

5. [Nnodu Okongwu was a Nigerian who in 1946 earned a PhD at New York University, but died shortly thereafter. Okechukwu Ikejiani (Nigeria) and Ako Adjei (Ghana) were close associates at Lincoln University with their classmate, Kwame Nkrumah. Adjei and Nkrumah were imprisoned together (part of the infamous "big six") by the British following the well-known shooting of ex-servicemen in Ghana in 1948, but later Nkrumah imprisoned Adjei on baseless charges of treason. K. A. B. Jones-Quartey became a famous journalist and activist, and professor of Adult Education at the University of Ghana with several publications to his credit. *Eds.*]

6. [In her legal action against Fisk University over her autobiography, Massaquoi claimed that Watkins physically assaulted her when she attempted to remove her autobiography from his safe. *Eds.*]

7. [*American Journal of Sociology.* Vol. 48, No. 6 (May 1943). *Eds.*]

CHAPTER 19

GOODBYE FRIENDS—YOU
SHALL BE HEARING FROM ME

"I have come that ye might have life and have it more abundantly."[1]
This biblical quotation is inscribed on the main building of the
Bethlehem Center, the settlement house in the slum area of
Nashville, Tennessee. The verse tells you vividly the origin of the center; it
was a gift of the "Methodist Mission Women as their Neighborly Service
To their Negro Friends." Mrs. Sawyer, a Negro woman of Nashville, felt
the need for wholesome recreation for the children in the Negro community and sought the aid of her white friend, Miss Haskins, who assisted
her in securing funds for her training school and recreational home for
her own people. From their humble efforts, the center was born and has
meant so much to the many children of the neighborhood.

When I was first told to live at the center, I never expected the work
would come to mean very much to me. Living with the missionaries,
especially Mrs. Foster Ethel Nagler and Miss Susie Peach Foster, I came
to learn that white people, even in America, can live above and without
prejudice. The fellowship with these two and with the rest of the other
members of the staff was perfect, as we all worked together for the common welfare of the children.

Of course, I can never forget the girls and the supervisors under whom
I worked, these being Miss Edwina Lowe and Mrs. Ollie Butler Moore.
Speaking of Mrs. Moore, I not only enjoyed working under her, but I
could not have a better friend in the whole of the United States. This also
applies to her husband, Mr. Sellers Moore. I have never gone to Ollie to
discuss a problem and not left enriched with a share of her vast experience, not only pertaining to my work, but to all of my own personal problems. I think that spiritually I am forever united with her for the better.

The Rev. and Mrs. Pitts, Mrs. Betty Curry, Mrs. Mildred Steele,
Miss Esther Cooper, Miss Alberta Jackson, and numerous others were
all the coworkers who helped make life beautiful during my stay at the
center. Miss Thelma Carmell provided not only for our physical needs,

but likewise was a friend who helped provide laughter. All of them contributed to make work and life a song of joy.

When I first moved to the center, I had no idea what I was going to do with the children, whose group leader I was to become. I had a club for homemakers, and I soon noticed that aside from cooking, the girls were often not inclined to want to sew or engage in activities that homemaking required. These girls, though, loved to sing and play games. After taking them to the playground one day, and seeing how much they enjoyed folk dances I taught them, I conceived the idea of making dancing a part of the group activities at the Bethlehem Center. Remembering how much I had wanted to be a part of that group of folk dancers at the Conservatory in my childhood, I did all I could to establish a folk dancing group for the children. From this one group, we developed into all types of dances, including African dances.

I also introduced a habit of telling them stories during craft sessions. I had them tell me stories too, telling them that I did not know any American folkstories. In this way, our Reading Room, my unique contribution to the establishment, was born. For, from a story here and a story there, more and more children came to the center on their own account. We were soon able to establish a Story Hour.

Aside from the pleasure of seeing how much the children enjoyed and reacted to stories that originated with other children of the world, I was satisfied to observe the children of the slum area become interested in reading. I would read a portion of a story before stopping at a point in the dramatization, when their curiosity had been brought to a peak. Then, I would tell them that it would be continued next time, referring them to the book that contained the story. The next time we would meet, someone would have read the story and was ready to complete it. I am hoping that through the Bethlehem Center Reading room, some boy or girl will someday find a story about a hero or heroine after whom he or she would like to pattern life. Even as I go back to Africa I will be happy to remember all the hours of toil and labor I put into the Reading Room—hours which were not at all expected of me.

I hope I have not given myself too much credit for the establishment of the Reading Room, because I can never thank the late Dr. Robert E. Park enough for all his suggestions and never-ceasing interests, once he learned of what I was doing. He was never too busy to listen, and I never left his office or home without a new idea about the method I was going to use. His account of what books he used to read as a child and where he obtained his ideal for his life's work, were all sources of inspiration to me during the whole period of its establishment. My numerous friends made while living on the Fisk campus—perhaps co-sufferers in various ways—have also all been sources of inspiration.

But during my stay, the whole of the Nashville public was kind to me in every respect. Father's former schoolmates, Mrs. Mattie Carr Chavis, Mrs. Green, Professor Talley, and others, all contributed to make me have and see in Nashville, what inspired father to write his poems of life in this city of the south, which I had enjoyed reading about so much in my childhood. The Nashville clubs were all pleasant in having me appear for them and share their lives and activities. I shall carry all the pleasant memories of people like Dr. and Mrs. J. T. Brown, Dr. and Mrs. W. A. Beck, and Rev. and Mrs. S. M. Dowell, and their daughter, Joy. There were Dr. and Mrs. Bone and their three daughters, and Mrs. Alma T. Watkins, who from the day of my arrival became an ever good friend. These and many others are the faces of friends that I have placed on the dresser of my heart. Last, but certainly not least, the woman with whom I have made my home during this last year here at Nashville, Mrs. Frankie McClain Wilson, along with her family and friends such as Mrs. Alice McClain Haynes and Mrs. Lena Watson. The individuals are all part of the picture that shall find its way back to the West Coast of Africa.

Of course, my friends in America are not all in Nashville. I am rich in friends and have found that that can mean more than having blood relatives around you. I think of my friends Miss Rose Lindsay, Miss Elizabeth Lindsay, Miss Katie P. Barbee, Miss Gwendolyn Chambliss, and numerous others, whose homes in Illinois have been mine. I shall never forget the year father died, when Miss Barbee, or "Philly," who felt so sorry for me invited me to speak at her school. This began the most beautiful of my contacts here in the United States. After my appearance before the school, and visiting the classes of Love Joy High, Mound City, Illinois, the Lindsays staged a bridge party for me. I knew fairly well how to play bridge, but never had I played with changing table partners, and that night I won the highest prize for the evening. Mound City, Mounds, Cairo, Carbondale, and all the small southern Illinois towns became a second Njagbacca for me. From the then principal of the high school, Professor Simms, and all the Negro community around that section, I know and love all of them. Yes, southern Illinois is also my home.

Now, it will be useless to try to share with you all of my varied experiences while covering the thirty-two states in the Union, which I happen to have visited in some way. Some day, I shall share my impressions of your schools, rural towns, religious groups, and beliefs in articles with you. I would like to take leave of you now.

I guess, though, that I shouldn't do so without giving you a key to my future, as well as one to my impressions, very briefly. I have learned in America to see why superlatives are used. This vast country has everything good and evil. It has sympathetic men and women, who can be as selfish as they can be kind. There is, in the words of Goethe, "much light," but also "much shade." But in spite of all this, freedom here is incomparable; no wonder then that the Negro can be lynched, and yet a Negro can stand and sing "My Country 'Tis Of Thee." There is very much to learn from the United States, if we can scratch the varnish off the surface and take the woodwork that is solid and not rotten. In doing this, we would have imitated and inherited one of the greatest civilizations that the world has ever known.

As for plans for my future, if I cannot obtain a ship home soon, so I shall be in school at Boston University for another ten months or so. My advisor and friend, Dr. Booth, professor at the institution, has kindly assisted me in making this possible. Also with the assistance and guidance of Mr. Roland Hayes and his amiable wife, I shall be a ready woman to return to my own homeland, and put into practice whatever I have stored up from my sojourn in America and from other places I have visited in the world.

I now take leave of not only the friends and people I know, but also those invisible friends of the radio and the theater, who in no small way have also contributed to my knowledge of the American way of life.

Goodbye friends for a while; you shall be hearing from me.

Note

1. John 10:10 (*Holy Bible*, KJV).

INDEX

Notes: Illustrations, photographs, or figures in the text are indicated by an f. Notes are indicated with an n. Some people appear under first name only, if a surname was not available.

CPSIA information can be obtained at www.ICGtesting.com
Printed in the USA
LVOW04*1432240914

405673LV00012B/136/P

9 780230 609587